BUSINESS ECONOMICS IN A RAPIDLY-CHANGING WORLD SERIES

STRATEGIC ECONOMICS OF NETWORK INDUSTRIES

Business Economics in a Rapidly-Changing World Series

Joint Ventures, Mergers and Acquisitions, and Capital Flow
James B. Tobin and Lawrence R. Parker (Editors)
2009. ISBN: 978-1-60692-795-3

Mark to Market Accounting Standards: A Study by the SEC
Brian N. Brinker (Editor)
2009. ISBN: 978-1-60741-994-5

Mark to Market and Fair Value Accounting: An Examination
James W. Curtis (Editor)
2009. ISBN: 978-1-60741-996-9

Strategic Economics of Network Industries
Hans Gottinger
2009. ISBN: 978-1-60741-345-5

BUSINESS ECONOMICS IN A RAPIDLY-CHANGING WORLD SERIES

STRATEGIC ECONOMICS OF NETWORK INDUSTRIES

HANS GOTTINGER

Nova Science Publishers, Inc.
New York

LIBRARY OF CONGRESS CATALOGING-IN-PUBLICATION DATA

ISBN: 978-1-60741-345-5

Published by Nova Science Publishers, Inc. ✦ New York

CONTENTS

PREFACE

Network economies on different aggregate levels play an important role in policy guidance and management of large interconnected systems. They consist of systemic parts that relate to competitive and cooperative interactions reinforced by technology driven characteristics.

This text should be of interest to policy makers , industry consultants and students of industrial economics and management alike who feel attracted and pay attention to strategic and structural elements of network economies. The book is also designd as a text for a course in business strategy as supplementary to industrial organization. In contrast to strategy texts that tend to do comprehensive covering of descriptive material we identify and focus on specific issues that offer analytical insights and have direct relevance in industry analysis.

The selection of the material springs from academic and consultancy work in ICT related network industries . Some of the industry-specific observations, insights and experiences derive from my economic consultancy work with STRATEC, Germany (http://stratec-con.com). The central theme is the interplay of competition and cooperation along vertical and horizontal industry lines This forms the core base of business strategy relating to the growth of business and complementary activities through innovation, mergers and related strategic choices.

Another feature of this approach is to link strategic considerations to the particular issues concerned rather than to come up with a grand , comprehensive, fully integrated plan which fails to adapt to specific firms in different network industries.

On this point each chapter appears self-contained .

In a specific network industry context , for example, we observe that strategy is about complementarity that form increasing returns mechanisms. Here we find valuable insights into elements of business strategy, how they have been designed and successfully implemented in ongoing industry formation and (re)structuring. Some of the strategic situations encountered require the use of game theory as an analytical tool.

In those situations strategizing involves several players aware of each other and considering how others (rivals, partners) will behave. Their collective outcome will tend to equilibrium behavior. This concept has the advantage to show situations in which no one could do better , given the behavior of others. Here the logic of best response , how a firm should behave given the expectation about rivals' behavior is a valuable tool for the design of strategy.

Wherever possible I have reduced the mathematics to the bare minimum but there are a number of topics where for deeper understanding mathematical modeling cannot be avoided .In most cases I have relegated this to Appendices.

To facilitate orientation and selection for the interested reader I have provided Chapter 0 as an integrated overview and summary of subsequent chapters (1-9) .

ACKNOWLEDGMENTS

Much of the work for this book derives from a set of courses given on the topic at Hitotsubashi University, Tokyo, in fall and spring 2006/2007, and earlier at National Univ. of Singapore, 2004/2005. Some parts have been presented at international conferences at the UAEU, Dubai , Univ. of Naples, Italy the European Univ. Institute, Florence and National Taiwan Univ. I am grateful to the students and conference participants of the various institutions for their feedbacks.

A large number of people have provided me with thoughtful comments and advice about this project. I particularly want to single out Sadao Nagaoka, Hajime Eto,

Makoto Takashima , Masanao Aoki (Tokyo), A. Sharaawi (Dubai), Alfredo DelMonte (Napoli),C. Deissenberg (Aix), Ray Schwendner (Munich).

I want to thank Celia Umali (Univ. of Nagasaki) for her detailed and thorough reading and correction of the manuscript.

Munich. Jan. 2009

INTRODUCTION AND OVERVIEW

This book highlights the interface issues of competition, cooperation and strategy in an evolutionary dynamic economy exemplified in the context of industry specific concerns in network industries .

The core of chapters 1 to 3 emphasizes the linkage between high speed technological competition , and its extension to vertical integration along the supply chain and cooperative ventures on strategic positioning of the firm. This results in several interesting insights. This preview concludes by emphasizing the analytical , strategic and practical implications and providing directions for future industry analysis.

The conceptual framework, model formulation and insightful analytical results provide a strong groundwork to integrate the role of operations with the overall strategic business of an enterprise. Specifically, the context of product development and collaboration allows an examination of important aspects from research and development (R&D), marketing, strategy, organizational analysis and operations management.

The first chapter (HSTC) relies on (stochastic) differential game analysis in symmetric and asymmetric rivalrous situations in that it extends the modeling of R&D based competition beyond conventional models found in the economics and marketing literature. Specifically, an investigation of continuous incremental improvement of product quality by means of investments in innovation provides a setting for evaluating R&D policies which remain unaddressed in models examining patent racing. Although, organizational learning is not explicitly modeled, it is implicitly shown to be an important constituent of the overall dynamics. This conceptualization aids modeling efforts in product development to consider a holistic framework incorporating innovation, continuous improvement of quality and learning.

In highly competitive technological industries new challenges and opportunities are arising in the new product development arena. Driven by global markets, global competition, the global dispersion of scientific/engineering talent, and the advent of new information and communication technologies (ICT) a new vision of product development is that of a highly disaggregated , distributive process with people and organizations spread throughout the world. At the same time products are becoming increasingly complex requiring numerous engineering decisions to bring them to market. Competitive pressures mean that 'time to market' has become a key to new product success. However, at the same time it is important to keep the innovation and quality dimensions of the new product at their optimal level.

A central question to address is how should firms invest in innovation and what are the implications of such investments for competitive advantage? Understanding why a firm benefits from investments in innovation and quality illuminates issues of competitive strategy and industrial organization. In the field of competitive strategy, much attention has been devoted to the concept of core capabilities (Teece et al., 1997). Understanding how firms make optimal investments in the face of competition reveals the nature of competition and provides theoretical and managerial implications for developing core competence and dynamic capabilities.

In major parts of competitive analysis involving R&D decisions the focus is on breakthrough innovations which could create entirely new markets, for example, in studies featuring patent racing between competing firms. In more common competitive situations we observe firms, however, competing by investing in incremental improvements of products. It is an important aspect when innovation is considered to be manifested in product quality, process improvements and in the overall quality culture of an organization (Moss Kanter, 2006). For example, after product launch, incremental improvement of different aspects of product quality, improvements in various business processes and an incremental adoption of a quality culture are quite real-world phenomena. Thus innovation is conceptualized as being manifested in terms of quality. Moreover, the quality dimension extends to pursue continuous total quality improvement for the entire product life cycle. Some firms operate in a simultaneous product launch situation while others compete sequentially by adopting the role of leader or follower. The strategic implications in these diverse circumstances can be treated within a unified framework of dynamic stochastic differential games.

In recent years with the emergence of e-business and a supply chain view for product development processes, multiple firms with varying and at times conflicting objectives enter into collaborative arrangements. In such situations, the competitive strategy based on quality and innovation could potentially permeate in those collaborative setups. A recent example is the collaborative venture of Sony and Samsung to build a cutting edge plant for LCD flat screen TV though displaying ongoing fierce rivalry in new product launches in exactly the same product categories. When innovation and quality levels form the core of a firm's capabilities, each member in the supply chain would have an incentive to invest and improve their dynamic capabilities. This leads to tacit competition among collaborative product development partners by means of active investment in innovation and quality.

Although the forces of innovation are central to competition in young, technically dynamic industries, they also affect mature industries where life cycles historically were relatively strong, technologies mature, and demands stable.

A strategy for technology must confront primarily what the focus of technical development will be. The question is what technologies are critical to the firm's competitive advantage. In this context, technology must include the know-how the firm needs to create, produce and market its products and deliver them to customers. As a major step in creating a technology strategy it has to define those capabilities where the firm seeks to achieve a distinctive advantage relative to competitors. For most firms, there are a large number of important areas of technological know-how but only a handful where the firm will seek to create truly superior capability.

Having determined the focus of technical development and the source of capability, the firm must establish the timing and frequency for innovation efforts. Part of the timing issue involves developing technical capabilities, and the rest involves introducing technology into the market. The frequency of implementation and associated risks will depend in part on the nature of the technology and the markets involved (e.g. disk drive vs. automotive

Extending this argument to the upstream microprocessor industry also provides some technology), but in part on strategic choice. At the extreme, a firm may adopt a rapid incremental strategy, that is, frequent, small changes in technology that cumulatively lead to continuous performance improvement. The polar opposite might be termed the great leap forward strategy. In this approach, a firm chooses to make infrequent but large-scale changes in technology that substantially advance the state of the art (Gottinger, 2006, Chapt. 6)..

As an example of the importance of innovation strategy in product development we notice that IBM created and continues to dominate the mainframe segment , but it missed by many years the emergence of the minicomputer architecture and market. The minicomputer was developed and its market applications exploited by firms such as Digital Equipment Corp.(DEC) and Data General (DG.) back in the 1970s (Kidder, 1986)

Summarizing, in a mainstream scenario, high speed technological competition is likely to be driven by

a companies competing in fast changing, diverse networks, and
b companies confronted with ever shortening product/technology life cycles because of multiple interactions between current and emerging technologies and product diversity, or what may be circumscribed as 'combinatorial innovation' (Varian,2005).

A neat example is provided by Arthur(2000,p.3):

> "If you look at genomics , it is certainly heavily based on biology, but it is also highly dependent on digital computing .Genomics, then, is as much a manifestation of digital computing as it is a manifestation of molecular biology. What happens is that some of the new technologies become base technologies, and these give rise to manifestations, some of which themselves become base technologies. Manifestations then appear at an even faster rate."

To represent the features of leader-follower type in a sequence of technological racing we consider a class of differential games in which some firms have priority of moves over others.

The firm that has the right to move first is called the leader and the other competing firm is called the follower. A well-known example of this type of sequential move game is the Stackelberg model of duopoly. In this type of interaction the open-loop Nash equilibrium conditions in a sequential move game can be derived. It would lead to a comparison of the strategies of leader and follower. In some alternative context Dasgupta (1986) presents technological competition as bidding games in representing patent races but those games are differential game the dynamic change of a firm's conduct at each stage is at stake.

A second contribution (VCOSC) , Chapt. 2, uncovers the importance of asymmetries by investigating the difference between firms in terms of key parameters. Moreover, for the examination of inter-firm competition through product development, the context of simultaneous entry and sequential entry are treated separately. This allows a deeper understanding of the implications of information asymmetry and commitment which have been regarded as important determinants in the context of game-theoretic studies.

The study of innovation based competition has often considered aspects related to patent races and incremental product-process innovation to achieve distinctive advantage. However, recently innovation-based competition has become an aspect of buyer-supplier relationships. There are many instances in manufacturing where one finds situations of lock-ins created by innovative suppliers. For example, in the computer industry Intel and Microsoft as suppliers of microprocessor and operating systems, respectively, to desktop manufacturers like IBM , Hewlett-Packard and Dell illustrate such innovation-based lock-ins. Indeed, there exists an evolving power structure (dubbed 'channel power') in a supply chain driven by innovation competence of its members. This chapter focuses on innovation-based buyer-supplier competition as addressed strategically by Porter (1979) which lately applies to competition on a value chain (Porter and Teisberg, 2006, Chapt.4).

A business context is envisaged in which, at any given point in time of the relationship, both the buyer and the supplier could be pursuing innovation simultaneously. We recognize that the primary motivation for such investments in innovation by members of the supply chain is to increase their differential or relative channel power in the supply chain. Also in a situation where the buyer is locked in by a supplier, the buyer may actively pursue the creation of a substitute technology by investing in innovation. The primary motivation for the buyer in this case would be to eliminate the technology lock-in and become independent.

In such circumstances, firms enter the crossroads of a very delicate strategic supply chain relationship. Specifically, a strategy ought to be in place to defend the ability to appropriate and accumulate value by ensuring that the suppliers of the resources that the firm chooses not to own are not able to put themselves in a position to leverage value to the firm. The PC industry provides an excellent example of power diffusion up the supply chain. In 1981, IBM designed product, process and supply chain such that it sources the microprocessors from Intel and the operating system from Microsoft. The outcome was an outstanding successful product design but a disastrous supply chain design for IBM.

Today, the power of Intel in the supply chain for PCs is undisputed but continues to be challenged by Advanced Micro Devices (AMD).The new innovations that occur in this industry are to a great extent defined by this upstream supplier of microprocessors. The lesson learnt is to beware of the 'Intel Inside' syndrome (Fine,1999).

Extending this argument to the upstream microprocessor industry also provides some interesting observations. During the 1960s, the practice of second sourcing whereby innovative firms license production of one or more manufacturers that can act as a second source of any new product had already developed. It was alleged that some sole suppliers of semiconductors 'exploited' their customer firms once they had locked in their product designs to that of the supplier's product. This feature of the industry profoundly affected the evolution of market structure, for it opened up a new and attractive strategy for second sourced suppliers. A firm would enter as a second sourcer and learn to produce high volumes efficiently while offering a leading edge product identical to that of t he innovating firm. Once this hurdle was surmounted, it could use its growing cash flow to support a larger R&D effort with a view to developing its own next generation products. For example, AMD operated as a second sourcer in its early years, achieved considerable success, and later on more than half a dozen companies were second sourcing AMD's product (Sutton, 2001).

A differential game formulation, as applied to an innovation race (Gottinger, 2006) and high speed technological competition (Chapt. 1) is used to examine the competition between the buyer and the supplier. Investigation of this type of buyer-supplier competition would lead to a better understanding of the dynamics of collaboration among supply chain partners. An interesting aspect of the problem is the fact that the supplier must take into account the inherent incentives for the buyer to develop a 'backstop' technology which can be substituted for the supplied component. The supplier with the knowledge of this intent of the buyer acts such that the profits are maximized before the invention of substitute technology by the buyer. The time when such innovation materializes is uncertain, but can be affected by R&D efforts.

The model formulation is related to a case in the economics of exhaustible resources. Harris and Vickers (1995) analyze a dynamic game between a resource-exporting country and an importing country that is seeking to invent a substitute technology. They address a central question in the economics of exhaustible resources concerning incentives for the discovery of reproducible 'backstop' technologies to substitute for finite natural resources that are being depleted. Importing countries are motivated to discover backstop technologies not only to overcome the problem that resource stocks are finite, but also to reduce dependence upon resource producers, who often enjoy a considerable degree of monopoly power over them.

The third contribution (COOPET) , Chapt. 3, presents the competitive role of innovation among collaborating firms. The models provide reasoning for inter-firm incentives in forming collaborative arrangements for product development. The dynamics of relationship among supply chain partners is viewed in terms of their respective innovation competence. It is emphasized that varying power arrangements in a supply chain leads to different implications for investments in innovation by buyer and supplier. The incentive for buyer and supplier to strategically maneuver their overall innovation levels by appropriate investments is highlighted.

The purpose of this chapter is to provide a strategic framework and insights regarding power and competition in a collaborative supply chain setup. It builds on strategic thinking specifically in the context of collaboration. In particular, Williamson's (1975; 1985, 1999) transaction cost approach provides a conceptual grounding for understanding the fundamental basis on which relationship between buyer and supplier takes place. With multiple firms constituting a supply chain, investments by supply chain partners have implications that transcend the traditional cost minimization or revenue/profit maximization objectives. In present dynamic environments, firms are investing in risky innovations and associated strategies to gain first-mover advantage (Gottinger, 2006). But also in high technology industries more firms strategically decide to enter a collaborative relationship. In a joint product development context, many firms outsource the manufacturing process of components which would be used in the final product (Besanko, et al., 1999, Chapt. 2). At times, this outsourcing goes beyond just the manufacturing of a fully specified component to allowing and expecting the supplier to build resource competence through active innovation.

An example can be found in the supply chain of automobiles (Clark and Fujimoto, 1991, Chapts.5, 6). Automobile production begins with design, which consists of three main elements. The first element is the concept itself, thereafter, the design of the vehicle can be usefully divided into the macro-design (the development of the basic chassis, sub-assembly and component specification) and the micro-design (the development to agreed specifications of the vehicle's constituent components). The first two elements of design tend to be undertaken by the car assembler. In particular, the assembler takes charge of concept origination. In the face of intense competition, however, the costs associated with developing new vehicle prototypes have increasingly forced car assemblers to source the design of sub-assemblies and components (the micro-design) from external suppliers. The degree to which such outsourcing is undertaken by assemblers varies between different firms.

The assemblers who outsource the micro-design to external suppliers have a motivation to let these suppliers grow larger so that the supply bases can be brought up to global standards. These larger suppliers would then be required to take full responsibility for the design of sub-assemblies and for the coordination of the second and third-tier component manufacturers that contribute to the product.

The strong market position of these sub-assemblers is further enhanced by product specialization. No single supplier produces all types of sub-assembly. For example, Bosch, which is the world's largest automotive equipment manufacturer, targets its efforts on starter systems, spark plugs, braking systems, lighting and windscreen wipers.

The net result of market consolidation is that the supply of particular sub-assembly systems has become concentrated amongst just a handful of manufacturers.

In such circumstances, firms enter the crossroads of a very delicate strategic supply chain relationship. Specifically, a strategy ought to be in place to defend the ability to appropriate and accumulate value by ensuring that the suppliers of the resources that the firm chooses not to own are not able to put themselves in a position to leverage value from the firm. The PC industry provides an excellent example of power diffusion up the supply chain. In 1981 IBM designed product, process and supply chain such that it sources the microprocessors from Intel and the operating system and application software from Microsoft. The outcome was a phenomenally successful product design but a disastrous supply chain design for IBM. Today, the power of Intel in the supply chain for PCs is undisputed. The new innovations that occur in this industry are to a great extent defined by this upstream supplier of microprocessors. The lesson learnt is to be aware of the "Intel inside" syndrome (Fine, 1999). Also in the context of anti-trust analysis evidence of vertical innovation and its impact on competitive positioning has previously been shown by Fisher et al (1983) in detail.interesting observations. During the 1960s, the practice of second sourcing already developed whereby innovative firms license production to one or more manufacturers that can act as a second source of any new product . It was alleged that some sole suppliers of semiconductors "exploited" their customer firms once they had locked in their product designs to that of the supplier's product. This feature of the industry profoundly affected the evolution of market structure, for it opened up a new and attractive strategy for second sourced suppliers. A firm would enter as a second sourcer and learn to produce high volumes efficiently while offering a leading edge product identical to that of the innovating firm. Once this hurdle was surmounted, it could use its growing cash flow to support a larger R&D effort with a view to developing its own next generation products. For example, Advanced Micro Devices (AMD) operated as a second sourcer in its early years. The company's president once described its strategy as one of "planting cash crops" with a payback period of a few months and moving to longer-term projects only as cash flows grew (Wilson, Ashton and Egan 1980, pp.58-9). AMD's annual R&D budget in the early 1970s stood at 6 million dollars compared to Intel's 193 million dollars (Dorfman 1987, pp.211). By 1975; however, AMD could launch its own (4-bit) microprocessor (Wilson, Ashton and Egan 1980, pp.96). By providing a family of compatible devices, AMD achieved considerable success, and by 1978 half a dozen companies, were now second sourcing AMD's product (Sutton 2001).

With increasing formation of collaborative supply chain networks, research regarding channel power and lock-in circumstances in a supply chain is of paramount importance. Cox et al. (2002) highlight the need to undertake rigorous analytical research in this sphere of supply -and value chain networks to augment our understanding of power regimes. The results of an analytical research could potentially provide understanding of the types of countervailing strategy to shift the balance of power in a supply chain.

Chapter 3 analytically examines this issue using a differential games based approach. A model of competitive dynamics between a supplier and a buyer is presented using stochastic processes and differential games. It analyzes the context of buyer-supplier competition, by adapting and building on Browne (2000); which is primarily targeted towards investigation of portfolio investment strategies in finance. In this work, the analysis and theoretical results in Browne (2000) are extended to gain insights associated with strategic supply chain management. Also we draw from a specialized survey of results by Karatzas (1990)

Throughout we assert that the competitive strategy based on innovation could potentially permeate into collaborative setups aimed towards dispersed product development. The existing literature on supply chain management doesn't explicitly consider the implications of innovation and quality based competitive strategies in a collaborative supply chain context. Two theoretically insightful models have been presented that provide motivation and a starting point for further work to explicitly consider competition among buyer and supplier in supply chains. The notion of lock-ins and power shifts is implicit in the model development and has implications for the future modeling in this area.

Finally, from a methodological standpoint, the chapter provides motivation to use game-theoretic analytical studies to investigate some of the interesting questions in operations and strategic management. It extends the research on innovation and quality-enabled competition by considering dynamic models of competition utilizing a differential game approach. The theory of differential games originated as an extension of optimal control theory (which is concerned with one-person dynamic optimization problems in continuous time). These analytical tools of differential games are therefore influenced by those of optimal control (e.g., maximum principles, Hamilton-Jacobi-Bellman equations of dynamic programming, state space analysis). However, differential game theory has long since transcended its origins in one-person dynamic optimization and has moved on to become a subclass in its own right of the broader field of dynamic game theory.

The use of differential games is now more common among researchers in economics, marketing and management science. However, the use of such an approach to examine issues related to strategic supply chain management is quite sparse, in particular in the form of non-zero sum. By explicitly considering strategic issues in operations and supply chain management, this work enhances the existing methodological foundations in this field. It is emphasized that the competitiveness achieved with operations is deeply rooted in core capabilities and relates to the dynamic capabilities view of the firm .It is asserted that the key operations constructs and variables ought to he viewed from a strategic framework and differential games provide one of the tools for a rigorous treatment of the problem context.

Managerial Dimensions

The analytical results provide insights into managerial implications regarding strategic issues concerned with product development and supply chain planning. The conceptual framework provides a foundation for managers to view competitive advantage emanating from product development in a more integrated manner.

The results of HSTC point towards a time variant innovation investment strategy. It suggests that firms competing by means of new product development must choose instantaneous investment in innovation such that it increases with time. The quality manifestations exhibit an increasing trajectory. In a symmetric competition, the investment profile of the leader is sigmoidal while that of the follower is convex increasing. 'T'he impact of such an investment profile is aptly reflected in the quality improvement trajectory.

The results provide implications for a firm for innovation investments by considering their relative strengths and weaknesses. The exploration of firm asymmetries provide some interesting implication that a firm should consider when competing via new product development. The results can be translated into executable decisions for investments. These results provide insights to evaluate different scenarios for pursuing strategies which would lead to best market outcome.

Chapts. 1 and 2 provide a way of thinking about business strategy and operational alignment in a collaborative network. The results provide directions for strategies to be adopted in a supply chain context. These are becoming increasingly important in the present business environment, where many firms are joined together in a collaborative network. In industries driven by innovation ,e,g. semi-conductors or biotechnology, having the control on the overall innovation levels that drive the technology landscape could mean a strong strategic advantage for one partner over other contributing firms.

Innovation competence plays an important role in this approach on a supply chain relationship. In Chapt. 2 the specific scenario modeled is representative of practical situations. As an example, it can be observed that IBM is actively involved in creating quantum computers. One reasoning for investments in quantum computers could be an extension of technology landscape. However, equally important is the realization that a success of such an endeavour could lead to a lock-out of Intel from this newly formed market for quantum courputers. The simplistic model used in Chapt. 3 allows for an exploration of such a situation. The stationary Markov perfect Nash equilibrium investment strategy of the buyer and supplier is found to be time invariant and is characterized by the parameters in the model. An interesting insight obtained as a result of analysis of the model is that the supplier can influence the motivation of the buyer to invest in substitute technology. The underlying mechanism can be translated into pricing strategy that results in a long-term buyer-supplier relationship.

The analysis of a model of buyer-supplier relationship in Chapt. 3 allows to investigate a more generalized setup of buyer-supplier innovation-based competition. The aspect of channel power is tightly integrated in the analysis to understand the complex behavioral aspects using a simple framework. These results indicate that structural risk plays an important role in innovation investment decisions. Moreover, the variance in wealth formation is an important indicator of how much to invest. These results are quite intuitive and enable managers to objectively resolve some of these strategic decisions.

The propositions provide insights into the dynamics of relationship between a buyer and a supplier firm. These propositions present the role and responsibility of buyer in creating motivation for the supplier to collaborate. The importance of critical assets is aptly amplified in the results. The possession of critical assets, often observed with the upstream partner gives the supplier a potential to achieve relative market closure through a position of dominance over competitors. It is likely that a firm in possession of such a critical asset also has the potential to achieve effective leverage over collaborating partner--' and suppliers. The responsibility of the buyer is to create a delicate balance between managing supplier and customers. Similar to the conceptual development the results suggest that for a buyer that wishes to be successful an understanding must be developed about how to own and control critical assets that provide opportunities to create customer dependency and 'lock-in ' .A competence in procurement management forms the cornerstone for success of long term business strategy.

EXTENSIONS

Many extensions can be considered for this theme and some of them are discussed below as potential further directions in managerial economics.

First; within the framework of HSTC the model can be extended by evaluating the improvement in product quality with learning effect. The learning effect is very well documented in the literature and the extension to incorporate learning effects is straightforward. Specifically, learning can be used to characterize the dynamics of evolution of product quality and in the characterization of costs associated with innovation investments.

For analytical simplicity the revenue function is treated as a salvage value. As an extension the incorporation of the dynamics of evolution of revenue in the analysis of the model can be explored. In the sequential play game, the state dynamics of the follower can be considered to be dependent on the state of the leader at previous time instant. This modification would allow for analysis of a model in which the leader uses open-loop Nash equilibrium strategy for innovation investments whereas the follower would adopt a Markovian Nash equilibrium strategy. Additional insights can be gained by this modification for leader-follower competitive dynamics in new product development.

Firm asymmetries can be explored by considering multiple parameters at the same time. This would enable a richer understanding of the strategies that a leader and a follower should adopt based on their strengths and weaknesses.

The competitive dynamics of buyers and suppliers are explored. The essays present the competitive role of innovation among collaborating firms. The research asserts that the buyer and the supplier could be in a competitive relationship due to efforts in innovation. Existing literature in operations management doesn't explicitly consider the implications of innovation based competitive strategies in a collaborative supply chain context. Models are presented that provide motivation to explicitly consider such competitive situations. The notion of lock-in and channel power is implicit in the model and presents an approach for theory-building activities in this area.

We know that the model presented derives from a simplified version of the dynamics between a buyer and a supplier. The constraints placed on different parameters and the context of a monopoly supplier and a buyer facing perfect competition is an approximation for analytical convenience. However, this enables a theoretical investigation of some important aspects underlying buyer-supplier relationships. Specifically, the research provides a way of thinking about business strategy in collaborative networks. These are becoming increasingly important in the present business environment, where many firms are part of a collaborative network. In industries driven by innovation for example, semiconductors and biotechnology, having control over the overall innovation levels could mean a strong strategic advantage for one partner over other contributing firms. At the same time, the firm already having the channel power can take some actions that would enable a long-term relationship built on trust based governance.

Several extensions could be considered to better represent such'co-opetitive' relationships between collaborating firm. Given the objective interests, it is necessary for collaborating partners to know how far the other side is prepared to concede before it is no longer profitable to be in a relationship. Information about the cost structures of the collaborating partners and their relative utility from the exchange relationship is critical to an understanding of power in exchange relationship. Hence, one of the extension of the problem is to consider aspects of information asymmetry. The two key problems generated by private information and imperfect observability are - adverse selection and moral hazard. The adverse selection is a condition of supplier opportunism that occurs prior to a signing of a contract. Moral hazard on the other hand refers to supplier opportunism that occurs once the buyer has signed a contract.. A rational buyer tries to possess information that counters the above motives on the part of suppliers. Aspects related to detailed price comparison between the supplier; its competitors and the range of substitutes provides means to investigate buyer strategies. An investigation of the implications of threat by buyer of placing the contract elsewhere to get additional price concessions from its preferred supplier can be carried out.

The assumptions made in the models and the constraints put on variables can be relaxed to obtain a better representation. A scenario with multiple suppliers/buyers enables enrichment of the findings . The result regarding guidelines for price bandwidth to create long-term relationships can be explored in further detail. The implications on profits by adopting a strategy for long-term relationship can be compared and contrasted with those of adopting the Markov-perfect Nash equilibrium strategies. The insights obtained from this approach also provide a background for future studies in supply chain contracts. The problem context and results clearly demonstrate the competitive role of innovation between the buyer and the supplier. It provides a rationale for investigation of supply chain contracts by explicitly considering the evolution of innovation competence and critical assets of collaborating partners.

In Chapt. 3 (SCOOP), the stochastic differential game model considers the Brownian motion for the evolution of wealth for supplier and buyer. These Brownian motions can be treated to be autocorrelated to investigate the associated implications of investment strategy. The model can be extended to examine a sequential game and the associated investment strategy for buyer and supplier. Another extension to the model is consideration of spill-over effects. The spill-over of knowledge created by investments in innovation is common in literature pertaining to economics and management science. Such a spill-over of knowledge may provide some interesting results regarding buyer-supplier power structure and investment strategy.

The results obtained in these chapters provide grounding for hypothesis for future empirical studies. The availability of secondary data could aid in validating the results and thereby fulfilling the theory testing requirement. Primary data can be collected based on the insights generated from this study to explore some of the psychological aspects involved with inter-firm competition in product development. The aspect of buyer-supplier relationship as reflected by the psychological school of thought can be integrated with the results in this study by using survey data from buyer and supplier firms involved in collaborative product development.

Finally, from a methodological standpoint, the analysis can adopt classical game theory and evolutionary game theory to broaden the scope of investigation. Complex adaptive systems based approach can be used to simulate the models in this study. The results obtained from this analytical study may aid in defining key relationships among agents, and can enhance our understanding of supply chain dynamics.

COOPERATIVE VENTURES

Shifting our attention to cooperative ventures (COOP) and (TCRDCOOP), Chapts 4 and 5, on the R&D dimension between firms we will see that those complement (not substitute) the competitive path.

Inter-firm relationships in thc R & D first stage are often assumed to be either cooperative or non-cooperative, while a second stage product market is usually characterized by a non-cooperative Cournot competition. Most of the present R & D literature concentrates on the comparison of the pure cooperative case to the pure non-cooperative first stage, given Cournot competition in the product stage. Such frameworks may not be applicable to situations where either: (a) the firms' technology is determined by a mixture of independent R & D and cooperative research joint ventures (RJV), or (b) product market competition is not Cournot. A model of research joint venture operating competitively in a differentiated product market would allow participating firms to engage in independent R & D in addition to that performed jointly. Co-operative R&D is thought to be socially beneficial for several reasons:

(i) RJVs can alleviate the under-provision of R&D effort that results from technological spillovers and other sub-optimal R&D decisions.

(ii) Cooperation can lead to greater dissemination of R&D results. It can improve R&D efficiency through good research design and information sharing, avoiding needless duplication of resources.

(iii) Cooperative R&D enables the firms to share risks, to exploit synergies, pool different complementary assets, and exploit increasing returns to scale in R&D. It can enable firms to overcome a cost-of-development barrier impenetrable to any one of them alone.

After Schumpeter (1942) emphasized the importance of technological progress for economic growth, much attention has centered on the relationships between product market structure and technological progress. However, the relationship between market structure and technological progress is still an open question. The ambiguity regarding this relationship also results in difficulties in analyzing the benefits and costs of R & D competition. It is difficult to determine whether cooperation in R & D will result in collusion in the production stage or how the concentration ratio will affect R & D investment. Instead of analyzing a complete set of interactions, economists have tackled the issues related to cooperative R & D by adopting a two stage model and concentrating their attention on the effects of R & D competition before considering the competitive interactions of firms in the product market. They explicitly or implicitly assume that symmetric firms are effectively prohibited from collusion. Grossman and Shapiro (1986) and Katz (1986) first used this approach to analyze the effects of cooperative R & D. Grossman and Shapiro adopt the upstream and downstream perspective and describe the possible benefits and costs of a research joint venture. Katz proposes a four stage model in which R & D activities are specified by three stages. Using this model, he discusses the general effects of cooperative R & D. Both approaches emphasize the possibility that cooperation produces greater total R & D because it can internalize the spillover externality, thereby avoiding duplication of R & D efforts and thus decreasing each firm's R & D expenditure. They also note the possibility that a RJV may have an anti-competitive effect when product market competition is intensive and suggest that the negative effect of a RJV may be prevented by allowing the participating firms to engage in independent R & D.

D'Aspremont and Jaquemin (1988) develop a constructive model and prove that cooperative R & D produces greater R & D effort in equilibrium than non-cooperative R & D when the spillover rate is relatively high and the product market is modeled as a homogeneous goods Cournot competition. In this model, both firms in the cooperative R & D venture coordinate their R & D expenditure to maximize joint profits. D'Aspremont and Jacquemin show that while one might expect cooperation to lead to a reduction of R & D expenditure by avoiding wasteful duplication, in fact cooperation actually produces greater R & D when the spillover rate is relatively high. A limitation in their model is that the firms participating in the RJV do not share their R & D outcomes but rather simply coordinate their R & D spending. This naturally leads to the question of why the firms want to coordinate their R & D expenditure. Moreover, the coordination of R & D expenditure will not necessarily avoid duplication of R & D since the participants do not share the results. Kamien, Muller and Zang (1992) extend d'Aspremont and Jacquemin's model to the case when the R & D outcome is fully shared and still conclude that a RJV results in greater R & D output than non-cooperative R & D competition. Choi (1993) generalizes the model to the case where the R & D outcome is uncertain and finds the same outcome.

Alternative schemes of cooperative R & D can change R & D incentives and its social implications. Specifically, firms may spend at least as much in the cooperative stage as they would under the non-cooperative competition when RJV allows the participants to continue independent R & D. When independent R & D is allowed, both firms know that if cooperative R & D by RJV is not large enough, they will increase their R & D investment. But, mostly, independent R & D is less efficient than cooperative R & D because it is not shared and does not avoid the duplication on R & D investment. When cooperative R & D allows room for independent R & D, firms can save R & D by agreeing to increase their cooperative investment on R & D. Given the importance of governmental policy with respect to RJVs, understanding the implications of alternative RJV schemes seems to be a valuable one to explore. A scheme that includes research joint venture plays an important role in investment in process innovation. In fact, this analysis shows that when independent R & D is allowed, the level of R & D in the RJV is not lower than in the purely non-cooperative equilibrium. That is, if the RJV allows the parent firms to continue their independent R & D, the danger of the collusive reduction in R & D is unlikely to be serious. Even if member firms' products are close substitutes, an antitrust authority need not worry about the anti-competitive risk of RJVs as long as the RJVs allow participants to continue independent R & D.

Lastly, we examine how changes in the model's parameters affect R&D effort levels in each scheme. Specifically, a comparative static analysis is performed to determine the effect of the spillover rate ,the internal spillover rate and the cost of R&D on innovative activities. Most writers acknowledge the possibility that the intensity of competition in product markets, the rate of spillover, the efficiency of sharing cooperative R&D and the expensiveness of R&D costs play important roles with respect to R&D investment decisions. Since the framework of this chapter allows one to analyze these relationships, it is possible to provide clues to addressing these questions.

Chapter 5 (TCRDCOOP) is concerned with technological competition when firms can share both the cost and the outcome of innovative activity. Since innovative investments are often very expensive and accumulated knowledge has a tendency to leak to others , firms may have an incentive to conduct their innovative activities cooperatively. Cooperation in R&D among competing firms can produce more rapid technological progress. But cooperation in R&D may not always produce a better social outcome . The potential gain from R&D will be dissipated to consumers if price competition in the product market is intense. That is, the incentives to innovate depend on the degree of product differentiation. If the products are less substitutable, the profit incentive dominates each firm's willingness to invest in R&D and it leads to the result that the currently less advanced firm engages in more R&D. If the products are very substitutable, then the competitive incentive determines the outcome of the technological competition so that the currently more advanced firm increases its superiority in technology.. Hence the rate of product differentiation is shown to be an important determinant predicting the outcome of technological competition.

Asymmetries between firms are frequently observed in market competition as for example in the case that one firm has a more advanced technology. If there exists some difference between firms, it will certainly affect the incentives to engage in innovative activity. The asymmetries between those firms will generate different incentives to introduce new technology. Since the outcome of technological competition has an obvious effect upon the firms' market positions, firms need to take account not only of the immediate profits that it brings but also the advantage that it may confer in subsequent competition when later innovations are expected. To explore this we first construct a two period model and ask how the existence of such subsequent innovative opportunities affects the outcome of technological competition.

The analysis uncovers two different forces on determining the incentives to innovate. The competitive incentive is defined as the difference between a firm's profits if it innovates and the profits it would make if its rival innovated instead. The profit incentive is determined by calculating the increase in a firm's 'profits if it alone were investing in R & D. Given those forces, we explore how the incentives to innovate depend on the degree of product differentiation or niche building in product markets.

An alternative outcome could be expected with technological competition when firms can share both the cost and the outcome of innovative activity. The majority of models consider the case that there is only one winner in the technological competition. But alternative models develop technological competition in which each firm engaging in R & D can obtain a patent on a cost reducing technology. Since innovative investments are often very expensive and knowledge has a tendency to leak to others, firms may have an incentive to conduct their innovative activities cooperatively.

Cooperation in R & D among competing firms can produce more rapid technological progress. Since the new technology is shared among competitors through cooperative R & D, firms can avoid the duplication of R & D. The cooperation in R & D can also be a solution to the leakage of information. Since knowledge is inherently a public good, the research done by one firm can be used by another firm even though the latter does not have permission to use the inventive output. Cooperation in R & D is a solution to this problem because cooperative research agreements can internalize spillover externalities. But cooperation between firms' R & D activities may not always produce a better social outcome. The potential gain from R & D will be dissipated to consumers if price competition in the product market is intense. This creates the potential collusive reduction in R & D. That means, firms could use a cooperative agreement in R & D as a vehicle to slow the pace of technological innovation.

In exploring the relationship between technological competition and product differentiation we ask how the rate of product substitutability influences technological progress. The number of firms in the market determines the intensity of price competition. But market competition is also affected by the degree of product differentiation. When the products in the market are less substitutable, the participants in the market will experience less competition. Instead of asking how the incentive to innovate is affected by the increase in the number of firms in the market, which is a common theory in analyzing the relation between R&D and product differentiation (Suzumura, Chapt.4), we consider the question of how the incentive to innovate is related to the degree of product differentiation.

When two products are close substitutes, technological competition is intensified and it drives the market 'to be monopolized' by a firm. If two products are less substitutable, the firms have greater monopolistic power over customers. This discourages a firm from stealing its rival firm's customers through innovation and the market keeps its competitive structure unchanged. It also turns out that the effect of a spillover externality on technological progress is dependent on the closeness of the two products. As stated earlier, knowledge is inherently a public good and it is difficult to prevent its use by others. The analysis shows that the incentives to innovate are generally reduced as the rate of such leakage of knowledge increases. However, when products are very different, the firm that has less of an incentive to innovate has a tendency to raise its R & D effort as the spillover rate increases. The increase in the spillover rate helps the firm that has less of an incentive to improve its marginal contribution of technological progress and compensates for the reduction in its own competence.

COMPETITION AND COOPERATION IN NETWORK MARKETS (CCNM)

Many high technology industries are characterized by positive network externalities. Firms essentially compete and cooperate on R&D and the production of goods and services that share a network. Some models of competition contain special features that apply equally well to network markets. One is the uncertainty in technological development or uncertainty in the realization of a firm's R&D effort. The other is the dynamic nature of price competition between firms in the presence of network effects.

Firms compete with each other over an extended period of time and must therefore strategically choose prices as the market shares of the firms evolve.

Most existing models of network markets focus on only one of the two features. Further, almost all the models have the commonality that one firm captures the market instantaneously and sells to all consumers from then on (the 'winner-takes-all' market) . However, the history of high technology industry abounds with instances where rival firms (and technologies) have had extended battles for providing the industry standard (Uttenback, 1994).

In network markets evolution of market share is a very interesting phenomenon especially in the face of uncertainty about future product quality. Chapter 6 (CCNM) also attempts to provide a framework that could capture the richness of market share evolution in the presence of network externalities.

We are looking into the following situation: "Firms that are not leaders in network industries generally have little hope of reaching that status unless they come up with a major innovation – one that can defeat the natural advantage that network effects bestow on the industry leaders. Incremental innovation – making slight improvements in the leaders' products – will not enable a small firm to overtake a leader that enjoys the benefits of network economies. …It is not atypical for a fringe firm that invests heavily to displace the leader by leapfrogging the leader's technology …" (Evans and Schmalensee, 2001,pp. 10-12)

This situation described may also be encountered in 'dynamic oligopoly' where exogeneously emerging new technologies are rapidly eroding costs or where market structure responds endogeneously to intense racing behaviour (Shapiro,1989,Sec.5, Baumol, 2002,Chapts. 1, 4).

We are encountering the problem of tradeoff between 'network dominance' and 'radical innovation' that could tip the market the other way, with a significant caveat added that breakthrough R&D is highly uncertain. From a strategic perspective, in this environment, for any two firms of asymmetric size, both compete dynamically over prices to win market share. In this dynamic process there are two ways to achieve (temporary) monopolistic status. The 'smaller' firm can use dynamic pricing competition to delay the time in which the 'larger' firm wins a critical market share in the hope to hit the innovation first and displace it. If the innovator is 'patient' and the probability of innovation and the discount factor are sufficiently high, there is an equilibrium in which duopoly persists (no firm achieves a critical market share) until one of the two firms wins the race for innovation.

We briefly summarize a historical example from markets for IT products. In the personal computer (PC) operating system market. Microsoft products (MS DOS and Windows) have been dominating the market since the mid 1980s. An operating system is the fundamental program that controls the allocation and use of computer resources. Thus, the utility that operating systems provide to consumers depends on the number of compatible applications. As a general rule an application that relies on a specific operating system will not function on another operating system unless it is ported to that specific operating system. Therefore, because of its dominance, the majority of applications have been written to run on Microsoft operating systems (MS DOS). The domination of MS DOS has become even stronger since the arrival of Windows 95 in the PC operating system market. This, in turn, has provided a great indirect positive network externality to PC owners who adopted Windows 95 as an operating system. Many other firms, such as IBM and BEA Systems, Inc., introduced their own operating systems and tried to compete with Windows. These products, however, lacked sufficient compatible applications to efficiently compete with Microsoft products. The lack of compatible applications prevented enough application developers and consumers from regarding OS/2 Warp or BeOS as a viable alternative to the dominant incumbent, Windows. This obstacle prevented these potential entrants from obtaining a sizable market share. Their failure to enter the market successfully, however, was not due to the inferior quality of their operating systems. In fact, OS/2 Warp was reported to be at least as good as Windows, and BeOS offers superior support for multimedia applications and systems security. If consumers who use multimedia applications frequently adopt Windows at the expense of BeOS, they have to give up the convenience that is provided by BeOS. Thus, for multimedia specific users, adopting BeOS as their operating system at the expense of another operating system might provide the highest utility. Nevertheless, the lack of compatible applications, which in turn implies the lack of positive network externality, has prevented consumers from adopting OS/2 Warp or BeOS. As a conclusion, the positive network externality for the dominant incumbent (Windows) has worked as an entry barrier against entrants (OS/2 Warp or BeOS) which do not have network externality. Such an entry barrier could only be overcome by a radical innovation, virtually leapfrogging the dominant incumbent.

Open Source Technologies (OST)

In OST, Chapter 7, we focus on a contestable market with network externalities engaging an incumbent and an entrant. The incumbent, unlike the entrant, already has an installed base of consumers. We look at decision situations of firms regarding how proprietary they want to make their technology , either through patent protection or through development in open source systems (OSS). We explicitly model the direct and indirect effects of network externalities. For example, more software companies are willing to produce programs for an operating system (OS) if it has a larger consumer base. This increased competition could lead to an improvement of the quality of the OS. The model predicts that using open source technologies is likely to enhance the rate of R&D , and consequently the quality of the product.. An incumbent that would choose this strategy is likely to deter entrance of a market for internet browsers between Microsoft and Netscape. Netscape had a major head start on Microsoft, controlling 90 percent of the browser market by 1996 before Microsoft started aggressively selling in the market. With the entry of Microsoft, both firms engaged in a race to have the best available product.

Given the intense competition between the two firms, by the end of 1997 Microsoft was pricing the Internet Explorer free. In contrast, Netscape was charging corporations licensing fees for using their browser. By the end of 1997, Microsoft had stolen a large chunk of Netscape's market share. Netscape eventually followed suit and started giving away its browser free.The extended battle between Microsoft and Netscape had its toll on the profits of both companies. In 1998 Netscape came up with a new strategy and decided to release its source code, the actual line of programming language, for the Netscape Communicator. This allowed users and developers to look inside the workings of the browser, to modify the software and even to redistribute the new version under their own brand name, provided that the modified source code was also freely available. The whole idea is to turn the entire internet community into a vast research division for Netscape browser.

The term 'open source software' has been widely used in the popular and professional literature. Instead of keeping their technology proprietary, the firms will distribute it freely. It newcomer because it can play out its advantage of a larger network.

Cooperative R&D is a crucial phenomenon both from the point of view of the individual firm and the economy as a whole. Since innovation could be regarded as a public good, society as a whole benefits from innovation. However, the private benefits to a firm from innovating are likely to be different from the social benefits. In the absence of any mechanism preventing it, the benefits to an innovating firm are likely to be quickly dissipated by the entry of other imitating firms. In such a scenario, firms are unlikely to innovate. Thus according to conventional thinking, firms need to have some sort of reward for innovating. Intellectual property rights such as patents and copyrights provide this compensation. A big portion of the R&D literature has focused on the optimal patents' duration and breadth and the incentive of firms to innovate.

However, a different trend has emerged these days especially with the increasing proliferation of hi-tech (network) industries. Instead of trying to get exclusive ownership rights, an increasing number of firms are making their technology freely available i.e., their technology is no longer proprietary i.e. 'open source' (Cane, 2004).

In the so-called browser war, in the 1990s, we have witnessed intense competition in the is this phenomenon that Chapter 7 attempts to explore. We wish to study the decisions of firms whether to keep their technologies proprietary or not.

Even though the whole unorthodox open approach may seem counterintuitive, Netscape was not the only one who employed it. Apache, a program for serving world wide web sites, and Sendmail, a program that routes and delivers internet electronic mail, are examples of free open source programs that dominate the market. Open source approaches have been expanded to the biotechnology and health care industries. . Linux, an increasingly popular operating system created in 1991 is another classic example of successful open source software. Many of the programmers and software designers advocating OSS may share a utopian vision of software development, or they may simply want to prove themselves to be better than software giant Microsoft. However, the whole idea of OSS may not be so anti-capitalistic as it seems. It is hard to believe that profit-aiming firms will employ the OSS strategy without considering more pragmatic matters. .As recently being pointed out, 'open source software' such as Linux refers to freedom of choice not free prices. (Cane, 2004) The emergence of OSS as an observable phenomenon may be because the markets under consideration are no longer conventional markets. These markets exhibit "network externalities"- a market has network externalities when buyers of a good exert positive benefits on the other users of the same good. For instance consumers are likely to value computer hardware more the more users of the hardware there are. This could be because there is likely to be a better support system the larger is the network of consumers buying the product. Similarly, it is more likely for improved software to get written for the computer hardware the bigger is the network of consumers buying it. But network externalities can be working both ways, positive or negative, for example, incompatibility with network systems on a rival operating system (such as MS Office) is a major obstacle in the OSS pursuit of the desktop though low prices for OSS products would be a strong incentive to switch and for new customers to enter.

In such a market time is of utmost importance in the race for product improvement. Firms cannot afford to let their competitors get ahead in the race for technological innovation since that would give them the added advantage of a bigger network. Also, consumers in these markets tend to exhibit a very high level of loyalty. That is because learning to use the product involves a cost. Once a consumer becomes familiar with particular software, she is unlikely to switch to a completely different brand performing the same tasks. Instead, she would rather purchase new releases of the same brand even though there can be various close substitutes with similar qualities available in the market. This enhances the effect of network externalities in the long run. Further, OSS *can* feasibly translate into better quality in markets such as those for computers.

The effect of OSS on product improvement is two-pronged. Making the technology freely available means that there can be more people directly working on improving the product. For example, ever since Linux went fully OSS, thousands of programmers have volunteered elaborate improvements of their own design for no more reward than the respect of the geek subculture. It is like expanding the R&D department, so larger improvements in quality can be realized. Second, there is likely to be a better supply of complementary goods. For instance giving out the source code for an operating system is likely to lead to more software being developed for it, which is in essence equivalent to having a better quality operating system i.e., consumers now find this more attractive.

On the other hand, making technology freely available means a loss in license fees. There is also the fear of technology being stolen. But in a market with network externalities, if the firm giving away its technology already has a sufficiently big network then it is more difficult for other firms just entering the market to steal the technology and get ahead since they would also have to overcome the network advantage of the existing firm (Gottinger, 2003). Besides in this digital era, the relative ease of creating software with similar functionalities using different programming codes has made the whole idea of keeping technology proprietary less relevant.

We can thus think of OSS as increasing the rate of product improvement or increasing the success rate of R&D. We model OSS via license fees and assume that OSS increases product development deterministically.

A lower license fee represents a less proprietary technology. A zero or negative license fee means that the technology is totally non-proprietary. Positive license fees represent a proprietary technology - the firm is not willing to freely distribute its technology. The more ‘open’ a firm is the higher is its rate of R&D - in our model R&D translates directly into the quality of the product. The greater the R&D, the higher is the quality of the product. OSS improves the quality of the product in our model by increasing the supply of people or firms working on improving the product.

We look at a market with network externalities with an incumbent and an entrant. The incumbent, unlike the entrant, already has an installed base of consumers. Our objective is to explore the decisions of the firms regarding how proprietary they want to make their technology, i.e., how copyright or ‘open’ to make their product. The decision of copyright or open mentioned above, is modelled via license fees. We wish to see whether the incumbent could use ‘open’ as an entry deterring strategy. We also compare the incumbent's decision with that of a monopoly's.

In modeling the direct and indirect effects of network externalities, as in most models, we have the network term showing up in the consumers' utility; the bigger the network, the better off the consumers are. Consumers prefer to use a popular word processor because they know the format of their work can be easily transported to other users' computers. This is the direct effect of network on consumers' utilities. In our model there is also an indirect effect of network externalities - a bigger network translates into better quality. For example, more software companies are willing to produce programs for an operating system if it has a larger consumer base. That is because the downstream software companies thus can tap into this larger network of customers. This improves the quality of the operating system.. This is the indirect effect of network on consumers' utilities.

Increasing Returns Mechanism (IRM)

Most industrial sectors of highly industrialized economies are not perfectly competitive. They are usually formed by a small number of big firms with non-negligible market share. Besides being prevalent in the economy, big firms cluster around concentrated industrial structures which exhibit a skewed distribution of firm size and market share. This situation may be brought about by the intrinsic potential of dynamic technological competition to end up in (temporary) technological monopoly, so in those cases industrial competition may start out symmetric but end up asymmetric.

In IRM, Chapter 8, we show how the competitive process proliferates in increasing returns industries (IRIs) where the total of all unit activities linked together yield a higher return than the sum of the individual unit activities operating separately. This creates synergies inside and outside an industry to what is known as a scope economy. For this to be happening we must show that a variety of increasing returns mechanisms combine to enable the effect of an increasing returns industry.

We propose an integrated framework going beyond previous attempts by W. Brian Arthur (1994) to provide tools and insights for explaining competition among skewed industrial structures. However, this is only a tentative step toward attempting to explain the path-dependent, indeterminate, suboptimal, locking-in nature of technological competition under increasing return .We partially review the literature on the dynamics of technological diffusion, substitution, and competition. The purpose of this review is to show that we cannot accurately understand industrial competition without taking into account the self-reinforcing nature of commercial success in most emerging markets. We enrich increasing returns mechanisms by incorporating a set of stronger, yet neglected, increasing returns mechanisms, i.e., reputation effects, infrastructure effects and positive network externalities into a preliminary framework model. The resulting theoretical structure, we will argue, captures the interdependent and cumulative character of the three aspects of industrial competition: the number and size of firms, skewed industrial structures, and the nature of technological competition.

The increasing returns discussion in economics has provided important insights into the characteristics and dynamics of modern industrial economies. However, the discussion on policy applications has (mis)led some authors and policy analysts to conclude that a completely *new economy* is emerging and that it obeys a set of rules, which are totally different from those that apply to traditional sectors of the economy. While it is undeniable that the increasing return paradigms remain fairly new and revolutionary and while there is no doubt that this paradigm is key to our understanding of new industrial sectors, and their sustaining role in productivity growth, we should clarify its proper role in industrial structure and growth of the economy. Referring to Arrow's (1993, p.403) dictum : ' ... that if there are increasing returns , then the processes of capital formation and labour force growth result eventually in a steady exponential growth in per capita income' such a process could be equally well applied to corporate , industrial and economic growth of a national economy. At this stage we are most concerned about the catalytic role of technological competition in increasing returns industries. Increasing returns industries are nowadays most likely to be identified with high technology industries, in particular with information, communication and health care related industries (Gottinger, 2003). As an example, in a corporate context, how to unlock increasing returns in its global operations, consider General Electric (GE). It constantly evolves its portfolio to drive growth despite its large size and already significant presence in major markets. It encourages its executives and business units to take an expansive view of its markets as a means of unlocking growth initiatives that a product centric view would miss. Often, when its market share exceeds l0 percent, it seeks to redefine the market more broadly to include adjacent products or services . This continual questing lies behind successful moves from manufacturing to services , that has allowed it to keep growing in complementarizing given industrial markets .For those industries Shapiro and Varian (1999) have suggested a combination of supply-side scale economies and demand-side scale economies to explain the intrinsic aspects of technological competition. It appears however that this way of seeing technological competition is too simple to capture the variety and complexity of real-world businesses in those industries Thus we suggest a general framework to describe technological competition in what we are going to call the *increasing returns economy.*

INTERNET COMPETITION (IC)

Competition in the internet commons provides a universal case of competition in the media, advertising and entertainment industry (Chapt.9). Massive complexity makes traditional approaches to resource allocation impractical in modern distributed systems such as the Internet. Traditional approaches attempt to optimize some system-wide measure of performance (e.g. overall average response time, throughput etc.) Optimization is performed either by a centralized algorithm with complete information , or by a decentralized consensus based algorithm.The current and future complexity of resource allocation problems described makes it impossible to define an acceptable system-wide performance metric. What single, system-wide performance metric adequately reflects the performance objectives of multimedia server and an online transaction processing system? Centralized or consensus based algorithms are impractical in dynamic systems owned by multiple organizations.

Resource allocation complexity due to decentralizations and heterogeneity is also present in economic systems. In general, modern economies allocate resources in systems whose complexity overwhelms any algorithm or technique developed for computer systems. Here we discuss the similarities between complex distributed systems and economies. Competitive economic models could provide algorithms and tools for allocating resources in distributed computer systems. There is another motivation that has come about due to the commercialization of the Internet.

The debate has begun in the area of multiple Quality of Service (QoS) levels and pricing. How should pricing be introduced to provide many service levels in the Internet? Should pricing be based on access cost or should it be based on usage and QoS received by the end user? Will usage based pricing help the Internet economy grow, help in accounting, improve the efficiency of the Internet, and make users benefit much more? Similar issues are being investigated in the ATM networking community. We address some of the issues of QoS and pricing, and efficient allocation of resources (computational resources)in networks and systems. With advances in computer and networking technology, numerous heterogeneous computers can be interconnected to provide a large collection of computing and communication resources . These systems are used by a growing and increasingly heterogeneous set of users which are identified with the present Internet. A macroscopic view of distributed computer systems reveals the complexity of the organization and management of the resources and services they provide. The complexity arises from the system size (e.g. no. of systems, no. of users) and heterogeneity in applications (e.g. online transaction processing, e-commerce, multimedia, intelligent information search) and resources (CPU, memory, I/O bandwidth, network bandwidth and buffers, etc.)

The complexity of resource allocation is further increased by several factors. First, in many distributed systems, the resources are in fact owned by multiple organizations.

Second, the satisfaction of users and the performance of applications is determined by the simultaneous application of multiple resources. For example, a multimedia server application requires I/O bandwidth to retrieve content, CPU time to execute server logic and protocols, and networking bandwidth to deliver the content to clients. The performance of applications may also be altered by trading resources. For example, a multimedia server application may perform better by releasing memory and acquiring higher CPU priority , resulting in smaller buffers for I/O and networking but improving the performance of the communication protocol execution .

Finally, in a large distributed system , the set of systems, users and applications is continuously changing. In this chapter we address some of the issues of Quality of Service (QoS) and pricing, and efficient allocation of resources (computational resources) in networks and systems.

. Boston: Harvard Business School Press

REFERENCES

Arrow, K.J. (1993), 'Innovation and Increasing Returns to Scale', in *Endogeneous Growth and Innovations*, London: MacMillan, 403-408

Arthur,W.Brian (2000), 'Myths and Realities of the High-Tech Economy', Talk given at Credit Suisse First Boston (CSFB) Thought Leader Forum, Sept. 10

Baumol,W.J. (2002), *The Free-Market Innovation Machine: Analyzing the Growth Miracle of Capitalism*, Princeton and Oxford: Princeton Univ. Press

Besanko,D., Dranove, D. and Shanley, M. (1999), *Economics of Strategy*, New York: John Wiley & Sons

Browne,S. (2000), 'Stochastic Differential Portfolio Games', *Journal of Applied Probability.* 37,126-147

Cane, A. (2004), 'No free lunch, no free software' , *Financial Times.* March 31

Choi,J.P (1993), "Cooperative R&D with Product Market Competition", *International Journal of Industrial Organization.* 11, 553-571

Clark,K.B. and Fujimoto,T. (1991), *Product Development Performance*, Boston, Ma.: Harvard Business School Press

Cox, Andrew; Ireland, P., Lonsdale,C., Sanderson,J., Watson,G. (2002), *Supply chains, markets and power: Mapping buyer and supplier power regimes.* London: Routledge

Dasgupta, P.(1986), 'The Theory of Technological Competition', in K. Binmore and P. Dasgupta (eds.), *Economic Organizations as Games.* Oxford: Basil Blackwell, 139-164

Dasgupta, P.;Stiglitz ,J.(1981), 'Resource Depletion under Technological Uncertaintv', *Econometrica.* 49, 85-104.

D'Aspremont,C. and A. Jacquemin (1988), "Cooperative and Noncooperative R&D in Duopoly with Spillover", *American Economic Review.* 78, 1133-37

Dockner,E., Jorgensen,S.; VanLong, N. and G. Sorger (2000), *Differential Games in Economics and Management Science.* Cambridge: Cambridge Univ. Press

Dorfman,N.(1987), *Innovation and Market Structure: Lessons from the Computer and Semiconductor Industries.* Boston: Ballinger

Evans,D.S. and R. Schmalensee (2001)'Some Economic Aspects of Antitrust Analysis in Dynamically Competitive Industries', National Bureau of Economic Research, Cambridge, MA. Working Paper 8268, http://www.nber.org/papers/w8268

Fine,C,H, (1999), *Clockspeed: Winning Industry Control in the Age of Temporary Advantage.* New York: Perseus

Fisher,F.M., Gowan,J. and Greenwood,J.E.(1983), *Folded, Spindled and Mutulated, Economic Analysis and U.S. v. IBM*, Cambridge,Ma: MIT Press

Gottinger, H.W. (2003), *Economies of Network Industries* , London: Routledge

Gottinger,H.W. (2006), *Innovation, Technology and Hypercompetition*, London: Routledge

Grossman, G.M. and Shapiro,C. (1986),"Research Joint Venture: An Antitrust Analysis", *Journal of Law, Economics and Organization.* 2,315-337

Kamien,M.I. , Muller,E. and Zang,I. (1992), "Research Joint Ventures and R&D Cartels", *American Economic Review.* 82, 1293-1306

Katz, M.L.. (1986),"An Analysis of Cooperative Research and Development", *Rand Journal of Economics.* 17, 527-543

Katz,M. And C. Shapiro (1992)'Product Introduction with Network Externalities', *The Journal of Industrial Economics.* 40, 55-83

Harris,C., and Vickers,J.(1995),'Innovation and natural resources: A dynamic game with uncertainty',*The Rand Journal of Economics.* 26(3), 418-430

Kidder, M (1986), *The Soul of a New Machine.* New York: Norton

Moss,Kanter,R.(2006), 'Innovation: The Classical Traps', *Harvard Business Review.* Nov. 2006, 72-83

Porter,M. E.(1979),'How Competitive Forces shape Strategy', Chapt 1 in *On competition*, Boston: Harvard Business School Press, 21-38

Porter, M.E. and Teisberg, E.O. (2006), *Redefining Health Care: Creating Value Based Competition on Results*

Robson,A.J.(1990),'Duopoly with Endogeneous Strategic Timing: Stackelberg Regained', *International Economic Review.* 31, 25-35

Schumpeter,J.A.(1942), *Capitalism, Socialism and Democracy.* New York: Harper

Sutton, J.(2001), *Technology and Market Structure.* Cambridge, Ma: MIT Press

Shapiro, C. (1989) ,"Theories of Oligopoly Behavior", in *Handbook of Industrial Organization.* Vol. 1,

R. Schmalensee and R.D. Willig, eds., Amsterdam: North Holland, 329-414

Suzumura, K (1995), *Competition, Commitment and Welfare.* Oxford: Clarendon Press

Teece, D.J., Pisano, G. and A. Shuen (1997), 'Dynamic Capabilities and Strategic Management', *Strategic Management Journal.* 18(7), 509-533

Uttenback,J.M. (1994) *Mastering the Dynamics of Innovation.* Boston: Harvard Business School Press

Varian,H R., Farrell,J. and Shapiro,C. (2004),The *Economics of Information Technology.* Cambridge: Cambridge Univ. Press

Vickers, J. (1986), "The Evolution of Market Structure When There is A Sequence of Innovations', *Journal of Industrial Economics.* 35, 1-12.

Williamson, O.E. (1975), *Markets and Hierarchies: Analysis and Anti-trust Implications.* The New York: The Free Press

Williamson, O.E. (1985), *The Economic Institutions of Capitalism.* New York: The Free Press

Williamson, O.E. (1999),'Strategy Research: Governance and Competence Perspectives', *Strategic Management Journal.* 20, 1087-1109

Wilson, R., Ashton,P. and Egan,T.(1980), *Innovation, Competition, and Government Policy in the Semiconductor Industry.* Lexington, Ma.: D.C. Heath

Chapter 1

1. HIGH SPEED TECHNOLOGY COMPETITION (HSTC)

1.1. INTRODUCTION

In highly competitive technological industries new challenges and opportunities are arising in the new product development arena. Driven by global markets, global competition, the global dispersion of scientific/engineering talent, and the advent of new information and communication technologies (ICT) a new vision of product development is that of a highly disaggregated , distributive process with people and organizations spread throughout the world. At the same time products are becoming increasingly complex requiring numerous engineering decisions to bring them to market. Competitive pressures mean that 'time to market' has become a key to new product success. However, at the same time it is important to keep the innovation and quality dimensions of the new product at their optimal level.

A central question to address is how should firms invest in innovation and what are the implications of such investments for competitive advantage? Understanding why a firm benefits from investments in innovation and quality illuminates issues of competitive strategy and industrial organization. In the field of competitive strategy, much attention has been devoted to the concept of core capabilities (Teece et al., 1997). Understanding how firms make optimal investments in the face of competition reveals the nature of competition and provides theoretical and managerial implications for developing core competence and dynamic capabilities.

In major parts of competitive analysis involving R&D decisions the focus is on breakthrough innovations which could create entirely new markets, for example, in studies featuring patent racing between competing firms. In more common competitive situations we observe firms, however, competing by investing in incremental improvements of products. It is an important aspect when innovation is considered to be manifested in product quality, process improvements and in the overall quality culture of an organization (Moss Kanter, 2006). For example, after product launch, incremental improvement of different aspects of product quality, improvements in various business processes and an incremental adoption of a quality culture are quite real-world phenomena. Some firms operate in a simultaneous product launch situation while others compete sequentially by adopting the role of leader or follower.

The strategic implications in these diverse circumstances can be treated within a unified framework of dynamic stochastic differential games.

In recent years with the emergence of e-business and a supply chain view for product development processes, multiple firms with varying and at times conflicting objectives enter into collaborative arrangements. In such situations, the competitive strategy based on quality and innovation could potentially permeate in those collaborative setups. A recent example is the collaborative venture of Sony and Samsung to build a cutting edge plant for LCD flat screen TV though displaying ongoing fierce rivalry in new product launches in exactly the same product categories. When innovation and quality levels form the core of a firm's capabilities, each member in the supply chain would have an incentive to invest and improve their dynamic capabilities. This leads to tacit competition among collaborative product development partners by means of active investment in innovation and quality.

Although the forces of innovation are central to competition in young, technically dynamic industries, they also affect mature industries where life cycles historically were relatively strong, technologies mature, and demands stable.

A strategy for technology must confront primarily what the focus of technical development will be. The question is what technologies are critical to the firm's competitive advantage. In this context, technology must include the know-how the firm needs to create, produce and market its products and deliver them to customers. As a major step in creating a technology strategy it has to define those capabilities where the firm seeks to achieve a distinctive advantage relative to competitors. For most firms, there are a large number of important areas of technological know-how but only a handful where the firm will seek to create truly superior capability.

Having determined the focus of technical development and the source of capability, the firm must establish the timing and frequency for innovation efforts. Part of the timing issue involves developing technical capabilities, and the rest involves introducing technology into the market. The frequency of implementation and associated risks will depend in part on the nature of the technology and the markets involved (e.g. disk drive vs. automotive technology), but in part on strategic choice. At the extreme, a firm may adopt a rapid incremental strategy, that is, frequent, small changes in technology that cumulatively lead to continuous performance improvement. The polar opposite might be termed the great leap forward strategy. In this approach, a firm chooses to make infrequent but large-scale changes in technology that substantially advance the state of the art (Chapt.7).

As an example of the importance of innovation strategy in product development we notice that IBM created and continues to dominate the mainframe segment , but it missed by many years the emergence of the minicomputer architecture and market. The minicomputer was developed and its market applications exploited by firms such as Digital Equipment Corp.(DEC) and Data General (DG.) back in the nineteen seventies.

Summarizing, in a mainstream scenario, high speed technological competition is likely to be driven by

a companies competing in fast changing, diverse networks, and

b companies confronted with ever shortening product/technology life cycles because of multiple interactions between current and emerging technologies and product diversity, or what may be circumscribed as 'combinatorial innovation' (Varian,2005).

A neat example is provided by Arthur(2000,p.3):

> "If you look at genomics , it is certainly heavily based on biology, but it is also highly dependent on digital computing ...Genomics, then, is as much a manifestation of digital computing as it is a manifestation of molecular biology. What happens is that some of the new technologies become base technologies, and these give rise to manifestations, some of which themselves become base technologies. Manfestations then appear at an even faster rate."

To represent the features of leader-follower type in a sequence of technological racing we consider a class of differential games in which some firms have priority of moves over others.

The firm that has the right to move first is called the leader and the other competing firm is called the follower. A well-known example of this type of sequential move game is the Stackelberg model of duopoly. In this type of interaction the open-loop Nash equilibrium conditions in a sequential move game can be derived. It would lead to a comparison of the strategies of leader and the follower.

In what follows, Section 1.2 presents the essence of leader-follower type interactions through the format of a differential game which is accommodated to a competitive market situation in Section 1.3. The properties of their interactions are derived in Section 1.4. Section 1.5 handles various market asymmetries in the leader follower type situation.

Finally, Section 1.6 summarizes and draws up conclusions and directions for future research.

1.2. A Differential Game Formulation

For our modelling effort we follow the notations and symbols as explained below.

N: number of firms, *T*: finite time horizon for the strategies, *i,j:* superscripts to denote competing firms in a duopoly, *t:* an instant of time in the dynamic game setup, *u(t):* investments in innovation effort (expenditure per unit time), *R(t)*: net revenue rate for the firm at t, R_o product category net revenue rate for the existing product, R_l : product category net revenue rate for the new product, x_o: quality level of the existing product.

Several examples illustrate the importance of innovation and quality as competitive weapons. In the computer mainframe arena IBM replaced Remington Rand and Sperry Univac as market leader in the 1950s, and its subsequent growth outperformed its competitors so rapidly that in 1963 its data process revenues were four times larger than the combined revenues of its eight main rivals in the US market (Hofmann, 1976).

In the model we assume that enhancements of quality are achieved by climbing a performance ladder that may squarely embrace technology but could expand to other criteria uniquely identified with quality. Let the quality of the product at time *t* be *x(t)*. In the context of total quality management , as quality levels increase it becomes even more difficult to climb the performance ladder. The hypothesis behind the formulation is that a firm needs to make higher innovation investments targeted towards improvement of quality. To capture this dynamics a negative feedback effect of the present state quality on the rate of change of product quality ($x^{\bullet}(t)$) is considered. The state dynamics is

$$x^{\bullet}(t) = K[u(t)]^{\alpha} - Lx(t) \tag{1}$$

where K is proportional to the level of capital investment in development technology and L is the proportionality constant for the influence of present quality on the speed of further quality improvements, α is the innovation resource productivity parameter.

Based on (1) the quality of the product at time t is

$$x(t) = x_o \int_0^t [K[u(s)]^{\alpha} - Lx(s)]\, ds \tag{2}$$

The product quality provides a means for evaluating the product's attractiveness in the market in the presence of other competing products. The firm's market share is a function of both its own product quality and the product quality of rivals.(The initial product quality x_o may reflect the reputational capital of the firm, either low or high, and may induce her to different innovation investment efforts) The difference lies in the planning horizon. In this competitive setup, the planning horizon extends beyond the date of launch and the competing firms continue investing in product-process innovation until the end of the growth phase of a product. Further,

$$R(t) = \begin{cases} R_0 \cdot \dfrac{x_0}{x_0^i + x_0^j}, & 0 \le t < T_p, \\ R_1 \cdot \dfrac{x^i(T)}{x^i(T) + x^j(T)}, & T_p \le t < T, \end{cases} \tag{3}$$

The cumulative development cost of the new product at time t is given as:

$$TC(t) = \int_0^T \{u(s)\}\, ds \tag{4}$$

the firm's cumulative profit at time t is determined as follows,

$$T\Pi(t) = TR(t) - TC(t), \tag{5}$$

where $TR(t)$ *and* $TC(T)$ are total revenues and costs at time t, respectively. The total revenue function is given by:

$$TR(t) = \int_0^T R(s)\, ds \tag{6}$$

where $R(\cdot)$ is given in (3). The firm's decision set is $\Delta = \{u(t)\}$. Notice that the firm pre-commits on the date of product launch T_p. The cumulative profit function, $T\,\Pi(\delta)$, is defined as the total profit by end of the window of opportunity with decision $\delta \in \Delta$. The firm's decision problem can be stated as,

$$\max_{\delta \in \Delta} T\Pi(\delta) = TR(\delta^*) - TC(\delta^*) = T\Pi^*(\delta^*) \tag{7}$$

The combination of equations (1) through (6) generates an explicit representation of firm i's cumulative profit by the end of time horizon. This substitution yields:

$$T\Pi^*(\delta^*) = \max_{\delta \in \Delta}[R_0 \cdot \frac{x_0}{x_0^i + x_0^j} \cdot T_p + R_1 \cdot \frac{x_0 + \int_0^T K_1[u(s)]^\alpha - Lx(s)ds}{x_0 + \int_0^T K[u(s)]^\alpha - Lx(s)ds + x^j(T)} \cdot (T - T_p) - - \int_0^T \{u(s)\}ds] \tag{8}$$

where $x_0{}^j$ and $x^j(T)$ respectively are the quality of existing and new products of the competitor. Considering a duopoly, the optimization problem written above can be reformulated as a differential game problem with state variable for the firm i (the competing firm is represented by superscript j) given as $x^i(t)$; the control variable $u^i(t)$. In the terminology used in optimal control and differential games, the salvage term for firm i,

$\Phi^i(T, x(T))$ is defined as follows:

$$\Phi^i(T,x(T)) \triangleq R_0 \cdot \frac{x_0^i}{x_0^i + x_0^j} \cdot T_p^i + R_1 \cdot \frac{\left\{x_0^i + \int_0^T K_1[u^i(s)]^{\alpha^i} - L_1 x^i(s)ds\right\}(T - T_p)}{x_0^i + \int_0^T K_1[u^i(s)]^{\alpha^i} - L_1 x^i(s)ds + x^j(T)} \tag{9}$$

where

$$x^j(T) = x_0^j + \int_0^T \left[K_2[u^j(s)]^{\alpha^i} - L_2 x^j(s)\right]ds \tag{10}$$

1.3. A Sequential Differential Game between Two Competing Firms

We extend the conceptualization of a hyper-competitive scenario by considering a sequential differential game as being representative of a leader-follower or incumbent-entrant competitive situation. The game is characterized by information asymmetry where the follower is aware of the innovation and quality levels of the leader`s products. The motivation for considering this scenario is its close correspondence with many real life competitive cases in high technology markets which recur in Chapt. 7 .Knowing the investment strategy of the leader , the rival firms can formulate their own strategies. Therefore, the firm acting as a leader chooses a decision path that maximizes the objective for all conceivable responses that can be taken by the follower(s). In the case of sequential games a hierarchical play differential game approach is used to model the competitive situation and to obtain the open-loop Stackelberg Nash equilibrium. The issue of subgame perfectness and commitment is extremely important in these solutions.Adding to the previous notation we let T_p, date of product launch by leader, $T_p + \tau$, date of product launch by follower. The leader is represented by the superscript i and the follower is represented by the superscript j. Since it is a sequential game the time of product launch for the two players is such that the leader launches the product at time T_p. Later, the follower launches the product after time τ at $T_p + \tau$. A continuous improvement in the product is considered and therefore the entire time interval $t \in [0,T]$ for the leader , and $t \in [T_p,T]$ for the follower needs to be optimized. The state dynamics of the leader is

$$x^{\bullet i}(t) = K_1[u^i(t)]^\alpha - L_1x^i(t) \tag{11}$$

The rate of quality improvement $x^{\bullet i}(t)$ increases with investments $u^i(t)$. The factor $L_1x^i(t)$ suggests a natural decay in quality in the absence of any investments. The differential game formulation for leader is:

$$max\ T\Pi^i\ (u^i(t),T_p) = -\int_0^T \{(u^i(s)\}ds + \Phi^i(T, x^i(T)\} \tag{12}$$

with the first component under the integral identifying the investment costs and the second the returns on investment (ROI)

where $\Phi^i(T, x^i(T)$ is defined as

$$\Phi^i(T, x^i(T) \cong R_0 \cdot x_0^i/(x_0^i + x_0^j) \cdot T_p^i + R_1 \cdot x^i(T)(\tau)/(x^i(T)+x_0^j) + \\ + R_1 \cdot x^i(T)(T - T_p - \tau)/(x^i(T)+x^i(T)) \tag{13}$$

subject to

$$x^\bullet(t) = K_1[u^i(t)]^\alpha - L_1x^i(t)\ ,\ x^i(0) = x_0^i\ ,\ T\ fixed,\ x^i(T)\ free. \tag{14}$$

Next, the follower's problem formulation is discussed. Owing to the sequential nature of the game , the information about the leader's quality and about the leader's investments is known to the follower.

Specifically, it is assumed that the knowledge gained by the leader's investments "spills over" to the follower's quality improvement dynamics. It is plausible to assume that in the context of a leader-follower competition, the level of quality improvements of the follower indeed depends not only on its own innovation efforts but also on the knowledge pool available because of the leader's investments. The fact that the leader often cannot wholy conceal his efforts nor can he credibly announce the commitment he has made, make the situation quite complicated. To address these issues fully in this context would require a subtle and rich analysis of games with incomplete information (Robson, 1990).

A formal treatment of "spillover effects" would enrich this model .The spillover effect is modeled by considering a linear additive term $M_2u^i(t)$. The follower`s state dynamics is

$$x^{\bullet j}(t) = K_2[u^j(t)]^{\alpha} - L_2x^j(t) + M_2u^i(t) \tag{15}$$

It is assumed that the spillover is a function of the investments made by the leader $u^i(t)$. In this term M_2 is some number which quantifies the amount of spillover from the leader to the follower. The term $M_2u^i(t)$ would restrict the analysis to the case where the follower emulates the innovation and product quality of the leader , as opposed to setting his own technology and quality standards. Now with all considerations wrapped up, a leader-follower dynamics can be stated..

The follower's differential game formulation is given as:

$$\begin{aligned} max\, T\Pi^j(u^j(t),T_p) &= -\int_{T_p}^{T}\{u^j(s)\}ds + \Phi^j(T,x^j(T)) = \\ &= -\int_0^{T-T_p}\{u^j(s+T_p)\}ds + \Phi^j(T,x^j(T)) \end{aligned} \tag{16}$$

where $\Phi^j(T, x(T))$ is defined as,

$$\begin{aligned} \Phi^j(T,x(T)) \underline{\underline{\Delta}}\, R_0 \cdot \frac{x_0^j}{x_0^i + x_0^j} \cdot T_p + \\ + R_0 \cdot \frac{x_0^j}{x^i(T) + x_0^j} \cdot \tau + R_1 \cdot \frac{\{x^j(T)(T - T_p - \tau)\}}{x^i(T) + x^j(T)} \end{aligned} \tag{17}$$

subject to

$$x^j(t) = K_2\left[u^j(t)\right]^{\alpha} - L_2x^j(t) + M_2u^i(t) \tag{18}$$

where $M_2u^i(t)$ represent the spillover of knowledge, assumed to be a function of investments by the leader, M_2 is a small constant such that $0 < M_2 << 1$.

Furthermore, $x^j(0) = x_0^j$, T fixed, $x^j(T)$ free where

$$x^i(T) = x_0^i + \int_0^t \left[K_1 \left[u^i(s)\right]^{\alpha^i} - L_1 x^i(s) \right] ds \tag{19}$$

$$x^j(T) = x_0^j + \int_{T_p}^t \left[K_2 \left[u^j(s)\right]^{\alpha^j} - L_2 x^j(s) + M_2 u^i(s) \right] ds \tag{20}$$

In this type of competitive game with a lagged response of the follower we would approach a catchup equilibrium as displayed in Fig. 2.1

1.4. Analysis of the Model and Discussion

A conventional tool for solving the problem is the application of Pontryagin's maximum principle for open-loop Stackelberg equilibrium conditions. Interested readers can refer Dockner et al. (2000) for details regarding Pontryagin's approach to solving sequential differential game problems. The equilibrium results are expressed in the form of properties as given below.

Equilibrium Results

Property 1. The maximized costate variables for the follower are function of time and are given by,

$$\lambda_1^* = \lambda_{01} e^{L_2 t} \tag{21}$$

$$\lambda_2^* = \lambda_{02} e^{L_1 t} \tag{22}$$

where λ_1^* and λ_2^* are the costate variables reflecting the marginal price for a unit increase in follower firm's own state and the state of the leader i, $\lambda_1(0) = \lambda_{01}$, $\lambda_2(0) = \lambda_{02}$ are known constants.

Property 2. The Stackelberg equilibrium investment by the follower in product development is given as:

$$u^j(t)^* = \left[K_2 \alpha^j \lambda_{01} e^{L_2 t}\right]^{\frac{1}{1-\alpha^j}} \tag{23}$$

Next the leader's problem is investigated. The leader knows the follower's best response to each control path $u^i(\cdot)$.

Property 3. The maximized costate variables for the leader are given by,

$$\psi_1^* = \psi_{01} e^{L_1 t} \tag{24}$$

$$\psi_2^* = \psi_{02} e^{L_2 t} \tag{25}$$

$$\psi_3^* = -\psi_{03} e^{-L_2 t} \tag{26}$$

where ψ_1^*, ψ_2^* and ψ_3^* are the costate variables reflecting the marginal price for a unit increase in the leader's own state, the state of the follower and the costate of the follower. ψ_{01}, ψ_{02} and ψ_{03} are constants.

Property 4. The Stackelberg equilibrium investment by the leader in product development is given as:

$$u^i(t)^* = \left[\frac{K_1 \alpha^i \psi_{01} e^{L_1 t}}{1 - M_2 \psi_{02} e^{L_2 t}}\right]^{\frac{1}{1-\alpha^i}} \tag{27}$$

Property 5. The equilibrium state trajectory of performance improvement of the follower is given as:

$$x^j(t) = \frac{e^{-L_2 t}}{L_2}\Big[L_2 x_0^j + (-1 + e^{L_2 t}) M_2 \left[\frac{K_1 \alpha^i \psi_{01} e^{L_1 t}}{1 - M_2 \psi_{02} e^{L_2 t}}\right]^{\frac{1}{1-\alpha^i}} + \\ + (-1 + e^{L_2 t}) K_2 (K_2 \alpha^j \lambda_{01} e^{L_2 t})^{\frac{\alpha^j}{(1-\alpha^j)^2}}\Big] \tag{28}$$

Property 6. The equilibrium state trajectory of performance improvement of the leader is given as:

$$x^i(t) = \frac{e^{-L_1 t}}{L_1}\left[L_1 x_0^i + (-1 + e^{L_1 t}) K_1 \left[\frac{K_1 \alpha^i \psi_{01} e^{L_1 t}}{1 - M_2 \psi_{02} e^{L_2 t}}\right]^{\frac{\alpha^i}{1-\alpha^i}}\right] \tag{29}$$

For the analysis, assuming behavioural interchangability between leader and the follower we can expect a corresponding convergence path for both leader and follower.

The first observation is that the costate variable of both the leader and the follower increases more rapidly with time.

The marginal utility of a unit increase in quality, exhibits a convex increasing trajectory. With comparable values of parameters the plot of the costate trajectory of the follower has an upward exponential drift with time. The plot begins at time $t = T_p$, since the follower initiates product development activities only after the leader has already launched the product. Regarding the costate trajectory of the leader we see that ψ_l represents marginal utility from a unit increase in quality of the leader's product .The costate variable for both the leader and the follower firm increase for the entire planning horizon. This follows since the leader and follower are competing on the basis of their quality levels. Firms increase their market shares based on their relative quality to that of the competitor's. After launch the product faces its introduction and growth stage.

In these phases, maintaining higher quality becomes even more important since the product sales are directly influenced by product quality. This leads to a convex increasing trajectory for the costate variable. Thus, as a second observation:

The investment in innovation made by the follower increases more rapidly with time.

The investment strategies of the follower are purely a function of its own costate variable. The follower's costate variable increases in a convex fashion. This in turn results in a convex increase in follower's control trajectory. With identical parameter values we can derive that the follower compensates for a delayed entry into the market by increasing its investment intensity. Such an increase in investment results in increased quality and therefore high total revenue for the follower. Thus we observe:

The investment in innovation made by the leader initially increases rapidly with time but later increases at a decreasing rate.

The leader's investment trajectory is sigmoidal or S-shaped. Because of the nature of the game, the leader enters the market before the follower. While formulating his equilibrium investment strategy, the leader takes into account the evolution of his own costate and also the costate of the follower.

Being early in the market, the leader takes into account all possible courses of action that a follower may choose.

We note that the leader's rate of investment increases in the initial phase and then starts to decrease. That is, the leader *capitalizes* on the advantage of early market entry by increasing the intensity of investments and gaining a high market share. Subsequently, after the follower's entry, the leader reduces the intensity of investments and thereby reduces the amount of spillover that is potentially possible.

When the parameter values of the leader and follower are identical, the follower invests higher than the leader.

In the course of time initially the follower maps its investment strategy to that of the leader. However subsequently the leader starts reducing the rate of investments, while the follower continues with the high investment rate based strategy.

As a further observation, the rate of increase of the follower's product quality increases with time.

The quality of follower's product increases for the entire time-horizon. Moreover, this increase is a convex function. As can be inferred from the problem formulation, the quality level of the follower is a function of investments made by the leader and the follower. Specifically, the quality trajectory is influenced by both the convex profile of investments made by the follower and also by the spillover effect of the investments made by the leader. This results in a convex increase in quality improvements. The state trajectory is therefore upward sloping in convex form.

The follower starts accruing revenue only after $T_p + \tau$, where T_p is the date of launch of the leader. In the game context of quality-based competition, the follower compensates for the delayed entry by increasing the quality levels at a fast rate.

The rate of increase of the leader's product quality decreases with time.

The leader's investment trajectory follows an S-shaped trajectory. In the problem formulation the leader's quality improvement is only a function of its own investments. Moreover, it is assumed that the leader doesn't obtain the advantages of spillover of knowledge gained by the follower's investments.

Furthermore, the leader needs to deliberately avoid maintaining very high investments to ensure that the follower doesn't achieve huge gains from spillovers. Under such a setup it must be noted that the leader chooses an S-shaped trajectory for investments. In such an investment profile the investment increases rapidly in the initial phase but then eventually tapers off. Corresponding to this investment profile, the rate of quality improvement is high in the initial phase but then eventually the rate of improvement starts decreasing. Thus, the quality trajectory of the leader is concave. This leads to another observation.

When the parameter values of the leader and follower are identical, the quality of the follower's product is higher than that of the leader's product.

With identical parameter values the follower and leader are perfectly symmetric in their capabilities.

Moreover, the leader has the advantage of earlier market entry, whereas the follower obtains the gains of information asymmetry and the associated knowledge spillovers from the leader. It is reasonable to assume that the follower employs his inherent competence and the benefit of spillover of knowledge from the leader's investments to increase quality at a much faster rate. Under such circumstances the overall gain and loss in the competitive game is dictated by the relative revenues achieved and the costs incurred by the two players. With higher investments than the leader the follower incurs higher costs. At the same time these investments also lead to higher quality levels and therefore revenues for the follower. In the event of the value of R_l being very high the follower wins the game while the results favour the leader if R_l is low.

1.5. Asymmetries in Firm Capabilities

We now turn to firm asymmetries and their implications. It is likely that firms take up the role of leader and follower based on inherent strengths and weaknesses. In this type of situation, firm asymmetries would turn technically into a non-zero sum differential game whose structure has been studied by Yao and Weyant (2004). Therefore, an explicit consideration of firm asymmetries is very important and could potentially lend more insights in a sequential game setup.

In practical termsAsymmetries may be addressed in at least four ways:

First, it is possible that organizational approaches and techniques (such as total quality management) can be used to make the product development process more cost-efficient and effective. This would influence the value of the resource productivity parameter α.

Second, it is possible to have an advantage in product development by making capital investment in technology development. This is equivalent to considering asymmetries in the value of K.

Third, it is possible that the obsolescence parameter of firms denoted by L is different.

Finally, different values of M suggest different levels of spillover of knowledge from the leader's investments to the follower. The firm with higher value of L has a higher obsolescence or decay in quality.

We restrict assessment of asymmetries by considering different values for the parameters: (α^i and α^j),

(K_1 *and* K_2), (L_1 *and* L_2) and (M_1 *and* M_2).

Innovation Resource Productivity

Parameters α^i and α^j denote the innovation resource productivity parameter of the two firms. An asymmetry could result if the competing firms have differing capabilities in making a productive use of investments. The skill set of employees, training and development activities, the quality culture are some of the reasons for such an asymmetry. For example,(α^i = 0.2) > (α^j = 0.1) suggest that firm i has a higher innovation productivity over j. An investigation of different values of α suggest that the firm with higher innovation productivity also invests a higher amount in product development. From the results we observe that the follower has a relatively higher level of investments in innovation as compared to the leader. Therefore, an increase in the value of α of the follower will only result in making these investments still higher. Instead, an increase in leader's α would provide some interesting insights in that it will show that the leader sails ahead with the follower having no chance in catching up. It clearly shows that the leader has a higher investment than that of the follower for almost the entire planning horizon. As can also be noted , the quality of the leader's product is always higher than that of the follower. Hence an asymmetry in terms of resource productivity parameters provides a totally different result than what was observed when the competing firms were symmetric. It suggests that the leader with an advantage in terms of early market entry as well as a higher level of resource productivity indeed continues having higher revenues. Under this situation the leader doesn't worry much about the spillover to the follower since its own resource productivity enables attaining higher revenues by increasing quality levels relative to that of the follower. With a high value of R_I it can be conjectured that the result favours the leader.

Capital Investment Parameters

Firm asymmetries can be analyzed by evaluating different values for K and the implications on control and state trajectories. K_I *and* K_2 are proportional to the level of capital investment in development technology by the two competing firms. If $(K_1 = 20) > (K_2 = 10)$, it suggests that the leader i has higher levels of capital investment in development technology as compared to the follower *j*.

The implications of a higher value of *K* for the leader can easily be derived. The parameter *K* exerts a positive effect on innovation investments. Similar to the conjecture regarding different values of α, the intuition behind this effect is that with a higher level of capital investments in development technology, a firm targets the investments towards increasing the product quality. Thus with a higher value of K the investment by the leader is relatively higher than that of the follower for most part of the planning horizon.

However, in the latter part of the planning horizon, the follower's investment in fact shoots up while that of the leader tapers off. Such an investment profile would have an impact on the state trajectory.

Furthermore, the product quality of the leader is higher than that of the follower for most part of the planning horizon. Eventually, at the end of the planning horizon, the high growth in the follower's investment results in higher quality than that of the leader.

In the model, the relative difference *in* resources due *to* strategic investments is captured in asymmetries in the value of *K*. Given adequately high values of R_I, the leader i would have relatively higher profits than the follower j.

The Obsolescence Parameter

L_1 and L_2 characterize the decay or in other words the obsolescence effect of quality. Different values of L_1 and L_2 help evaluate the difference among the two firms regarding this effect. $(L_I = I) > (L_2 = 0.7)$ suggests that the obsolescence effect for leader i is higher than that for the follower j. An investigation into the dynamics of innovation investments reveals that with higher value of the parameter L, a firm would make higher level of investments.

Interestingly, with a difference in L_1 and L_2 the shape of investment trajectory of the leader is now convex. That is when the leader faces a high obsolescence effect the investments are increased at a faster rate to ensure an increasing state trajectory. However, as opposed to parameter a and K such an increased control trajectory doesn't translate into higher quality. In fact, in this situation, the leader has lower product quality in spite .of higher investments. A high decay effect puts the leader into a disadvantageous position. In such a situation, under equilibrium control the leader always loses the competitive game.

Spillover Factor M_2

M_2 characterizes the amount of spillover from the leader to the follower. In this section the impact of reduction of the spillover factor M_2 is considered. Evidently in this case the leader would be less worried about the amount of advantage the follower obtains from the leader's own investments. If the spillover effect is low, the leader pursues investments more aggressively, consistent with the incentive enhancement of spillover effects in the context of network externalities (Saaskilahti, 2006). Under such circumstances, the control trajectory of the leader is also convexly increasing and is only marginally lower than that of the follower.

Regarding the impact of such investments on the state trajectory , the quality of the follower is higher than that of the leader and both obtain a convex increasing state trajectory. But unlike α, K and L, a different value of M_2 doesn't correspond to any advantage related to resources, core competence or dynamic capabilities. This is purely an exogenously defined variable based on technology and industry types. Under changed circumstances with respect to M_2 the leader doesn't really gain much in the competitive game. The results in fact point to the follower winning the game due to much higher levels of quality and only marginally higher levels of investments.

1.6. Conclusions and Extensions

There is apparently a paradox in trying to assess, both empirically and theoretically, the impact of competitive pressure on innovation and growth. On one hand, according to the tradition originating in Schumpeter (1942) the prospective reward provided by monopoly rent to a successful innovator is required to stimulate sufficient R&D investment and technological progress.

On the other hand, the incentives to innovate are weaker for an incumbent monopolist than for a firm in a competitive industry (Arrow, 1962). When competition is intense in the product market, innovation may even be seen as the only way for a firm to survive. In neo-Schumpeterian models of endogenous growth(Grossman and Helpman, 1991; Aghion and Howitt, 1992), innovation allows a firm in an industry to take the lead and gain profit. But the monopoly rent enjoyed by the winner is only temporary, and a new innovator, capitalizing on accumulated knowledge, is always able to "leapfrog" the leader unless the leader is endowed with advantages of firm asymmetries.

In the recent research literature, Aghion, Harris and Vickers (1997), and Aghion, Harris, Howitt and Vickers (2001), supposing a duopoly in each sector, both, at the research and production levels, have introduced what they call "step-by-step innovation," according to which technological progress allows a firm to take the lead, but with the lagging firm remaining active and eventually capable of catching up. This model has been extended by Encaoua and Ulph (2000), allowing for the possibility that the lagging firm leapfrogs the leader, without driving it out of the market. Here we adopt a simplified approach to consider spillover effects. Griliches(1979) lays out the conceptual framework and provides an early discussion of the importance of spillover effects of R&D. Later in 1992, Griliches reviewed the recent empirical evidence on spillovers, and tentatively concluded that spillover effects may be substantial.The model can be extended by evaluating the improvement in product quality with learning effect . This effect is very well documented in the literature and thus the extension to incorporate learning effects is straightforward. Specifically, learning can be used to characterize the dynamics of evolution of product quality and the characterization of costs associated with innovation investments.

For analytical simplicity the revenue function is treated as a salvage value. As an extension the incorporation of the dynamics of revenue in the analysis of the model can be explored. In the sequential play game , the state dynamics of the follower can be considered to be dependent on the state of the leader at previous time instant.

This modification would allow for analysis of a model in which the leader uses open-loop Nash equilibrium strategy for innovation investments whereas the follower would adopt a Markovian Nash equilibrium strategy.

Additional insights can be gained by this modification for leader-follower competitive dynamics in new product development.

Firm asymmetries can be explored by considering multiple parameters at the same time. This would enable a richer understanding of the strategies that a leader and a follower should adopt based on their strengths and weaknesses.

The conventional approach used in innovation and R&D research viewed the process as one with constant returns, competitive output and factor markets and no externalities. However, such a framework doesn't offer a full explanation of productivity growth. For a better understanding it therefore becomes very important to consider increasing returns to scale, R&D spillovers and other externalities and disequilibria.

REFERENCES

Aghion,P. , Harris, C. and J. Vickers (1997), 'Competition and Growth with Step-by-Step Innovation: An Example', *Review of Economic Studies.* 41, 771-782

Aghion,P., Harris, C., Howitt, P.. and J. Vickers (2001), 'Competition, Imitation and Growth with Step-by-Step Innovation', *Review of Economic Studies.* 68, 467-492

Aghion, P. and P. Howitt (1992), 'A Model of Growth through Creative Destruction", *Econometrica.* 60, 323-352

Arrow, K. (1962), 'The Economic Implications of Learning by Doing', *Review of Economic Studies.* 29, 155-173

Arthur,W.Brian (2000), 'Myths and Realities of the High-Tech Economy', Talk given at Credit Suisse First Boston (CSFB) Thought Leader Forum, Sept. 10

Dockner,E., Jorgensen,S.; VanLong, N. and G. Sorger (2000), *Differential Games in Economics and Management Science.* Cambridge: Cambridge Univ. Press

Encaoua, D. and D. Ulph (2000), 'Catching-up or Leapfrogging', *Cahiers de la MSE. 5, 10-22*

Griliches, Z. (1979), 'Issues in Assessing the Contribution of Research and Development to Productivity Growth', *The Bell Journal of Economics.* 10(1), 92-116

Griliches, Z (1992), 'The Search of R&D Spillovers', *The Scandinavian Journal of Economics.* 94, S29-S47

Grossman, G. and Helpman, E.(1991),*Innovation and Growth in the Global Economy.* Cambridge, Ma.:MIT Press

Hoffman, W.D.(1976), 'Market Structure and Strategies of R&D Behavior in the Data Processing Market – Theoretical Thoughts and Empirical Findings', *Research Policy.* 5, 334-353

Moss Kanter,R.(2006), 'Innovation: The Classical traps', *Harvard Business Review.* Nov. 2006, 72-83

Robson,A.J.(1990),'Duopoly with Endogeneous Strategic Timing: Stackelberg Regained', *International Economic Review.* 31, 25-35

Saaskilahti,P. (2006),'Strategic R&D and Network Compatibility', *Economics of Innovation and New Technology.* 15(8), 711-733

Schumpeter, J.A.(1942), *Capitalism, Socialism and Democracy.*, New York: Harper

Teece, D.J., Pisano, G. and A. Shuen (1997), 'Dynamic capabilities and strategic management', *Strategic Management Journal.* 18(7), 509-533

Varian,H R., Farrell,J. and Shapiro,C. (2004),The *Economics of Information Technology.* Cambridge: Cambridge Univ. Press

Yao,T. and J. Weyant (2004), 'Strategic R&D Investments under Uncertainty in Information Technology" , Dept. of Management Science and Engineering, Stanford University, Palo Alto, Ca., Working Paper

APPENDIX

Mathematical Preliminaries, Definitions and Theorems

This section covers some of the salient analytical aspects specific to a sequential play game.

For a finite horizon T let L and F denote the leader and follower respectively. Let x denote the vector of state variables, u^L the vector of control variables of the leader, and u^F the vector of control variables of the follower. Assume $x \in R^n$, $u^L \in R^{mL}$ *and* $u^F \in R^{mF}$.

Definition 1. The initial value of the, follower's costate variable λ_i is said to be non-controllable if $\lambda_i(0)$ is independent of the leader's control path $u^L(t)$. Otherwise, it is said to be controllable.

The definition suggests that if the costate variable is controllable, the follower's control variable u^F (t) at. time t depends also on future values of u^L (.); that is, on values $u^L(s)$ with s > t.

Theorems and Proofs

Theorem 1. The maximized costate variables for the follower are a function of time and is given by

$$\lambda_1^* = \lambda_{01} e^{L_2 t} \tag{A 1}$$

$$\lambda_2^* = \lambda_{02} e^{L_1 t} \tag{A 2}$$

*where λ_1 * and λ_2 * are the costate variables reflecting the marginal price for a unit increase in the follower firm's own state and the state of the leader i ;*

$\lambda_1 (0) = \lambda_{01}$, $\lambda_2 (0) = \lambda_{02}$ *are constants.*

Proof: Stackelberg equilibrium conditions are derived by constructing the Hamiltonians. The analytical solution is derived for the follower firm *j* by writing the Hamiltonian as:

$$H^j = -\left[u^j(t)\right] + \lambda_1 \left[K_2 u^j(t)^{\alpha^j} - L_2 x^j(t) + M_2 u^i(t)\right] + \\ + \lambda_2 \left[K_1 u^i(t)^{\alpha^i} - L_1 x^i(t)\right] \tag{A 3}$$

The necessary conditions for optimality are:

$$H^j_{u^j} = 0 \; ; \tag{A 4}$$

$$\dot{\lambda}_1^* = -H^j_{x^j} \; ; \quad \dot{\lambda}_2^* = -H^j_{x^i} \tag{A 5}$$

$$x^j(0) = x_0^j \tag{A 6}$$

From (A 5)

$$\dot{\lambda}_1^* = L_2 \lambda_1 ; \quad \lambda_1^* = \lambda_{01} e^{L_2 t} \tag{A 7}$$

$$\dot{\lambda}_2^* = L_1 \lambda_2 ; \quad \lambda_2^* = \lambda_{02} e^{L_1 t} \tag{A 8}$$

where λ_1 *(0)* = λ_{01} is the known positive constant denoting the initial value of the costate λ_1 and λ_2 *(0)* = λ_{02} is a known negative constant denoting the initial value of the costate λ_2.

Theorem 2. The Stackelberg equilibrium investment by the follower in product development is given as

$$u^j(t)^* = \left[K_2 \alpha^j \lambda_{01} e^{L_2 t}\right]^{\frac{1}{1-\alpha^j}} \quad \text{(A.9)}$$

Proof: Differentiating (A3) with respect to $u^j(t)$, we obtain:

$$H_{uj} = -1 + \lambda_1 \alpha^j K_2 \left[u^j(t)\right]^{\alpha^j - 1} \quad \text{(A.10)}$$

By equating (A 10) to zero and some algebraic manipulations, the following expression is obtained for optimal effort in product development:

$$u^j(t)^* = \left[K_2 \alpha^j \lambda_1^*\right]^{\frac{1}{1-\alpha^j}} \quad \text{(A.11)}$$

Substituting the expression for λ_i in (A 11):

$$u^j(t)^* = \left[K_2 \alpha^j \lambda_{01} e^{L_2 t}\right]^{\frac{1}{1-\alpha^j}} \quad \text{(A.12)}$$

Theorem 3. The maximized costate variables for the leader are give n by,

$$\psi_1^* = \psi_{01}\, e^{L_1 t} \quad \text{(A.13)}$$

$$\psi_2^* = \psi_{02}\, e^{L_2 t} \quad \text{(A.14)}$$

$$\psi_3^* = -\psi_{03}\, e^{-L_2 t} \quad \text{(A.15)}$$

where ψ_1^* , ψ_2^* *and* ψ_3^* *are the costate variables reflecting the marginal price for a unit increase in the leader's own state.the state of the follower and the costate of the follower;* ψ_{01}, ψ_{02} *and* ψ_{03} *are constants.*

Proof. The Stackelberg equilibrium conditions are derived by constructing the Hamiltonian.

An analytical solution is derived for the leader firm I by writing the Hamiltonian as:

$$H^i = -\left[u^i(t)\right] + \psi\left[K_1 u^i(t)^{\alpha^i} - L_1 x^i(t)\right] + \\ + \psi_2\left[K_2 u^j(t)^{\alpha^j} - L_2 x^j(t) + M_2 u^i(t)\right] + \psi_3\left[\lambda_1 L_2\right] \quad \text{(A.16)}$$

The necessary conditions for optimality are

$$H^i_{u^i} = 0 \, ; \quad \text{(A.17)}$$

$$\psi_1^* = -H^i_{x^i};\ \psi_2^* = -H^i_{x^j};\ \psi_3^* = -H^i_{\lambda_1}; \tag{A.18}$$

$$x^i(0) = x_0^i \tag{A.19}$$

From (A .18)

$$\psi_1^* = L_1\psi_1;\ \ \psi_1^* = \psi_{01}\, e^{L_1 t} \tag{A.20}$$

$$\psi_2^* = L_2\psi_2; \qquad \psi_2^* = \psi_{02}\, e^{L_2 t} \tag{A.21}$$

$$\psi_3^* = -\psi_3 L_2;\ \psi_3^* = -\psi_{03}\, e^{-L_2 t} \tag{A.22}$$

where ψ_1^* , ψ_2^* *and* ψ_3^* are the costate variables reflecting the marginal price for a unit increase in the leader's own state, the state of the follower and the costate of the follower; ψ_{01}, ψ_{02} *and* ψ_{03} are constants.

Theorem 4. The Stackelberg equilibrium investment by the leader in product development is given as:

$$u^i(t)^* = \left[\frac{K_1\alpha^i\psi_{01}e^{L_1 t}}{1 - M_2\psi_{02}e^{L_2 t}}\right]^{\frac{1}{1-\alpha^i}} \tag{A.23}$$

Proof: Differentiating (A.3) with respect to $u^i(t)$, we obtain:

$$H_{u^i} = -1 + \psi_1\alpha^i K_1\left[u^i(t)\right]^{\alpha^i-1} + \psi_2 M_2 \tag{A.24}$$

By equating (A.24) to zero and some algebraic manipulations, the following is expression is obtained *for* optimal effort in product development:

$$u^i(t)^* = \left[\frac{K_1\alpha^i\psi_1^*}{1 - M_2\psi 2^*}\right]^{\frac{1}{1-\alpha^i}} \tag{A.25}$$

Substituting the expression for ψ_1^* *and* ψ_2^* in (A.25) yields

$$u^i(t)^* = \left[\frac{K_1\alpha^i\psi_{01}e^{L_1 t}}{1 - M_2\psi_{02}e^{L_2 t}}\right]^{\frac{1}{1-\alpha^i}} \tag{A.26}$$

Theorem 5. The equilibrium state trajectory of performance improvement of the Follower is given as

$$x^j(t) = \frac{e^{-L_2 t}}{L_2}\left[L_2 x_0^j + (-1+e^{L_2 t})\, M_2 \left[\frac{K_1 \alpha^i \psi_{01} e^{L_1 t}}{1 - M_2 \psi_{02} e^{L_2 t}}\right]^{\frac{1}{1-\alpha^i}} + \right.$$

$$\left. + (-1+e^{L_2 t}) K_2 \left(K_2 \alpha^j \lambda_{01} e^{L_2 t}\right)^{\frac{\alpha^j}{(1-\alpha^j)^2}} \right] \qquad \text{(A.27)}$$

Proof: The expression for the optimal state trajectory can be obtained by considering the state dynamics given in equation (11). Substituting $u^i(t) = u^i(t)^*$ and $u^j(t) = u^j(t)^*$ in (11) the following first-order differential equation can be obtained

$$x^j(t) = K_2\left[K_2 \alpha^j \lambda_1^*\right]^{\frac{\alpha^j}{1-\alpha^i}} - L_2 x^j(t)\,(T_p + \gamma - t) + M_2 \left[\frac{K_1 \alpha^i \psi_1^*}{1 - M_2 \psi 2^*}\right]^{\frac{1}{1-\alpha^i}} \qquad \text{(A.28)}$$

The first order differential equation can be solved with the initial condition $x^j(0) = x_0{}^j$ .The resulting expression for $x^j(t)^*$ is:

$$x^j(t) = \frac{e^{-L_2 t}}{L_2}\left[L_2 x_0^j + (-1+e^{L_2 t})\, M_2 \left[\frac{K_1 \alpha^i \psi_{01} e^{L_1 t}}{1 - M_2 \psi_{02} e^{L_2 t}}\right]^{\frac{1}{1-\alpha^i}} + \right.$$

$$\left. + (-1+e^{L_2 t}) K_2 \left(K_2 \alpha^j \lambda_{01} e^{L_2 t}\right)^{\frac{\alpha^j}{(1-\alpha^j)^2}} \right] \qquad \text{(A.29)}$$

Theorem 6. The equilibrium state trajectory of performance improvement of the leader is given as:

$$x^i(t) = \frac{e^{-L_1 t}}{L_1}\left[L_1 x_0^i + (-1+e^{L_1 t}) K_1 \left[\frac{K_1 \alpha^i \psi_{01} e^{L_1 t}}{1 - M_2 \psi_{02} e^{L_2 t}}\right]^{\frac{\alpha^i}{1-\alpha^i}} \right] \qquad \text{(A.30)}$$

Proof: The expression for the optimal state trajectory can be obtained by considering the state dynamics given in equation (14). Substituting $u^i(t) = u^i(t)^*$ in (14) the following first-order differential equation can be obtained:

$$x^j(t) = K_1 \left[\frac{K_1 \alpha^i \psi_1^*}{1 - M_2 \psi 2^*}\right]^{\frac{\alpha^i}{1-\alpha^i}} - L_1 x^i(t) \qquad \text{(A.31)}$$

The first order differential equation can be solved with the initial condition $x^i(0) = x_0{}^i$. The resulting expression for $x^i(t)^*$ is:

$$x^i(t) = \frac{e^{-L_1 t}}{L_1}\left[L_1 x_0^i + (-1 + e^{L_1 t})K_1\left[\frac{K_1 \alpha^i \psi_{01} e^{L_1 t}}{1 - M_2 \psi_{02} e^{L_2 t}}\right]^{\frac{\alpha^i}{1-\alpha^i}}\right] \tag{A.32}$$

Chapter 2

2. VERTICAL COMPETITION AND OUTSOURCING IN A SUPPLY CHAIN

2.1. INTRODUCTION

The study of innovation based competition has often considered aspects related to patent racing and incremental product-process innovation to achieve distinctive advantage.

Lately innovation-based competition has also become an aspect of buyer-supplier relationships. There are many instances in manufacturing where one finds situations of lock-ins created by innovative suppliers. For example, in the computer industry Intel and Microsoft as suppliers of microprocessor and operating systems, respectively, to desktop manufacturers like IBM and Dell illustrate such innovation-based lock-ins. Indeed, there exists an evolving power structure (dubbed 'channel power') in a supply chain driven by innovation competence of its members. This chapter focuses on innovation-based buyer-supplier competition as addressed strategically by Porter (1979).

A business context is envisaged in which, at any given point in time of the relationship, both the buyer and the supplier could be pursuing innovation simultaneously. We recognize that the primary motivation for such investments in innovation by members of the supply chain is to increase their differential or relative channel power in the supply chain. Also in a situation where the buyer is locked in by a supplier, the buyer may actively pursue the creation of a substitute technology by investing in innovation. The primary motivation for the buyer in this case would be to eliminate the technology lock-in and become independent.

We can look at how three diverse companies view their value chain in their degree of vertical integration.:

1. Staples in the office products industry saw a multistep, high-cost value chain . They envisioned a future in which immense customer and shareholder value could be created by shortening the chain to capture margin while offering small businesses lower prices, wider product selection and more convenience. Staples enabled this value proposition with a model that supported its retail stores with its own central distribution centers. The centers required greater operational scale but allowed Staples to eliminate middlemen and increase margin.

2. Consider how Intel developed its capabilities to sustain its growth path of innovation. Forced to exit the dynamic random access memory (DRAM) chip market in the late 1980s by Japanese competitors , Intel knew it had industry-leading logic circuit design skills but had been outclassed on its manufacturing platform. Each of its chip fabrica- tion plants , or 'fabs' , was different , requiring different processes and a new learning curve at each fab when new products were rolled out. In response , the company laun- ched a 'copy exactly' initiative to enable the transfer of new products and process flows into mass production with minimal variation.
3. Another example is Starbucks' actions to develop its capabilities in support of its path of channel innovation. The company has launched two initiatives: the first is to expand its food services account and the second to build its presence in grocery stores. To support the first initiative , the company has transitioned the majority of its food service accounts to broadline distribution networks and aligned its current food service sales, service and support resources with SYSCO Corporation, an established player in food service. To enable the second initiative, Starbucks is developing an alliance with Kraft Foods to market and distribute its whole bean and ground coffees to grocery stores.

In this context it boils down to how much integrated or disintegrated a company should become to maximize accumulated value in a value net. The Economist (2007) reports that the car industry is a case in point as an example of "the decomposition of the vertically integrated business model" from the one that used to be very integrated as part of a shift in a value net..

In such circumstances, firms enter the crossroads of a very delicate strategic supply chain relationship. Specifically, a strategy ought to be in place to defend the ability to appropriate and accumulate value by ensuring that the suppliers of the resources that the firm chooses not to own are not able to put themselves in a position to leverage value to the firm. The PC industry provides an excellent example of power diffusion up the supply chain. In 1981, IBM designed product, process and supply chain such that it sourced the microprocessors from Intel and the operating system from Microsoft. The outcome was an outstanding successful product design but a disastrous supply chain design for IBM. Today, the power of Intel in the supply chain for PCs is undisputed but still challenged by Advanced Micro Devices (AMD). The new innovations that occur in this industry are to a great extent defined by this upstream supplier of microprocessors. The lesson learnt is to beware of the 'Intel Inside' syndrome (Fine,1999).

Extending this argument to the upstream microprocessor industry also provides some interesting observations. During the 1960s, the practice of second sourcing whereby innovative firms license production of one or more manufacturers that can act as a second source of any new product had already developed. It was alleged that some sole suppliers of semiconductors 'exploited' their customer firms once they had locked in their product designs to that of the supplier's product. This feature of the industry profoundly affected the evolution of market structure, for it opened up a new and attractive strategy for second sourced suppliers. A firm would enter as a second sourcer and learn to produce high volumes efficiently while offering a leading edge product identical to that of the innovating firm. Once this hurdle was surmounted, it could use its growing cash flow to support a larger R&D effort with a view to developing its own next generation products. For example, AMD operated as a second sourcer in its early years, achieved considerable success, and later on more than half a dozen companies were second sourcing AMD's product (Sutton, 2001).

A differential game formulation, as aplied to an innovation race (Gottinger, 2006) and high speed technological competition (Chapt.1)) is used to examine the competition between the buyer and the supplier. Investigation of this type of buyer-supplier competition would lead to a better understanding of the dynamics of collaboration among supply chain partners.

An interesting aspect of the problem is the fact that the supplier must take into account the inherent incentives for the buyer to develop a 'backstop' technology which can be substituted for the supplied component. The supplier with the knowledge of this intent of the buyer acts such that the profits are maximized before the invention of substitute technology by the buyer. The time when such innovation materializes is uncertain, but can be affected by R&D efforts.

The model formulation is related to a case in the economics of exhaustible resources. Harris and Vickers (1995) analyze a dynamic game between a resource-exporting country and an importing country that is seeking to invent a substitute technology. They address a central question in the economics of exhaustible resources concerning incentives for the discovery of reproducible 'backstop' technologies to substitute for finite natural resources that are being depleted. Importing countries are motivated to discover backstop technologies not only to overcome the problem that resource stocks are finite, but also to reduce dependence upon resource producers, who often enjoy a considerable degree of monopoly power over them.

The organization of this chapter is as follows. A stochastic differential game model for supply chain technological competition is presented in the next section. In Section 3 the differential game is analyzed and the Markov-perfect Nash equilibrium results are given. Section 4 provides a discussion of results. The proofs of theorems are provided in the Appendix.

2.2. Differential Game Formulation

The notations and symbols used in the model are as follows:

S: subscript for the supplier firm
B: subscript for the buyer firm.
T: Finite time horizon for the strategies
t: An instant of time in the dynamic game setup
$u_B(t)$: Buyer's innovation effort (R&D expenditure per unit time)
$u_S(t)$: Supplier's production effort (Expenditure in production processes and resources per unit time)
$p(u_S)$: Price/ Inverse demand curve
$c_S(u_S)$: unit production cost to be incurred by the supplying firm
c_B: unit production cost to be incurred by the buying firm (Assumption $c_S > c_B$)
$c_U(u_B)$: Effort cost incurred by the buying firm for achieving the level of innovation that would be a perfect substitute for the supplier S's innovation
τ: random instant of time at which the level of innovation (breakthrough innovation) is reached

F(t): the probability that the buying firm B is successful in the innovation project by time t, that is $\Pr(\tau < t) = F(t)$

k_{01}: function representing the switching rate

x(t): state dynamics represented by remaining demand for the product

The context of buyer-supplier relationship that is based on innovation and quality parameters can be considered in the broad rubric of a resource-based view of a firm. Specifically, the vendor S is providing a resource in the form of innovation capabilities to the buyer firm B. There is a fixed known demand for the product. A one- to- one correspondence is considered such that for every product sold by the buyer to the final consumer, at least one component is required from the supplier. The supplier is assumed to be a monopolist and the buyer faces perfect competition in the final consumer market.

It is asserted that a one- to- one correspondence assumption helps in the analysis in two distinct ways.

First, this allows explicit examination of dependence between the two collaborating partners and the evolution of power structure based on innovation. Second, this lends analytical simplification for solving the problem. The supplier S is a monopoly producer of a product component for which the cost of production is $c_S(u_S) > 0$ per unit. Supplier S's rate of production is a function of production effort u_S and is assumed to be γu_S. For analytical simplicity γ is assumed to be equal to 1. The rate of production is defined as, u_S: $(0,\infty) \rightarrow [0, \bar{u}_S]$ The remaining market demand (measured as a percent of initial demand x_o) is the state variable for the problem. In the context of the model specification and the underlying assumptions, the remaining demand x is identical for the buyer and the supplier. This remaining demand , x, is assumed to be a function of the supplier's production rate and the rate of change of remaining demand is,

$$x^{\bullet}(t) = -\gamma\, u_S\,(x(t)) = -\, u_S\,(x(t))\ ;\ x(0) = x_o$$

As the production rate increases, the remaining market demand falls more rapidly. The price function of the buyer firm B, $p(u_S)$ is a function of the production rate of the supplier. The buyer invests to create a substitute technology which is assumed to enable production of the product component at a unit cost $c_B \leq c_S$. In the event of a successful creation of such a technology there will be no demand for the supplier's component. The investment policy in innovation chosen by B is denoted by $u_B : (0, \infty) \rightarrow [0, \infty)$. This investment represents the buyer's efforts in R&D and is a function of the remaining demand x(t). By investing in innovation, the buyer gains knowledge and the time path for the buyer's level of knowledge k(t) is given by,

$$k^{\bullet}(t) = u_B\,(x(t))\ ,\ k(0) = 0$$

The outcome of innovation investments is considered to be uncertain. Therefore, we assume that the R&D investments don't precisely determine the date of success of innovation. A natural and convenient way to represent uncertain innovation is to suppose that the instantaneous probability of the buyer B innovating, conditional on not having so far done so, is a function of its current R&D effort rate. This "hazard rate" approach, which derives from an exponential probability distribution, has been used by numerous authors, e.g. Dasgupta and Stiglitz (1981) , Harris and Vickers(1995) . The probability that the buyer B has innovated by t is assumed to take an exponential form, which is independent of the accumulated knowledge level, k(t).

$$F(t) / [1 - F(t)] = u_B (x(t)) \qquad (1)$$

where F(t) is the probability that the buyer B is successful in the innovation project by time t; that is $Pr(\tau < t) = F(t)$.

Let $\pi(u_S) = [p(u_S) - c_S(u_S)]\gamma u_S$ be the supplier's instantaneous profit function. This instantaneous profit function acts as the objective functional for the supplier. In the problem context, the buyer faces perfect competition. The buyer invests in innovation to become independent of the lock-in created by the supplier. Since the buyer is facing perfect competition, it maximizes consumer surplus. A figure representing the consumer surplus is provided in figure 1. Let the consumer surplus be denoted by $\sigma(u_S) = \int_0^{uS} p(y))dy - u_S p(u_S)$. After the successful invention of substitute technology, a new market is created for the buyer's product. Now, the buyer can gain discounted profits depending upon the price $p_B(u_B)$ and the variable cost of production $c_B(u_B)$ The payoff of the buyer firm B is $\int_0^{\tau} e^{-rt} [\sigma(u_S(x(t))) - c_U(u_B(x(t)))]dt + \int_{\tau}^{\infty} e^{-rt} \pi_B (u_B)dt$, where c_U is the buyer's cost of innovation effort, τ is the random time at which innovation occurs, $r > 0$ is the discount rate, p_B is the price that the buyer can charge for the product once the innovation materializes and $\pi_B (u_B)$ is the profit earned by the buyer after time τ. It is a function of the price charged and the variable cost of production. The payoff of the supplier firm S is $\int_0^{\tau} e^{-rt} \pi(u_S(x(t)))dt$.

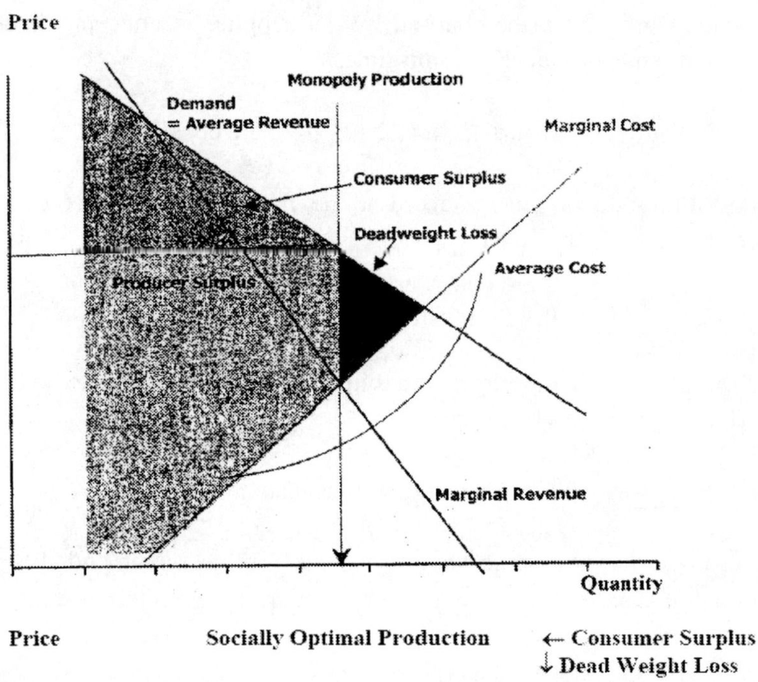

Figure 1. Monopoly Production and Price.

The strategies $u_S(.)$ and $u_B(.)$ constitute an equilibrium if and only if, for all $x_0 > 0$, taking $u_B(.)$ as given, the production effort $u_S(.)$ maximizes the supplier's payoff among all remaining strategies; and similarly, taking $u_S(.)$ as given, the innovation effort $u_B(.)$ maximizes the buyer' s payoff among all possible strategies. The following assumptions are considered for the inverse demand function, the profit function and the cost of effort function.

(i) The inverse demand function $p(u_S)$ is twice continuously differentiable on $[0, \bar{u}_S]$: $p' < 0$ on this interval; $p(0) > c_S \geq 0$; and $p(\bar{u}_S) = 0$. This assumption signifies that there is a finite price p(0) to sustain a profitable production, the inverse demand function is downward sloping, and that the total demand for the supplier's output at any given time is bounded by the maximum possible production rate $\bar{u}_S$

(ii) The profit function $\pi(u_S)$ is strictly concave on $[0, \bar{u}_S]$: $\pi'' < 0$, which is equivalent to $2p' + p''u_S < 0$.

(iii) The cost of production effort $c_S(u_S)$ is continuously differentiable on $[0, \bar{u}_S)$: $c_S(0) = 0$ on $[0, \bar{u}_S)$ and $c'_S(y)$ is a constant. The cost of innovation effort $c_U(u_B)$ is twice continuously differentiable on $[0, \infty)$; $c_U(0) = c'_U(0) = 0$; $c''_U > 0$ on $[0, \infty)$; and $c'_U(y) \to \infty$ as $y \to \infty$. This assumption suggests that costs increase and are strictly convex in effort. It also suggests that zero R&D effort is suboptimal and for the strategy u_B we can confine our interest to interior solutions.

In this market setting, it is assumed that the product enjoys a very large fixed demand. Furthermore, whatever is produced by the supplier gets sold and hence the production rate of the supplier equals the quantity demanded per unit time in the market. The inverse demand function or in other words the price charged by the supplier is conceptualized as a linear decreasing function of units produced per unit time.

$$p(u_S(x(t))) = a - b\gamma u_S(t) = a - bu_S(t); \quad a > c_S > 0,\ b > 0 \text{ are constants} \tag{2}$$

The variable cost of production is assumed to be linear and an increasing function of production effort u_S.

$$c_S = c_1 [u_S], \qquad c_1 > 0 \text{ is a proportionality constant} \tag{3}$$

The cost of effort function for the buyer is assumed to be strictly convex and increasing in innovation effort u_B

$$c_U = c_2 [u_B]^2, \qquad c_2 > 0 \text{ is a proportionality constant} \tag{4}$$

Note that this problem has the same state dynamics for the buyer and the supplier. The objective functional of supplier S is the expected profit until the random instant of time τ,

$$J^S(x) = E_{uB(.)}\int_0^\tau e^{-rt} [p(u_S(x(t))) - c_S(u_S)]\gamma u_S\, x(t))]dt$$
$$= E_{uB(.)}\int_0^\tau e^{-rt} [a - bu_S(x(t)) - c_1(u_S)(x(t))u_S(x(t))]\, dt \tag{5}$$

Note that the supplier S receives zero profit for $t > \tau$ (since demand vanishes). The objective functional of firm B is the expected gain from innovation efforts, given by

$$J^B(x,u_B) = E_{uB(.)}\int_0^{\tau} e^{-rt}\,[\sigma(u_S(x(t))) - c_U(u_B)(x(t))]dt + \int_{\tau}^{\infty} e^{-rt}\,\pi_B\,(u_B)dt$$
$$= E_{uB(.)}\int_0^{\tau} e^{-rt}\,[\sigma(u_S(x(t))) - c_2(u_B)(x(t))]^2 dt + \int_{\tau}^{\infty} e^{-rt}\,\pi_B\,(u_B)dt \quad (6)$$

where

$$\sigma\,(u_S(x(t))) = \int_0^{uS} [p(y)dy - u_S\,(x(t))p(u_S\,) = \int_0^{uS} [a - by]dy - u_S(x(t))\,[a - bu_S(x(t))] \quad (7)$$

is the surplus gained by the customers if the buyer firm B is able to accomplish the required innovation level.

The problem formulation for the supplier is:

$$J^S(x) = E_{uB(.)}\int_0^{\tau} e^{-rt}\,[p(u_S(x(t))) - c_S(u_S)]u_S x(t))]dt$$
$$= E_{uB(.)}\int_0^{\tau} e^{-rt}\,[a - bu_S(x(t)) - c_1(u_S)(x(t))]u_S(\,x(t))dt$$

subject to $x^{\bullet}(t) = -\,u_S\,(x(t))\,;\; x(0) = x_o$ (8)

The problem formulation for the buyer is,

$$J^B(x,u_B) = E_{uB(.)}\int_0^{\tau} e^{-rt}\,[\sigma(u_S(x(t))) - c_U(u_B)(x(t))]dt + \int_{\tau}^{\infty} e^{-rt}\,\pi_B\,(u_B)dt$$
$$= E_{uB(.)}\int_0^{\tau} e^{-rt}\,[\sigma(u_S(x(t))) - c_2(u_B)(x(t))]^2 dt + \int_{\tau}^{\infty} e^{-rt}\,\pi_B\,(u_B)dt$$

subject to $x^{\bullet}(t) = -\,u_S\,(x(t))\,;\; x(0) = x_o$ (9)

The differential game defined by (8) and (9) belongs to the class of piecewise deterministic games (Dockner et al. , 2000):. The game has two modes only: mode 0 is active before firm B has made the innovation and mode 1 becomes active if firm B succeeds in making the substitute technology. Thus, there can be at most one switch of mode. The switching time is the random variable τ, and the probability distribution of τ is F, as given in equation (1).

2.3. Analysis of the Model

The variables are written without the arguments for notational convenience. For example, $u_S\,(x(t)) = u_S$. In the game specified in equation (8) and equation (9), the nature of stationary Markov perfect Nash equilibrium conditions for the supplier and buyer are analyzed. Supplier S's stationary Markovian strategy for production effort $U_S(\,h, x)$ is a mapping $U_S : M \times (0, \infty) \rightarrow [0, \bar{u}_S]$, where M= {0, 1} is the set of modes. Buyer B's stationary Markovian R&D effort strategy $U_B(\,h, x)$ is a mapping $U_B : M \times (0, \infty) \rightarrow [0, \infty)$.

The solution approach in Harris and Vickers (1995) is adopted and is presented below.

Let the value functions of the supplier and buyer be defined as $V^S(h,s)$ and $V^B(h,s)$ respectively for $h \in M = \{0, 1\}$ and $x \in (0, 1)$. As required from the definition and theorem pertaining to piecewise deterministic differential games provided in the Appendix, these value functions are assumed to be bounded and continuously differentiable and for all $x \in [0, 1]$ that satisfy the Hamilton-Jacobi-Bellman (HJB) equations.

$$rV^S(0,x) = \max\{\pi(u_S) - u_S V_x^{\ S}(0,x) + U_B(0,x)[V^S(1,x) - V^S(0,x)] \mid u_S \in [0, \bar{u}_S]\} \quad (10)$$

$$rV^S(1,x) = 0 \quad (11)$$

$$rV^B(0,x) = \max\{\sigma(U_S(0,x) - c_u(u_B) - U_S(0,x)V_x^{\ B}(0,x) + u_B [V_x^{\ B}(1,x) - V_x^{\ B}(0,x)] \mid u_B \in [0,\infty]\} \quad (12)$$

$$rV^B(1,x) = \pi(u_B) \quad (13)$$

Equations (11) and (13) present the value functions for the supplier and the buyer once the system switches to mode 1. As reasoned earlier, the supplier's profit stream becomes zero after the switch as there will be no demand for supplier's product component. On the other hand, in the event of being successful in making the innovation; the buyer earns the present value of the constant stream of consumer surplus over an infinite interval of time. Additionally, irrespective of the system mode, it can be observed that the supplier's profit will become zero if there is no remaining demand. In the absence of any production by the supplier, it is assumed that the buyer gets a constant expected payoff V^B which is the optimal value of a one player stochastic control problem with buyer B as the decision maker. Hence, the value functions are subjected to two constraints,

$$V^S(h,0) = 0 , \forall h \in M$$
$$V^B(0.0) = \underline{V}^B$$

The maximizing sets of $u_S \in [0, \bar{u}_S]$ and $u_B \in [0,\infty)$ that maximize the respective value functions of the supplier and the buyer in equation (10) and (12) are denoted as $\Phi^S(x)$ and $\Phi^B(x)$, respectively. If $U_S(0,x) \in \Phi^S(x)$ and $U_B(0,x) \in \Phi^B(x)$ for all $x \in [0,1]$,and provided that the value functions can be found that satisfy HJB equations; then from the theorems on Markov games (Dockner et al., 2000), the strategy pair (U_S(h, x), U_B (h,x))is a stationary Markov perfect Nash equilibrium. To determine the value functions, the equations (10) and (12) can be rewritten as,

$$rV^S(0,x) = G^S (V_x^{\ S}(0,x)) - U_B(0,x)\, V^S(0,x) \quad (15)$$

$$rV^B(0,x) = \sigma(U_S(0,x)) - U_S(0,x)V_x^{\ B}(0,x) + G^B [\ \bar{V}^B - V^B(0,x)] \quad (16)$$

where,

$$G^S(z) = \max\{\pi(u_S) - u_S z \mid 0 \le u_S \le \bar{u}_S\}\ ;\ G^B(z) = \max\{z u_B - c_U(u_B) \mid 0 \le u_B\}$$

$$U_S(0,x)) = \operatorname{argmax}\{\pi(u_S) - u_S\, V_x^{\ S}(0,x) \mid 0 \le u_S \le \bar{u}_S\} \quad (17)$$

$$U_B(0,x) = \text{argmax } \{[\ V^B - V^B(0,x)]\ u_B - c_U(u_B) \mid 0 \le u_B\ \} \tag{18}$$

Solution of the system of autonomous nonlinear differential equations (15) - (18) leads to the determination of the two value functions. Substituting the expressions for the demand function and the cost of effort function from equations (2) and equation (4) ,respectively.

$$G^S(z) = \max\ \{a - bu_S - c_1\ u_S\ ]\ u_S - u_S\ z \mid 0 \le u_S \le \bar{u}_S\} \tag{19}$$

$$G^B(z) = \max\ \{zu_B - c_2(u_B)^2 \mid 0 \le u_B\ \} \tag{20}$$

$$U_S(0,x)) = \text{argmax } \{a - bu_S - c_1\ u_S\ ]\ u_S - u_S\ V_x^S(0,x) \mid 0 \le u_S \le \bar{u}_S\} \tag{21}$$

$$U_B(0,x) = \text{argmax } \{[\ \bar{V}^B - V^B(0,x)]\ u_B - c_2(u_B)^2 \mid 0 \le u_B\ \} \tag{22}$$

where,

$$\bar{V}^B = \pi(u_B)\ /r \tag{23}$$

2.4. Equilibrium Results

Theorem 1. If V^{S*} and V^{B*} denote the positive equilibrium value of the supplier and buyer firm , then

$$V^{S*} = \frac{a^2\sqrt{c_2}}{\sqrt{2\{8r(b+c_1)^2(\ \bar{V}^B+rc_2) - a^2b\}}} \tag{24}$$

$$V^{B*} = 2c_2r + \bar{V}^B - \frac{\sqrt{c_2}\sqrt{\{8r(b+c_1)^2(\ \bar{V}^B+rc_2) - a^2b\}}}{\sqrt{2}(b+c_1)} \tag{25}$$

constitute the equilibrium pair.

Theorem 2. If U_S^* and U_B^* denote the positive equilibrium control functions of the supplier and buyer firm, then

$$U_S^*(0,x) = \frac{a - V_x^S(0,x)}{2(b+c_1)} = \frac{a}{2(b+c_1)} \tag{26}$$

$$U_B^*(0,x) = \frac{\bar{V}^B - V^B(0,x)}{2c_2} = \frac{\sqrt{8r(b+c_1)^2(\bar{V}^B+rc_2)} - a}{2\sqrt{2(b+c_1)}\sqrt{c_2}} \quad (27)$$

Theorem 3 At equilibrium the remaining demand at time t can be expressed as:

$$x(t) = x_o = \frac{at}{2(b+c_1)} \quad (28)$$

where $x(0) = x_o$ is the initial remaining market demand.

2.5. Observations and Discussion

Observation 1. At equilibrium the supplier chooses a monopoly production rate.

The observation can be explained by exploring the monopoly production rate of the supplier in the given setting. The monopoly profit of the supplier π_m is

$$\pi_m = \max\,\{\pi(u_S)\,|\,0 \le u_S \le \bar{u}_S\} = \max\,\{[a - bu_S - c_1(u_S)]\,u_S \mid u_S \in [0, \bar{u}_S]\}$$

The corresponding production effort required to attain a monopoly profit is therefore, $u_{Sm} = \text{argmax}\,\{\pi(u_S)\,|\,0 \le u_S \le \bar{u}_S\} = \text{argmax}\,\{a - bu_S - c_1(u_S)\,]\,u_S \mid u_S \in [0, \bar{u}_S]\}$

Taking the first order condition leads to the monopoly production rate given by a $u_{Sm} = a/2(b+c_1)$

The supplier is assumed to be a monopoly. In the given setup the supplier employs monopoly production rate to gain as much of monopoly profits as possible before being locked out of the market. An illustration of such a monopoly production is provided in figure 2.

At equilibrium the supplier exercises monopoly power and allows the buyer to pursue creation of substitute technology. The supplier sets the monopoly production rate at the start of the game and it remains time invariant for the entire planning horizon. Next, the observation regarding innovation effort of the buyer is presented.

Observation 2.

i The innovation effort of the buyer increases with the potential value of time discounted profit $\bar{V}^B$ that the buyer can receive in the event of successful creation of substitute technology.

ii The monopoly production rate of the supplier exerts a negative effect on the buyer's innovation rate.

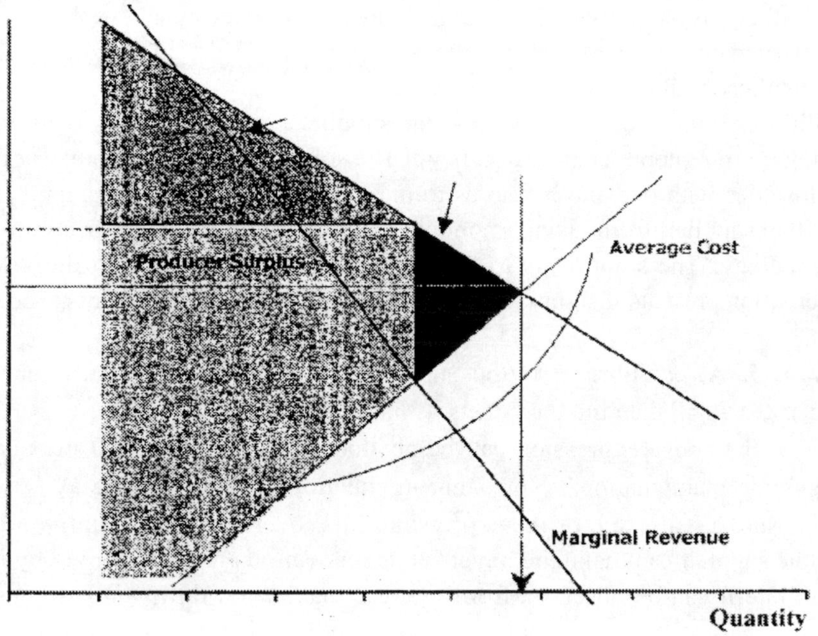

Figure 2. Price Range.

The observation stated in 2(i) is intuitive and can be observed from the expression for buyer's equilibrium control given in equation (27). The motivation for the supplier to invest in substitute technology would indeed be dependent on the discounted profits that the buyer can obtain in case the innovation is successful. The time of successful `invention' is uncertain but it can be influenced by the buyer's innovation efforts. This is expressed in equation (1). For observation 2(ii) the expression for equilibrium innovation rate by the buyer U_B^* is revisited. With some algebraic manipulations the equilibrium innovation rate of the buyer can be expressed as:

$$U_B^* = \sqrt{[(V^B + rc_2)/ c_2) - (U_S^*)^2/2\, c_2]} - r \qquad (29)$$

From the above expression it can be noted that the supplier's monopoly production rate exerts a negative effect on the buyer's innovation efforts. Observation 1 and 2 characterize the nature of equilibrium control of the buyer and the supplier. Indeed, in the given setting there exists no motivation for the two players to collaborate and each acts in its best interest. The supplier makes full use of the monopoly power and the buyer continues investments in innovation to create substitute technology.

However, as asserted by Schelling (1980,p.4) , if we confine our study to the theory of strategy, we seriously restrict ourselves by the assumption of rational behavior. The result obtained doesn't necessarily suggest "intelligent" behavior but the equilibrium results are suggestive of a behaviour motivated by a conscious calculation of advantages, a calculation that in turn is based on explicit and internally consistent value systems. Still, the assumption of rational behavior is a productive one as it gives us a grip on the subject. In the problem context the availability of equilibrium solution based on the assumption of rationality permits us to identify our own analytical processes with those of the hypothetical participants in a conflict. By further investigation of a certain kind of consisterrcy in the behavior of our hypothetical participants, we can examine alternate courses of behavior according to whether or not they meet those standards of consistency.

The equilibrium control of the buyer and the supplier presents a dilemma in achieving a long-term collaborative supply chain partnership. The solution for this dilemma for both firms is to create close ties with one another so as to minimize the risk of opportunism. These ties should deter the supplier from using monopoly power aud the buyer from investing in substitute technology. The solution is to build credible commitments into the relationship. The next observation presents insights for building such credible commitments.

Observation 3. At equilibrium if the supplier's production rate is such hat $U_S^* = \sqrt{2/b[(r\ \bar{V}^B + c_2)/ c_2) - r^2)]}$ then the buyer sets its innovation effort to zero.

Analytically, the above expression can be obtained by setting $U_B^* = 0$ in equation (29) and some algebraic manipulations. Note, that in equation (29) we require $(V^B + rc_2)/ c_2 > (U_S^*)^2/2\ c_2$ to ensure a real value of the expression. Moreover, it is also intuitive to note that the only way the supplier can make the buyer set its innovation efforts to zero is by increasing the production rate It can be observed from figure 2 that with a downward sloping demand curve, the price charged by the supplier decreases with an increase in its production. The inverse demand curve (price) of the supplier's product component is $(a - bu_S)$. The monopoly price charged by the supplier is therefore $p^* = a - b[a/ 2(b+c_1)]$.

With the changed production rate, the price becomes

$$\bar{p} = a - b[\sqrt{2/b[(r\ \bar{V}^B + c_2)/ c_2) - r^2)]}]$$

The observation suggests that there is a price bandwidth that the supplier can credibly commit to the buyer and achieve a long-term partnership. It can be reasonably asserted that based on the cost structures there is a $\underline{p}$ below which the supplier makes losses. Theoretically, at this price marginal cost equals average revenue. Therefore the price range that a supplier can charge and achieve a long-term relationship with the buyer can be given as $\underline{p} < p < \bar{p}$. With this price range the supplier can create a disincentive for the buyer to invest in substitute technology. In the problem context considered in this paper, the motivation for the supplier to adopt such a policy depends on two considerations. First, the price should be at least high enough to cover marginal costs. Second, if the supplier wishes to remove uncertainty in the relationship and intends to be the preferred partner for the entire planning horizon, the supplier will adopt this policy. Particularly the second consideration depends on the profits that can be earned for the time period $[0, \tau]$ using a monopoly pricing with the profits that can be earned for the entire planning horizon $[0, \infty)$ by judiciously choosing a price from the given range. The choice of price from the given range would be such that the supplier starts with a price $p = \bar{p}$ and gradually reduces it over time till it reaches $\underline{p}$.

It is important to note that in the problem context, time τ is not deterministic and is characterized by the hazard rate. The time instant τ could approach ∞ or alternately it could be very close to 0, depending on the outcome of innovation investments by the buyer. The pricing scheme obtained from this analysis provides implications for the supplier to create conditions for trust-based governance. The formation of buyer-supplier trust emanates from certain proactive measures taken by the collaborating partners as a part of their contract. Cox et al.(2002,p.14) suggest some other aspects for forming long-term relationships. To avoid potential conflict between a, buyer and a supplier due to relative difference in innovation competence, one approach is to have either the buyer or the supplier make dedicated investments. The other partner could protect its interest by posting a bond that it would forfeit if the partner investing in innovation acts opportunistically. The authors assert. "This bond, which is known in transaction cost parlance as a hostage, would be used to create a condition of bilateral dependency (more commonly referred to as interdependency").. Yet another approach to create conditions for interdependency is that both the collaborating partners invest in innovation. Such joint innovation activity strengthens the bond between collaborating firms and enables long-term relationship formation.

From the supplier's perspective an ideal contract is one that is large, relatively simple, and therefore cheap to service and that is likely to result in repeat business. The utility that a supplier attaches to a particular exchange relationship is typically highest in those instances that involve a key contract in a key segment. Along with the relative utility derived from the buyer's business, the supplier also considers the aspect of substitutability of a buyer's business. Specifically, the supplier considers the likelihood that it will be able to replace the buyer's business with an exchange of equivalent utility, if it loses the business. The answer depends on the market structure in which the supplier sells and on its competitive position relative to other suppliers. A higher frequency of transactions offers the supplier stability and certainty. From the buyer's perspective, creating conditions for repeat business allows the supplier to cover fixed and semi-fixed costs and justifies the supplier's investments in speculative investments.

REFERENCES

Cox, Andrew; Ireland, P. Lonsdale,C.Sanderson,J. ;Watson,G. (2002), *Supply Chains, Markets and Power: Mapping Buyer and Supplier Power Regimes*, London : Routledge

Dasgupta, P.;Stiglitz ,J.(1981), 'Resource Depletion under Technological Uncertaintv', *Econometrica* 49, 85-104.

Dockner,E., Jorgensen,S., Van Long, N., Sorger, G (2000), *Differential Games in Economics and Management Science* , Cambridge: Cambridge Univ. Press

The Economist (2007), 'Revving Up', A Special Report on Innovation, Oct.27, 6-10

Fine,C,H, (1999), *Clockspeed: Winning Industry Control in the Age of Temporary Advantage*, New York: Perseus

Gottinger,H.W. (2006), *Innovation, Technology and Hypercompetition*, London: Routledge

Harris, C., and Vickers,J.(1995),'Innovation and Natural Resources: A Dynamic Game with Uncertainty',*The Rand Journal of Economics* 26(3), 418-430

Porter,Michael E.(1979),'How Competitive Forces shape Strategy', Chapt 1 in *On Competition* , Boston: , Harvard Business School Press, 21-38

Schelling, T. (1980), *Strategy and Conflict,* Cambridge,Ma.: Harvard Univ. Press

Sutton, J.(2001), *Technology and Market Structure*, MIT Press: Cambridge,Ma.

APPENDIX

Proof of Theorem 1. .: From equations (19), (20), (21) and (22), the maximization of the expression in the right hand side leads to the expressions,

$$G^S(z) = (a - z)^2 / 4(b + c_1) \qquad \text{(A.1)}$$

$$G^B(z) = z^2 / 4c_2 \qquad \text{(A.2)}$$

$$U_S(0,x) = \frac{a - V_x{}^S(0,x)}{2(b+c_1)} \qquad \text{(A.3)}$$

$$U_B(0,x) = \frac{\bar{V}^B - V^B(0,x)}{2c_2} \qquad \text{(A.4)}$$

with $\bar{V}^B$ as a given pre-equilibrium level.

The system of autonomous nonlinear differential equations as specified in equations (15) and (16) can be analyzed by exploring the corresponding equilibrium points or critical points of the equations. These points are obtained by setting $V_x{}^S = 0$ and $V_x{}^B = 0$, respectively.

Equations (15) and (16) thus reduces to,

$$rV^S(0,x) = G^S(0) - U_B(0,x)\, V^S(0,x) \qquad \text{(A.5)}$$

and

$$rV^B(0,x) = \sigma(U_S(0,x)) + G^B[\,\bar{V}^B - V^B(0,x)] \qquad \text{(A.6)}$$

Substituting for G^S, G^B, $U_S(0,x)$, $U_B(0,x)$ from equations (A.1) – (A.4) , and solving for $V^S(0,x)$ and $V^B(0,x)$ leads to

$$V^{S*} = \frac{a^2\sqrt{c_2}}{\sqrt{2}\{8r(b+c_1)^2(\,\bar{V}^B+rc_2) - a^2b\}} \qquad \text{(A.7)}$$

and

$$V^{B*} = 2c_2r + \bar{V}^B - \frac{\sqrt{c_2}\sqrt{\{8r(b+c_1)^2(\,\bar{V}^B+rc_2) - a^2b\}}}{\sqrt{2}(b+c_1)} \qquad \text{(A.8)}$$

Proof of Theorem 2.

The equilibrium value of $U_S^*(0,x)$ is obtained by substituting $V_x^S(0,x) = 0$ and finding the argument u_S that maximizes the right hand side of equation (21). Similarly, the equilibrium value $U_B^*(0,x)$ is obtained by finding the argument u_B that maximizes the right hand side of equation (22) and substituting the equilibrium point $V^{B*}(0,x)$ from equation (25). Therefore, (26) and (27) follow.

Proof of Theorem 3.

The theorem follows by substitution of $u_S = U_S^*$ in the equation for state dynamics and solving the resulting first order differential equation $x^\bullet(t) = - U_S^* = - a/ 2(b+c_1)$ which leads to $x(t) = x_o - at / 2(b+c_1)$ where $x(0) = x_o$ is the initial remaining market demand.

Chapter 3

3. SUPPLY-CHAIN CO-OPETITION

3.1. INTRODUCTION

The purpose of this chapter is to provide a strategic framework and insights regarding power and competition in a collaborative supply chain setup. The chapter builds on strategic thinking specifically in the context of collaboration. In particular, Williamson's (1975; 1985, 1999) transaction cost approach provides a conceptual grounding for understanding the fundamental basis on which relationship between buyer and supplier takes place as well as the game-theoretic format of Brandenburger and Nalebuff (1998) are of relevance here. With multiple firms constituting a supply chain, investments by supply chain partners have implications that transcend the traditional cost minimization or revenue/profit maximization objectives. In today's dynamic environment, firms are investing in unpredictable innovations and associated strategies to gain the first-mover advantage.Today firms strategically decide to enter a collaborative relationship. In a joint product development context, many firms outsource the manufacturing process of components which would be used in the final product. At times, this outsourcing goes beyond just the manufacturing of a fully specified component to allowing and expecting the supplier to build resource competence through active innovation.

An example can be found in the supply chain of automobiles (Clark and Fujimoto,1991, Chapts.5,6). Automobile production begins with design, which consists of three main elements. The first element is the concept itself. Thereafter, the design of the vehicle can be usefully divided into the macro-design (the development of the basic chassis, sub-assembly and component specification) and the micro-design (the development, to agreed specifica-tions, of the vehicle's constituent components). The first two elements of design tend to be undertaken by the car assembler. In particular, the assembler takes charge of concept origination. In the face of intense competition, however, the costs associated with developing new vehicle prototypes have increasingly forced car assemblers to source the design of sub-assemblies and components (the micro-design) from external suppliers. The degree to which such outsourcing is undertaken by assemblers varies between different firms.

The assemblers who outsource the micro-design to external suppliers have a motivation to let these suppliers grow larger so that the supply bases can be brought up to global standards. These larger suppliers would then be required to take full responsibility for the design of sub-assemblies and for the coordination of the second and third-tier component manufacturers that contribute to the product.

The strong market position of these sub-assemblers is further enhanced by product specialization. No single supplier produces all types of sub-assembly. For example, Bosch, which is the world's largest automotive equipment manufacturer, targets its efforts on starter systems, spark plugs, braking systems, lighting and windscreen wipers.

The net result of market consolidation is that the supply of particular sub-assembly systems has become concentrated amongst just a handful of manufacturers.

With increasing formation of collaborative supply chain networks, research regarding channel power and lock-in circumstances in a supply chain is of paramount importance. Cox et al. (2002) highlight the need to undertake rigorous analytical research in this sphere of supply -and value chain networks to augment our understanding of power regimes. The results of an analytical research could potentially provide understanding of the types of countervailing strategy to shift the balance of power in a supply chain.

This paper analytically examines this issue using a differential games based approach.. A model of competitive dynamics between a supplier and a buyer is presented using the theory of stochastic processes and differential games. It analyzes the context of buyer-supplier competition, by adapting and building on Browne (2000); which is primarily targeted towards investigation of portfolio investment strategies in finance. In this work, the analysis and theoretical results in Browne (2000) are extended to glean insights associated with strategic supply chain management.

The organization of this chapter is as follows.The next section presents the model formulation. In the third section, the nature of the game is detailed. The model is analyzed in the fourth section and the results are presented in the form of theorems and propositions. Finally, the fifth section discusses the results. Proofs of the theorems and propositions is provided in the Appendix.

3.2. A Differential Game Model

The notations and symbols used in the model are as follows:

S: subscript for the supplier firm
B: subscript for the buyer firm
T: Finite time horizon for the strategies
t: An instant of time in the dynamic game setup
I(t): Risky innovation stock
J(t): Risk less "ordinary" stock
u(t): Investment in breakthrough innovation efforts (risky investments)
g(t): Investment in quality, labor and capital (risk-free investments)
W: Wiener process or Brownian motion
$\{\Omega, F(t), P\}$: Filtered probability space
F(t): P.-augmentation of the natural filtration $F^W(t) := \sigma(W_S{}^u, W_B{}^u ; 0 \leq u \leq t)$
θ: risk-adjusted return on investments in innovation

ρ: Correlation coefficient between the Wiener processes $W_B(T)$ and $Ws(T)$ for the buyer's and supplier's overall gain processes

r: Rate of return on risk-free investments

σ: A function defined on Ω

X_t^u : Overall gain at time t. It represents a diffusion process controlled by supplier X_t^{uS} and buyer X_t^{uB}.

$Zt^{uS,uB} := X_t^{uS}/ X_t^{uB}$ is a jointly controlled diffusion process which is a function of the investment policies u_S and u_B.

$\tau_y^{uS,uB} := \inf \{t > 0: Zt^{uS,uB} = y \}$.The first hitting time to the point y under the specific investment policies u_S and u_B.

$v^{uS,uB}(z)$: expected payoff function under the policy pair (u_S, u_B)

p(z) :"price" that a supplier can demand based on her overall wealth accumulation h(z) : a known function for z = a, z = b, with $h(b) < \infty$

Following Myerson (1991), we assume that the partnership formation game is such that each firm simultaneously announces the set of firms it wishes to ally with. Upon entering an alliance firms bargain over profit shares, and they write the results of the bargaining in a verifiable and enforceable contract. We can then assume that the compatibility costs are split evenly since bargaining can provide any other split through a transfer of profits.

The model considers two investment opportunities for the buyer and the supplier firm: investment in innovation stock I(t) and investment in risk free "ordinary" stock J(t). The growth process of innovation stock for the supplier and the buyer firm is assumed to follow a geometric Brownian motion and I(t) satisfies the stochastic differential equation for supplier S and buyer B.

$$dI_S(t) = \mu_S I_S(t)dt + \sigma_S I_S(t)\, dWs(t)$$
$$dI_B(t) = \mu_B I_B(t)dt + \sigma_B I_B(t)\, dW_B(t) \tag{1}$$

where μ_i, i = B. S are positive constants. The risk-free ordinary stock is assumed to evolve according to:

$$dJ_S(t) = rJ_S(t)dt$$
$$dJ_B(t) = rJ_B(t)dt \tag{2}$$

where $r \geq 0$. To avoid a trivial solution, we assume $\mu_i > r$, for i = S, B since if $\mu_i < r$ then the firms would invest in risk-free investments, which yield higher returns. Let the parameter θ_i denote the risk-adjusted excess return of innovation stock $I_i(t)$ over the risk-free rate of return, for i = S, B. Specifically,

$$\theta_i = (\mu_i - r) / \sigma_i \text{ for } i= S, B \tag{3}$$

Let $u_S(t)$ denote supplier's overall investments in innovation at time t under an investment policy $u_S = u_S(t)$, $t\geq 0$, and similarly, let $u_B(t)$ denote buyer's investments in innovation at time t under an investment policy $u_B = u_B(t)$, $t> 0$. It is assumed that both $u_S(t)$, $t> 0$ and $u_B(t)$, $t>0$ are suitable admissible F(t)- adapted control processes. In other words, $u_S(t)$, and $u_B(t)$, are nonanticipative functions that satisfy $\int_0^T u_S^2 dt$ and $\int_0^T u_B^2 dt < \infty$ for every $T < \infty$. The values of $u_S(t)$, and $u_B(t)$ are restricted to non-negative values.

Let X_t^{uS} denote the overall gain of the supplier firm at time t, if the firm follows policy $u_S = u_S(t)$, $t \geq 0$ with $x(0) = x_o$. This overall payoff includes monetary benefits associated with these investments , for example, increased revenue, profits and non-monetary benefits such as channel power owing to innovation. It is assumed that the proportion of investment not invested in innovation is put into risk free investment options. The evolution of the process can thus be obtained from (1) and (2) and using the definition in (3). The equation can be written as:

$$\begin{aligned} d X_t^{uS} &= u_S(t) X_t^{uS} dI_S(t) / I_S(t) + X_t^{uS} [1 - u_S(t)] dJ_S(t) / J_S(t) \\ &= X_t^{uS} [(r + u_S(t)\sigma_S \theta_S)dt + u_S(t)\sigma_S dW_S(t)] \\ & 0 \leq u_S(t) \leq 1 \ \forall t \end{aligned} \tag{4}$$

Analogously, the equation for the buyer can be obtained as follows:

$$\begin{aligned} d X_t^{uB} &= u_B(t) X_t^{uB} dI_B(t) / I_B(t) + X_t^{uB} [1 - u_B(t)] dJ_B(t) / J_B(t) \\ &= X_t^{uB} [(r + u_B(t)\sigma_B \theta_B)dt + u_B(t)\sigma_B dW_B(t)] \\ & 0 \leq u_B(t) \leq 1 \ \forall t \end{aligned} \tag{5}$$

These equations representing supplier's and buyer's individually controlled overall gain processes are similar to stochastic wealth equations familiar from financial economics (Huang and Litzenberger,1988; Fleming and Rishel, 1986, Chapt. V,§2).

In a supply chain environment the investments in innovation by buyer and supplier firm are expected to be correlated. To allow for this requirement, $W_S(t)$ is considered to be correlated with $W_B(t)$ with the correlation coefficient ρ , that is, $E(W_S(t),W_B(t)) = \rho t$. In this illustration we observe that Xt^{uS} is the diffusion process controlled by supplier and X_t^{uB} is the diffusion process controlled by the buyer firm. The jointly controlled diffusion process can thus be defined as $Zt^{uS,uB} := X_t^{uS} / X_t^{uB}$ where the supplier maximizes $Zt^{uS,uB} := X_t^{uS} / X_t^{uB}$ and the buyer minimizes $Zt^{uS,uB}$ by appropriate investments. It is a function of the investment policies u_S and u_B .Applying Ito's lemma (Malliaris and Brock,1982,p.80) and utilizing the results from (4) and (5) gives

$$d Zt^{uS,uB} = Zt^{uS,uB}[m(u_S(t), (u_B(t))dt + (u_S(t)\sigma_S dW_S(t) - u_B(t)\sigma_B dW_B(t)] \tag{6}$$

where the function $m(u_S(t), (u_B(t))$ is defined as

$$\begin{aligned} & m(u_S(t), (u_B(t)) \equiv m(u_S(t), (u_B(t)): \sigma_S, \sigma_B , \theta_S , \theta_B , \rho) = \\ & u_S(t)\sigma_S \theta_S - u_B(t)\sigma_B \theta_B + u_B(t)^2\sigma^2{}_B - \rho \sigma_S \sigma_B \theta_B u_S(t), u_B(t) \end{aligned} \tag{7}$$

The state dynamics of the stochastic differential game is given by equation (6). For the process Z(t) in equation (6) , let $\tau_y^{uS,uB} := \inf \{t > 0: Zt^{uS,uB} = y \}$ be the first hitting time to the point y under the specific investment policies u_S and u_B. For given number a, b where $a < Z_0 < b$, let $\tau := \min \{\tau_a^{uS,uB} , \tau_b^{uS,uB} \}$ denote the first escape time for the interval (a,b) under the policies u_S and u_B .The escape time signifies the point at which either the supplier or buyer gains channel power due to innovation capabilities.

The objective functional under the policies u_S and u_B are defined as:

$$v^{uS,uB}(z) = E_z\left(\int_0^\tau p(Zt^{uS,uB}) \exp\{(\int_0^t \lambda (Zr^{uS,uB})dr\}dt + \right.$$
$$\left. + h(Zt^{uS,uB}) \exp\{-(\int_0^t \lambda (Zr^{uS,uB})dr\}\right) \quad (8)$$

where $\lambda(z)$ is a given nonnegative function representing the discounting function. This function reflects a risk-adjusted discounting of the payoff function. For mathematical convenience we only consider the cases when the discounting function is a constant λ. The function p(z) is the "price" that a supplier can demand based on his overall wealth accumulation. We assume real bounded continuous functions , and h(z) is a known function for z = a or b , with $h(b) < \infty$. The function allows an investigation of discounted payoff and utility maximization games within the context of the above problem formulation . The supplier would choose a control function $u_S(t)$ in order to maximize $v(Zt^{uS,uB})$ while simultaneously the buyer would choose a control function $u_B(t)$ to minimize $v(Zt^{uS,uB})$.

Perfect, revelation of choices made by the buyer and the supplier firms is assumed. For the supplier firm the objective functional and state dynamics are

$$v^{uS,uB}(Zt^{uS,uB}) = \max E_z\left(\int_0^\tau p(Zt^{uS,uB}) \exp\{(\int_0^t \lambda (Zr^{uS,uB})dr\}dt + \right.$$
$$\left. + h(Zt^{uS,uB}) \exp\{-(\int_0^t \lambda (Zr^{uS,uB})dr\}\right)$$

subject to (6).

For the buyer, the objective functional and the state dynamics can be written as:

$$v^{uS,uB}(Zt^{uS,uB}) = \min E_z\left(\int_0^\tau p(Zt^{uS,uB}) \exp\{(\int_0^t \lambda (Zr^{uS,uB})dr\}dt + \right.$$
$$\left. + h(Zt^{uS,uB}) \exp\{-(\int_0^t \lambda (Zr^{uS,uB})dr\}\right)$$

subject to (6).

3.3. Nature of Games

Here we consider games related to the achievement of relative performance goals and shortfalls. Specifically, for numbers a, b with the associated condition, $aY_0 < X_0 < bY_0$, if the performance in terms of the objective of supplier is considered, upper performance goal b is said to have been reached if $X_t^{uS} = bY_t^{uB}$, for some $t > 0$ and that the lower performance shortfall level a occurs if $X_t^{uS} = aY_t^{uB}$, for some $t > 0$. In general the supplier wins if performance goal b is reached before shortfall level a is reached, while the buyer firm wins if the converse happens.

Two classes of games involving investments by supplier and buyer firms are considered. The first class of game considers the discounted payoff maximization (minimization) objectives. In this class, first a stochastic differential game is considered in which the supplier tries to maximize the expected discounted gain that is achieved upon outperforming the buyer in innovation capability. The buyer at the same time tries to minimize this expected discounted gain to be accrued by the supplier. Since the structure of the differential game is symmetric for both the buyer and the supplier, a straightforward inference can be made for the case when the buyer is investing in innovation to minimize the potential loss if the supplier outperforms. In this class of games, the ratio of the two gains processes $Zt^{uS,uB} := X_t^{uS}/ X_t^{uB}$ is a sufficient statistic to evaluate the investment strategies for the supplier and the buyer firms. This feature makes the objective functional to be dependent only on the gain process .

As an alternative formulation, the other game examined has time dependence that unlike the previous structure of the game allowing only one winner the results suggest the optimal strategies to be adopted by supplier and buyer firm have both firms try to outperform each other and thereby obtain overall surplus. In light of this argument, by making the strategies to be time-dependent, it shows that the relative utility gained by a supplier and buyer can be obtained at any time instant. In these types of games both buyer and supplier receive utility (or disutility) from the ratio of the gain processes (i.e., from the relative performance of their respective gains achieved by investment in innovation stock and in ordinary stock.) where the game is played for fixed duration of time. As in the previous class of games, in these games also the ratio $Zt^{uS,uB} := X_t^{uS}/ X_t^{uB}$ acts as the pertinent state variable.

Class 1: Discounted Payoffs

In this game, the supplier makes investments in innovation to maximize the expected discounted gains of reaching the upper goal b, while the buyer firm invests in innovation to minimize the potential gains by the supplier. For this game to have a solution we require the following condition to hold,

$$F^*(z) = \sup_{uS} \inf_{uB} E_z (e^{-\lambda\tau_b^{uS,uB}}) = \inf_{uB} \sup_{uS} E_z (e^{-\lambda\tau_b^{uS,uB}}) \text{, for } z < u \tag{9}$$

Since the objective is to reach the upper goal b, we can set h(b) = 1. This value models the situation where the supplier attains control of the channel power. This game has the structure of a nonlinear (Dirichlet) problem and therefore we can apply Theorem 1 of Browne (2000). Specifically, in equation (6) we can substitute a known discount .factor $\lambda(z) = \lambda > 0$. The following three cases are considered regarding the value of p(z):

Case A: p(z) = 0

In this case the supplier invests in innovation to maximize the terminal value of the objective functional by maximizing the gain process at the terminal time. The buyer on the other hand invests in innovation to minimize this terminal value. When the upper goal is reached the function h(z) takes the value h(b) = 1. This is manifested in the form of lock-ins and externalities that can be gained by the dominant partner.

Case B: p(z) = p, a constant price

In case B, a positive non-zero value of "price" p(z) is considered. In this case, the role of "price" in the nature of optimal control function is evaluated.

Case C: p(z) = a concave increasing function of z

In this case, the evolution of the "price" as a function of z is considered. The gains are manifested in the value of p which is a function of the joint gain process z at an instant of time in the game, and also on the terminal value of the objective functional.

Class 2: Utility-Based Games

In this class of game there is an explicit time dependence of the strategies by supplier and buyer firms. The objective functional is of the form given in the solution of a nonlinear (Cauchy) problem (as in Browne, 2000,Theorem 2) , and then the utility derived by the buyer and supplier firm is a function of the innovation level at an instant of time t. For this class of game, the following cases are investigated.

Case A': $\beta(z) = 0$, $\lambda(z) = \lambda$ and $U(z) = z^{\alpha}$, for $0< \alpha < 1$

In this case, the investments in innovation are aimed towards the terminal value of the game. In this game the function U(z) denotes the concave increasing utility a firm attains by investments in innovation whereas h(z) denotes a function that takes value at z = a and z = b. (A concave increasing utility function is quite widely used to represent the utility derived by investments in such strategic aspects as, innovation, quality, and advertising.)

Case B': $\beta(z)$ = a concave increasing function of z, $\lambda(z) = \lambda$ and $U(z) = z^{\alpha}$, for $0< \alpha < 1$

In case B', a positive discounting factor and a concave increasing payoff function $\beta(z)$ and utility function U(z) are considered.

3.4. Analysis of the Model

The proofs of the following theorems are given in the Appendix.

Discounted Payoffs

(1) Case A

Theorem 1. If the degree of market advantage of a supplier over a buyer denoted by δ satisfies the conditions $\delta^- > \delta > \delta^+$ where δ^-, δ^+ are as defined in the Appendix

$$\delta^-(\lambda) = (\rho/2)(1 - \sqrt{1 + 4\lambda/\theta_B^2}) \text{ and } \delta^+(\lambda) = (\rho/2)(1 + \sqrt{1 + 4\lambda/\theta_B^2}) \qquad \text{(A8)}$$

then the value of the discounted game (9) is given by

$$F^*(z) = (z/u)^{\eta+} \text{ for } z < u \quad (10)$$

η^+ is defined by

$$\eta^{+,-} = [\theta_B^2 (1 - \delta^2) \pm \sqrt{D}\,] / 2\,[\theta_B^2 (1 + \delta^2 - 2\,\rho\,\delta) + 2\,\lambda\,(1 - \rho^2)] \quad (A6)$$

and the associated saddle point is given by

$$u_S^*(z) = [\theta_S/\sigma_S]\,[(\rho/\delta - 1)\eta^+ - 1] / ((1 - \rho^2)(\eta^+)^2 - 1)],$$
$$u_B^*(z) = [\theta_B/\sigma_B]\,[(1 - \rho\delta)\eta^+ - 1] / ((1 - \rho^2)(\eta^+)^2 - 1)] \quad (11)$$

(2) Case B

Theorem 2. If the degree of market advantage of a supplier over a buyer δ satisfies the conditions $\delta^- > \delta > \delta^+$ where δ^-, δ^+ are as defined in (A8), then the value of the discounted game (9) is given by

$$F^*(z) = (z/u)^{\eta+} (1 - p/\lambda) + p/\lambda \text{ for } z < u \quad (12)$$

η^+ is defined in equation (A6) and the associated saddle point is given by (11)

(3) Case C

Theorem 3. If the degree of market advantage of a supplier over a buyer δ satisfies the conditions $\delta^- > \delta > \delta^+$ where δ^-, δ^+ are as defined in (A14), and θ_B, ρ satisfy the condition $\theta_B^2\,\rho^2 \geq 2$ then the value of the discounted game (9) is given by

$$F^*(z) = (z/u)^{\eta+} \text{ for } z < u \quad (10)$$

η^+ is defined in equation (A12) and the associated saddle point is given by (11).

Corollary: If $\theta_B^2\,\rho^2$ is equal to 2, the results are identical to that in Case A.

However, more generally the relationship between θ_B, the risk-adjusted return on investments in innovation for the buyer and ρ, the correlation coefficient between the Wiener processes $W_B(t)$ and $W_S(t)$ for the buyer's and seller's overall gain processes, can be written as $\theta_B \geq \sqrt{2} / \rho$.

Utility Maximization

(4) Case A'

Theorem 4. If the buyer and supplier are competing in utility maximization objective by maximizing the terminal value with investment in innovation and the discounting factor is λ, then the competitively optimal strategies are given as:

$$u_{SJ}^{*}(z) = [\theta_S/\sigma_S]\,[(\rho/\delta - 1)\alpha - 1] \,/\, (\,(1 - \rho^2)(\alpha^2 - 1)\,) \quad (13),$$

$$u_{BJ}^{*}(z) = [\theta_B/\sigma_B]\,[(1 - \rho\delta\,)\alpha - 1] \,/\, (\,(1 - \rho^2)\alpha^2 - 1)\,] \quad (14)$$

and the value of the game F* (t, z) is given by where $F\,(t, z) = e^{q(\alpha)(T-t)}z^{\alpha}$ where $q(\alpha)$ is

$$q(\alpha) := \alpha\,\theta_B^{\,2}\,[\,(\,1 - \delta^2) - \alpha(\,1 + \delta - 2\rho\delta)]/\,2\,[(1 - \rho^2)\alpha^2 - 1)\,] - \lambda$$

(5) Case B'

Theorem 5. If the buyer and supplier are competing in payoff maximization and terminal utility maximization objectives then the form of competitively optimal strategies are given by (13), (14), and the value of the game F* (t, z) is given by $F\,(t, z) = e^{q(\alpha)(T-t)}z^{\alpha}$ where

$$q(\alpha) := \alpha\,\theta_B^{\,2}\,[\,(\,1 - \delta^2) - \alpha(\,1 + \delta - 2\rho\delta)]/\,2\,[(1 - \rho^2)\alpha^2 - 1)\,] - \lambda + 1 \quad (15)$$

3.5. PROPOSITIONS

All proofs of the propositions will appear in the Appendix

Proposition 1. The solution to the differential game involving discounted payoffs yield highest value when $\delta \geq -\rho + \sqrt{\rho^2 + 1}$

Proposition 2. In a discounted payoff game, the complementarities and synergies in the investments in innovation are a function of who among the supplier and buyer exerts innovation based channel power.

Proposition 3. In a discounted payoff game, for negatively correlated gain processes, and for maximum value of the game (evaluated at $\lim_{\eta+\to 0}$), investments in innovation by a supplier firm would be strictly higher in case B than in the case A and case C, whereas the buyer will not make any investment in innovation in case B but would make investments $\lim_{\eta+\to 0} u_B^{*}(z) = \theta_B/\sigma_B$ in case A and case C.

Proposition 4. For discounted payoff game, in case B,

a. If the ratio, $\delta/\rho > 1$, both supplier and buyer firms would invest higher than in case A and case C;

b If the ratio is such that $0 < \delta/\rho < 1/2$, the buyer would make lesser investments (would make equal investment to case A and case C if $\delta/\rho = 1$) than those made in case A and case C, and the supplier would make no investments,

c If the ratio is such that $1/2 < \delta/\rho \leq 1$, the buyer would make lesser investments than those made in case A and case C. The supplier would make lower investments if the correlation coefficient $\rho = 1$(would make equal' investment to case A and case C if $\delta/\rho = 1$) and would make higher investments otherwise.

Proposition 5. In a discounted payoff game, investments in case A and case C would be identical when

$$\delta = -\rho + \sqrt{}\, \rho^2 + [2\,\lambda(1-\rho^2)+1]$$

In contrast to the discounted payoff maximization game, in utility maximization games, the competitively optimal controls for the supplier and buyer firm are identical in case A' and case B'. Analyzing the competitively optimal control functions for the supplier and buyer firm by taking $\lim_{\alpha\to 0}$ and $\lim_{\alpha\to 1}$ it can be observed that the resulting expressions are similar to those in the analysis of the discounted payoff game. Hence, the observations follow in the case of utility maximization game as well. The only difference lies in the value of the two games considered in case A' and case B'.

3.6. Discussion

We can derive from the above results that in all the cases pertaining to discounted payoff game as well as the utility maximization game, the investments made by the supplier and buyer in innovation are directly proportional to the risk adjusted returns of these investments. This result is quite intuitive because, if the firms can extract better returns from risk-free investments they would indeed do so. Moreover, these investments are also inversely proportional to the variability associated with the returns. Further exploration can be carried out by evaluating

$$\text{investments} \propto \theta_i/\sigma_i\,,\ i = B, S$$

Substituting $\theta_i = [\mu_i - r]\,/\,\sigma_i$, $i = B,S$ above leads to investments $\propto [\mu_i - r]\,/\,\sigma_i$, $i = B, S$

The expression suggests that a firm would consider investing in risky innovations if the risk-free rate of returns is high and if the variance in the evolution of innovation stock is low. The stationary Markov perfect Nash equilibrium results are time invariant and are characterized completely by the parameters of the model.

The impact of correlation between the growth of buyer's and supplier's innovation stock ρ and the power advantage δ cannot be straightforwardly conjectured from the equilibrium expressions. The propositions obtained from further analysis provide some implications of ρ and δ on the nature of relationship and innovation investment strategies.

By evaluating the expression in Proposition 1 with the equality sign, we note that when $\rho = 0$ we have $\delta > 1$. This implies that the degree of advantage of the supplier is either equal to or higher than that of the buyer. Therefore, when the investment plans are absolutely independent, the supplier gains the advantage in the relationship. This could be explained from the conjecture that the supplier may potentially invest into creating resources that could be supplied to other buying firms. The buyer's innovation investments on the other hand are geared towards creating value proposition for the final customers. In the long run therefore, the supplier channel power grows while the buyer's power depends on exogenous demand for resources developed through innovation investments.

For a perfect (positive) correlation (ρ=1) between the gain processes of the buyer and supplier we obtain $\delta > 0.414$. For such a situation, if $0.414 \leq \delta < 1$, the degree of advantage rests with the buyer and for $\delta \geq 1$, the supplier attains the degree of advantage. Perfect correlation is akin to the synergistic wealth formation by the supplier and the buyer. This is representative of the situations when the supply chain partners are collaborating in the "basic research" for creating a new product. The results intuitively suggest that with strong positive correlation between the wealth processes, both buyer and supplier firms could potentially attain the degree of advantage.

Finally, when the stochastic processes are negatively correlated, the supplier will always have higher degree of advantage than the buyer firm because now the value of δ is strictly greater than 1. An explanation for this is that with a negative correlation the two collaborating partners are creating substitute technologies. In such circumstance the result suggests that the gain that a supplier could achieve by creating technology which is potentially used by competitors of firm B, is higher than what the buyer could achieve by locking out the existing supplier.

Case B investigates a situation, in which there is a constant "price" charged by the supplier.

With a negatively correlated gain process it can be argued that the supplier would channel the payoffs into creating substitute products and innovation. By doing so, the supplier could potentially increase the market through other competing buyer firms. On the other hand, with no incentive to influence the "price", the buyer would set her innovation efforts to zero. In contrast, in case A the "price" is set to 0 and therefore both supplier and buyer firms target their innovation investments to gain channel power. In such a hypothetical situation the buyer and supplier would invest a positive amount to ensure that they attain the degree of advantage in the channel at terminal time. In case C, since the "price" is now influenced by the relative gain $Z^{uS,uB}$, the buyer has incentive to invest and compete in the collaborative setup.

From these cases, some inference can be made. First, the onus lies on the buyer to create conditions for the supplier so that the investments are synergistic. As could be observed, owing to the certainty of attaining the degree of advantage, the supplier firm would prefer an uncorrelated or negatively correlated gain process. This suggests that for any buying firm that wishes to be successful in a collaborative relationship, an understanding must be developed about how to own and control critical assets that provide opportunities to create customer dependency and supplier 'lock-ins'. Such understanding normally requires a competence in effective demand, supply, procurement and strategy management.

The results and the discussion connect well with the literature on core capabilities (Prahalad and Hamel 1990) . An uncorrelated or negatively correlated gain process associated with investments in risky innovation by the supplier and buyer firm implies that the responsibilities of the two firms in a partnership are set a priori. This is particularly relevant to cases when the supplier is chosen based on certain unique capabilities. These capabilities could be patented or possibly protected owing to high costs associated with replication. Similarly, a negatively correlated Brownian motion could be conceptualized as a situation in which one of the two supply chain partners is investing to create substitute technology. In light of the above argument, a supplier would gain by making investments in innovation that are independent of the investments made by the buyer. Furthermore, a supplier would also gain by making investments in innovations that are possible substitutes of the buyer's product-process portfolio. On the other hand, the buyer firm would never gain the degree of advantage if the investments in innovation are such that either they are uncorrelated with the investments made by the supplier or alternately, if the investments are potentially aimed at creating a substitute to the suppliers offering.

This can be interpreted in yet another way. We can infer from the results that a synergistic supply chain is dependent on the fact as to who among the supply chain partners actually commands the degree of advantage. In a supply chain where the supplier has the channel power owing to innovation, the innovation investment based gain processes are expected to be negatively correlated and the supplier and the buyer firms would be expected to invest in innovation to create substitutes. Whereas, in a supply chain where the channel power associated with innovation rests with a buyer, it is expected that the investments by the buyer and the supplier firm would be directed towards complementary gains. Although the gain process has been modeled as Brownian motion, the correlation between the gain processes of the buyer and supplier firm can be influenced by managerial actions. Specifically, when the buyer firm has the degree of advantage, the incentive for innovation for the supplier can be structured in such a way that the supplier would prefer considering synergistic and complementary innovation instead of substitutes.

If buyer firms intend to become effective in their ability to appropriate and accumulate value they must understand how to effectively manage the supply relationships (Cox et al. 2002) Therefore, in a collaborative context a competence in procurement management is at least as important for business success as effective demand and strategy management. To achieve sustainable business success, therefore, it is not enough to understand how to innovate with supply so that conditions are created for market closure to competitors. It is also essential to understand the power struggle over value appropriation and accumulation that occurs between buyers and suppliers at all stages in the supply chain networks that are created to produce products and services for final consumers.

There are several examples of strategies adopted by collaborating buyers to achieve sustained competitive advantage. For example, if a component or sub-assembly is considered commercially critical to a vehicle then, as a matter of routine, a Japanese assembler will take an equity stake in the supplier. Where an assembler does not own an equity stake in a supplier, however, it rarely opts to single source. Instead, it will choose to source from two suppliers simultaneously, so that, if one supplier underperforms. then it knows that the business will go instead to a second supplier. With such arrangements many of the opportunism found in a western context is reduced, because the Japanese assemblers insist upon cost transparency on the part of the Supplier as a precondition of signing a contract. Thus, because Japanese assemblers have fewer suppliers to manage, the costs associated with monitoring them for opportunism are correspondingly lower.

A plausible explanation for the failure of lean production in a European context might be the form of implementation (Cox et al. 2002). Japanese practice has been about creating complex networks of interlocking supplier dependencies as previously illustrated. The assembler dominates the sub-assembler, who in turn dominates the component manufacturer. This allows the assembler to drive its operational improvement program throughout the supply network. Many European assemblers, however, have simply outsourced the design, production and supply chain coordination of key sub-assemblies without bothering to ensure that the structures of power that will support such an enterprise are in place.

The economics literature makes an important distinction between information that is public and information that is private. The idea of public information broadly equates to the notion of common knowledge, which simply means something that is widely known. Private knowledge, by contrast, is information that is tightly controlled. In the buyer-supplier exchange, this refers to information that is only known by one of the contracting parties. The existence of such an information asymmetry could be the prerequisite of concealment and manipulation. Without this asymmetry, the objective interests of both parties are revealed and, power resources permitting, they can be aggressively pursued.

According to Williamson (1975. 1985) the risk of a buyer becoming dependent on a supplier was not a function of power, but occurred simply as a result of bad management. Ex post dependency, for example, was a. function of inadequate contracting that had left room for opportunism. A farsighted buyer should have appraised the circumstances that might placed it in a position of dependency. By learning from the experience, therefore, it should have been able to construct appropriate governance structures to avoid a repeat of the problem. If the buyer fails to display such iterative learning, at least behavior of its suppliers would reach such a level that its competitiveness and, ultimately, its survival would be threatened.

Specifically for earning rents the buying firm ought to develop critical supply chain assets. Cox et al. (2002) suggest that critical assets are based on supply chain resources that can be made relatively scarce, and that allow their owners both to close the market for this particular supply chain resource to other potential competitors; and to effectively leverage value from their downstream customers and upstream suppliers. The relative scarcity of the resources on which such assets are based implies that only a very small number of firms are likely to have them within any particular supply chain or market at any given time. Rents are earned through the continuous actualization of potential supply chain and market power. In other words, a firm earning rents will recognize that it has to focus on both supply chain and market power and will employ that power effectively. Essentially, there are three mechanisms through which firms without critical assets might seek to reconfigure the existing structure of power in any particular market, or supply and value chain. These are product innovation, process innovation and supply chain innovation.

Supply chain power is based upon owning or controlling a supply chain resource that combines high degrees of utility and scarcity for a buyer or a supplier in the context of a particular transaction. It is always this combination of the two variables that provide the basis for supply chain power. If, for example, a buyer is facing an extensive pool of interchangeable and openly competitive suppliers, it makes no difference how high the utility is of the resource that it is attempting to buy. In these circumstances none of the suppliers can exert supply chain power because the relative scarcity of the resource in question is low. None of the supplier in such situation would possess a critical asset because there is high imitability leading to a highly contested market. The possibility of supply innovation means that both dominant and dependent firms should be constantly aware that most power relations are unlikely to be permanent. There is a strong probability, particularly over the longer term, that potential competitors, as well as dependent buyers or suppliers, will attempt to reduce their vulnerability by searching for supply innovation, or by seeking out new suppliers or customers through product, process or supply chain innovation .

REFERENCES

Browne,S. (2000), 'Stochastic Differential Portfolio Games', *Journal of Applied Probability* 37,126-147

Clark,K.B. and Fujimoto,T. (1991), *Product Development Performance*, Boston: Harvard Business School Press

Cox, Andrew; Ireland, P., Lonsdale,C., Sanderson,J., Watson,G. (2002), *Supply Chains, Markets and Power: Mapping Buyer and Supplier Power Regimes*, London: Routledge

Dorfman, N.(1987), *Innovation and Market Structure: Lessons from the Computer and Semiconductor Industries*, Boston: Ballinger

Fine,C,H, (1999), *Clockspeed: Winning Industry Control in the Age of Temporary Advantage*, New York: Perseus

Fisher,F.M., Gowan,J. and Greenwood,J.E.(1983), *Folded, Spindled and Mutulated, Economic Analysis and U.S. v. IBM*, Cambridge,Ma: MIT Press

Fleming,W.H. and Rishel, R.W. (1986), *Deterministic and Stochastic Control,* 3rd ed., Berlin: Springer

Huang,C. and Litzenberger,R. (1988), *Foundations for Financial Economics,* New York : Elsevier

Malliaris,A.G. and Brock,W.A.(1982), *Stochastic Methods in Economics and Finance*, Amsterdam: North Holland

Molho, I.(1997), *The Economics of Information: Lying and Cheating in Markets and Organizations*, Oxford: Blackwell

Myerson,R.(1991), *Game Theory: Analysis of Conflict*,Cambridge,Ma.: Harvard Univ. Press

Prahalad, C.K. and Hamel,G.(1990), 'The Core Competence of the Corporation', *Harvard Business Review* , 79-91

Sutton, J.(2001), *Technology and Market Structure*, Cambridge, Ma.: MIT Press

Williamson, O.E. (1975), *Markets and Hierarchies: Analysis and Anti-trust Implications*, The New York: The Free Press

Williamson, O.E. (1985), *The Economic Institutions of Capitalism*, New York: The Free Press

Williamson, O.E. (1999),'Strategy Research: Governance and Competence Perspectives', *Strategic Management Journal* 20, 1087-1109

Wilson,R., Ashton,P. and Egan,T.(1980), *Innovation, Competition, and Government Policy in the Semiconductor Industry*, D.C. Heath: Lexington, Ma.

APPENDIX

Theorem 1. If the degree of market advantage of a supplier over a buyer denoted by δ satisfies the conditions $\delta^- > \delta > \delta^+$ where δ^-, δ^+ are as defined by

$$\delta^-(\lambda) = (\rho/2)(1 - \sqrt{1 + 4\lambda/\theta_B^2}) \text{ and } \delta^+(\lambda) = (\rho/2)(1 + \sqrt{1 + 4\lambda/\theta_B^2}) \quad \text{(A1)}$$

then the value of the discounted game (9) is given by

$$F^*(z) = (z/u)^{\eta+} \text{ for } z < u \quad \text{(10)}$$

η^+ is defined through

$$\eta^{+,-} = (\theta_B^2(1 - \delta^2) \,{}^+_-\, \sqrt{D})\,/\,2[\theta_B^2(1 + \delta^2 - 2\rho\delta) + 2\lambda(1 - \rho^2)] \quad \text{(A2)}$$

and the associated saddle point is given by

$$u_S^*(z) = [\theta_S/\sigma_S]\,[(\rho/\delta - 1)\eta^+ - 1]\,/\,((1 - \rho^2)(\eta^+)^2 - 1)\,,$$

$$u_B^*(z) = [\theta_B/\sigma_B]\,[(1 - \rho\delta)\eta^+ - 1]\,/\,((1 - \rho^2)(\eta^+)^2 - 1)$$

Proof: In this case Theorem 1 is applied with $\lambda(z) = \lambda > 0$, $p(z) = 0$ and setting $h(b) = 1$. Specifically, according to Theorem 1, Browne (2000), $F^*(z)$ must be a fast increasing concave solution to

$$(zF_z(z)^2/\,2\Gamma F(z))\,\theta_B^2[(1 - \delta^2)F_z(z) - (1 + \delta^2 - 2\rho\delta)(F_z(z) + z\,F_{zz}(z))] - \lambda\,F_z(z) = 0\,,$$

$$\text{for } z < u \text{ with } F^*(b) = 1 \quad \text{(A3)}$$

Γ denotes the differential operator defined by $\Gamma\psi(z) := (1 - \rho^2)\,[\,\psi_z(z) + z\,\psi_{zz}(z)]^2 - \psi_z(z)^2$

Solutions of the nonlinear Dirichlet problem of (A3) are of the form $(z/b)^\eta$ where η is a root to the quadratic,

$$\eta^2[\theta_B^2(1 + \delta^2 - 2\rho\delta) + 2\lambda(1 - \rho^2)] - \eta\theta_B^2(1 - \delta^2) - 2\lambda = 0 \quad \text{(A4)}$$

The discriminant of this quadratic is

$$D = [\theta_B^2(1 - \delta^2)]^2 + 8\lambda\,[\theta_B^2(1 + \delta^2 - 2\rho\delta) - 2\lambda(1 - \delta^2)\,] \quad \text{(A5)}$$

which is positive. It can be observed that (A4) admits two real roots $\eta^+(\lambda,\delta,\rho)$ and $\eta^-(\lambda,\delta,\rho)$ where

$$\eta^{+,-} = [\theta_B^2(1 - \delta^2) \pm \sqrt{D}\,]\,/\,2\,[\theta_B^2(1 + \delta^2 - 2\rho\delta) + 2\lambda(1 - \rho^2)] \quad \text{(A6)}$$

Since $\lambda > 0$ and $\theta_B^2 (1 + \delta^2 - 2 \rho \delta) + 2 \lambda (1 - \rho^2) > 0$ we have $\eta^- < 0 < \eta^+$. However, since we require $F_z > 0$, and $2F_z+zF_{zz} > 0$, only the positive root η^+ is relevant. Note that for concavity we require an additional condition that $\eta^+ < 1$. Therefore, we must have the following condition,

$$Q_2(\delta) := \delta^2 \theta_B^2 - \delta\rho\theta_B^2 - \lambda\rho^2 > 0 \tag{A7}$$

This equivalence condition follows from the elementary fact that for the quadratic equation a $x^2 + bx + c$, with $a > 0$, the requirement that the larger root be less than 1, is equivalent to the requirement that $a + b + c > 0$. Applying this fact to equation (A4) the condition $Q_2(\delta) > 0$ is obtained. The equation $Q_2(\delta) = 0$ admits two roots,

$$\delta^-(\lambda) = (\rho/2)(1 - \sqrt{(1 + 4\lambda/ \theta_B^2)}) \text{ and } \delta^+(\lambda) = (\rho/2)(1 + \sqrt{(1 + 4\lambda/ \theta_B^2)}) \tag{A8}$$

Equation $Q_2(\delta) > 0$ holds only for $\delta < \delta^-(\lambda)$ and $\delta > \delta^+(\lambda)$ With no discounting, (A8) yields $\delta^-(\lambda) = 0$ and $\delta^+(\lambda) = \rho$. Through the value of the optimal portfolio strategies (Browne,2000,Theorem 1)

$$u_{Sv}^*(z) = [\theta_S/\sigma_S]\, [\psi_z(z)/\Gamma\psi(z)]\, [(\rho/\delta - 1)(\psi_z(z) + z\psi_{zz}(z) - \psi_z(z))]$$
$$u_{Bv}^*(z) = [\theta_B/\sigma_B]\, [\psi_z(z)/\Gamma\psi(z)]\, [(1 - \rho\delta)(\psi_z(z) + z\psi_{zz}(z) - \psi_z(z))] \tag{A9}$$

the competitively optimal control functions for innovation strategies for the supplier firm and the buyer firm can be obtained as:

$$u_S^*(z) = [\theta_S/\sigma_S]\, [(\rho/\delta - 1)\eta^+ - 1] / ((1 - \rho^2)(\eta^+)^2 - 1)] ,$$
$$u_B^*(z) = [\theta_B/\sigma_B]\, [(1 - \rho\delta)\eta^+ - 1] / ((1 - \rho^2)(\eta^+)^2 - 1)] \tag{A10}$$

Theorem 2. If the degree of market advantage of a supplier over a buyer δ satisfies the conditions $\delta^- > \delta > \delta^+$ where δ^-, δ^+ are as defined in (A8), then the value of the discounted game (9) is given by

$$F^*(z) = (z/u)^{\eta+} (1 - p/\lambda) + p/\lambda \text{ for } z < u \tag{12}$$

η^+ is defined in equation (A6) and the associated saddle point is given by (11), or equivalently, (A10).

Proof: In this case $\lambda(z) = \lambda > 0$, and $p(z) = p$. For this case, $F(z)$ must be a fast increasing concave solution to (A3) with $F^*(b) = 1$. This problem has a solution which is of the form,

$$\{ (z/b)^{\eta+} (p/\lambda) + (z/u)^{\eta+} (1 - z/u)^{\eta+}) \}$$

where η^+ is defined in equation(A6). Substituting this expression in equations (A9), respectively, of Theorem 1, the competitively optimal investment strategies for the supplier and buyer firm can be obtained as (A10).

Theorem 3. If the degree of market advantage of a supplier over a buyer δ satisfies the conditions $\delta^- > \delta > \delta^+$ where δ^-, δ^+ are as defined in (A14), and θ_B , ρ satisfy the condition $\theta_B^2 \rho^2 \geq 2$ then the value of the discounted game (9) is given by

$$F^*(z) = (z/u)^{\eta+} \text{ for } z < u \tag{10}$$

η^+ is defined in equation (A12) and the associated saddle point is given by (11).

Proof: In this case Theorem 1 is applied with $\lambda(z) = \lambda > 0$, $p(z)$ = a concave increasing function of z and setting $h(b) = 1$. Specifically, according to Theorem 1, Browne (2000), $F^*(z)$ must be a fast increasing concave solution to (A3).

To make the problem stated in equation (A3) easy to solve we consider a particular functional form of p. Specifically we consider $p(z) = (z/b)^{\eta+}$ where η^+ is the positive root of the quadratic

$$\eta^2[\theta_B^2 (1 + \delta^2 - 2 \rho \delta) + 2 \lambda (1 - \rho^2)] - \eta\theta_B^2 (1 - \delta^2) - (2\lambda - 1) = 0 \tag{A11}$$

The solution of the Dirichlet problem (A3) with p(z) as defined is also of the form $(z/b)^{\eta+}$. The discriminant of equation (A11) is:

$$D = [\theta_B^2 (1 - \delta^2)]^2 + 4 (2\lambda - 1) [\theta_B^2 (1 - \delta^2 - 2 \rho \delta) - 2\lambda (1 - \delta^2)]$$

The positive root of equation (A11) is

$$\eta^+ = [\theta_B^2 (1 - \delta^2) \pm \sqrt{D}\,] / 2 [\theta_B^2 (1 - \delta^2 - 2 \rho \delta) + 2 \lambda (1 - \rho^2)] \tag{A12}$$

For concavity,, we require an additional condition $\eta^+ < 1$. This also ensures that the expression for p(z) above is concave as required for the analysis. Therefore we must have the following condition

$$Q_2(\delta) := \delta^2 \theta_B^2 - \delta\rho\theta_B^2 - \lambda\rho^2 + 1/2 > 0 \tag{A13}$$

The equation $Q_2(\delta) = 0$ admits two roots

$$\delta^-(\lambda) = (\rho/2)(1 - \sqrt{}\,(1 + (4\lambda/\,\theta_B^2)(\lambda - 1/2\rho^2)) \text{ and}$$
$$\delta^+(\lambda) = (\rho/2)(1 + (4\lambda/\,\theta_B^2)(\lambda - 1/2\rho^2)) \tag{A14}$$

$Q_2(\delta) > 0$ holds only for $\delta^-(\lambda) > \delta$ and for $\delta^+(\lambda) < \delta$. With no discounting it can be noted from equation (A14), that $\delta^-(0) = (\rho/2)(1 - \sqrt{}\,(1 - 2/\,\theta_B^2\rho^2)$ and $\delta^+(0) = (\rho/2)(1 + \sqrt{}\,(1 - 2/\,\theta_B^2\rho^2)$

To ensure a real value for δ^- and δ^+, the following condition is imposed on the possible values of θ_B and ρ:

$$\theta_B^2\rho^2 \geq 2 \tag{A15}$$

Applying equation (A9) of Theorem 1, the competitively optimal control function for innovation strategies for the supplier firm and the buyer firm can be obtained through (A10)

Corollary: If $\theta_B^2\rho^2$ is equal to 2, the results are identical to that in case A. However, more generally the relationship between θ_B, the risk-adjusted return on investments in innovation for the buyer and ρ, the correlation coefficient between the Wiener processes $W_B(t)$ and $W_S(t)$ for the buyer's and seller's overall gain processes, can be written as $\theta_B \geq \sqrt{2} / \rho$.

Theorem 4. If the buyer and supplier are competing in utility maximization objective by maximizing the terminal value with investment in innovation and the discounting factor is λ, then the competitively optimal strategies are given as:

$$u_{SJ}^*(z) = [\theta_S/\sigma_S]\,[(\rho/\delta - 1)\alpha - 1] \,/\, (\,(1-\rho^2)(\alpha^2 - 1)\,) \quad (13),$$

$$u_{BJ}^*(z) = [\theta_B/\sigma_B]\,[(1 - \rho\delta\,)\alpha - 1] \,/\, (\,(1-\rho^2)\alpha^2 - 1)\,] \quad (14)$$

and the value of the game F* (t, z) is given by where $F(t, z) = e^{q(\alpha)(T-t)}z^{\alpha}$ where $q(\alpha)$ is

$$q(\alpha) := \alpha\,\theta_B^2\,[\,(1 - \delta^2) - \alpha(\,1 + \delta - 2\rho\delta)]/\,2\,[(1-\rho^2)\alpha^2 - 1)\,] - \lambda \quad \text{(A16)}$$

Proof. Let $F^*(t,z)$ denote the value of this game – should it exist. Therefore, we have

$$F^*(t,z) = \mathrm{Inf}_{uB}\mathrm{Sup}_{uS}\, F^{uS,uB}(t,z) = \mathrm{Sup}_{uS}\mathrm{Inf}_{uB}\, F^{uS,uB}(t,z) \quad \text{(A17)}$$

In this case, by Theorem 1, $F^*(t,z)$ must be a fast increasing concave solution to

$$F(t,z) + (z\,F_z^2\,(t,z)/\,2\Gamma F(z))\,\theta_B^2[(1-\delta^2\,)F_z(t,z) - (1+\delta^2 - 2\rho\delta)(\,F_z(t,z) + z\,F_{zz}(t,z))] - \lambda\,F_z(t,z) = 0 \quad \text{(A18)}$$

The value function F(t, z) is obtained as

$$F(t, z) = e^{q(\alpha)(T-t)}z^{\alpha} \quad \text{(A19)}$$

where $q(\alpha)$ is defined by (A16).

Substituting the values in a nonlinear Cauchy problem (Browne, 2000, Theorem 2) we obtain the competitively optimal strategies (13) and (14)

Theorem 5. If the buyer and supplier are competing in payoff maximization and terminal utility maximization objectives then the form of competitively optimal strategies are given by (13), (14), and the value of the game F* (t, z) is given by $F(t, z) = e^{q(\alpha)(T-t)}z^{\alpha}$ where

$$q(\alpha) := \alpha\,\theta_B^2\,[\,(1 - \delta^2) - \alpha(\,1 + \delta - 2\rho\delta)]/\,2\,[(1-\rho^2)\alpha^2 - 1)\,] - \lambda + 1 \quad (15)$$

Proof. The proof proceeds like the one in Theorem 4 except that F* (t, z) must be a fast increasing concave solution to an added term of (A18)

$$F(t,z) + (z F_z^2 (t,z) / 2\Gamma F(z))\, \theta_B^2 [(1 - \delta^2) F_z(t,z) - (1 + \delta^2 - 2\rho\delta) (F_z(t,z) + z F_{zz}(t,z))] + \beta(z) - \lambda F_z(t,z) = 0 \qquad \text{(A20)}$$

For mathematical convenience, the functional form of $\beta(z)$ is considered identical to $F(t,z)$. $\beta(z)$ is therefore assumed to be $e^{q(\alpha)(T-t)} z^{\alpha}$. Since α is assumed to be strictly between 0 and 1, the concavity requirement for $\beta(z)$ is satisfied. Substituting the values in the nonlinear Cauchy problem , the competitively optimal strategies are obtained as in (13),(14).

Proposition 1. The solution to the differential game involving discounted payoffs yield highest value when $\delta \geq -\rho + \sqrt{\rho^2 + 1}$.

Proof. Evaluating the implications of the different cases in discounted payoff objectives, we observe that the solutions in Case A and Case C have equivalent representations

$F^*(z) = (z/u)^{\eta+}$ for $z < u$.

The corresponding solution for Case B is

$F^*(z) = (z/u)^{\eta+} (1 - p/\lambda) + p/\lambda$ for $z < u$ .Both of these expressions yield the highest value of 1 when $\lim \eta^+ \to 0$. This implies $\theta_B^2 (1 - \delta^2) \pm \sqrt{D} = 0$.

After some algebraic manipulations the following expression is obtained, $\theta_B^2 (1 - \delta^2 - 2 \rho \delta) = 2 \lambda (\rho^2 - 1)$. Since the right hand side of the above expression is less than or equal to 0, the following relation need to hold, $\delta^2 + 2 \rho \delta - 1 \geq 0 \Rightarrow \delta \geq -\rho \pm \sqrt{\rho^2 + 1}$

Since, the value of δ should be positive, only the positive root is relevant, that is, $\delta \geq -\rho \pm \sqrt{\rho^2 + 1}$ (A21)

Proposition 2. In a discounted payoff game, the complementarities and synergies in the investments in innovation are a function of whom among the supplier and buyer exerts innovation based channel power.

Proof: (A21) can be rewritten as

$$\rho \geq (1 - \delta^2)/2\delta \qquad \text{(A22)}$$

Analyzing (A22) with equality sign, it can be observed that if the supplier has a higher degree of advantage (and therefore, $\delta > 1$) then the Brownian motion leading to gain process from innovation for the buyer and supplier is expected to be negatively correlated. On the other hand, if the degree of advantage is in favour of the buyer firm (and $\delta < 1$) then the stochastic process is expected to be positively correlated.

Proposition 3. In a discounted payoff game, for negatively correlated gain processes, and for maximum value of the game (evaluated at $\lim_{\eta+\to 0}$), investments in innovation by a supplier firm would be strictly higher in case B than in the case A and case C, whereas the buyer will not make any investment in innovation in case B but would make investments $\lim_{\eta+\to 0} u_B^*(z) = \theta_B/\sigma_B$ in case A and case C.

Proof: The value of η^+ is such that $0 < \eta^+ < 1$. For u_S^* and u_B^* in Theorem 1 and 2, we consider $\lim_{\eta+\to 0}$ and $\lim_{\eta+\to 1}$. For case A and case C, this leads to $\lim_{\eta+\to 0} u_S^* = \theta_S/\sigma_S$ and $\lim_{\eta+\to 0} u_B^* = \theta_B/\sigma_B$. For case B the expression reduces to

$\lim_{\eta+\to 0} u_S^* = \theta_S/\sigma_S\,[(2 - \rho/\delta)/\rho^2)]$ and $\lim_{\eta+\to 0} u_B^* = \theta_B/\sigma_B\,(\delta/\rho)$.

In all three cases , the investments in innovation by supplier and buyer firm are directly proportional to the risk adjusted return on these investments. However, in case B the optimal investments also depend on correlation between the gain processes and on the degree of advantage between the buyer and supplier firm. Specifically, if the gain processes are negatively correlated, then in case B, the investments in innovation by the supplier are strictly greater than that in case A and case C. However, with negative correlation, the investment in innovation by the buyer would be equal to zero, since the value of control has lower bound by zero and negative values are not permitted.

Proposition 4. For discounted payoff game, in case B,

a If the ratio, $\delta/\rho > 1$, both supplier and buyer firms would invest higher than in case A and case C;

b If the ratio is such that $0 < \delta/\rho < 1/2$, the buyer would make lesser investments (would make equal investment to case A and case C if $\delta/\rho = 1$) than those made in case A and case C, and the supplier would make no investments,

c If the ratio is such that $1/2 < \delta/\rho \leq 1$, the buyer would make lesser investments than those made in case A and case C. The supplier would make lower investments if the correlation coefficient $\rho = 1$(would make equal' investment to case A and case C if $\delta/\rho = 1$) and would make higher investments otherwise.

Proof: For case A and case C, we have $\lim_{\eta+\to 0} u_S^* = \theta_S/\sigma_S$ and $\lim_{\eta+\to 0} u_B^* = \theta_B/\sigma_B$. These expressions do not depend on ρ. However, for case B the expressions reduce to $\lim_{\eta+\to 0} u_S^* = \theta_S/\sigma_S\,[(2 - \rho/\delta)/\rho^2)]$ and $\lim_{\eta+\to 0} u_B^* = \theta_B/\sigma_B\,(\delta/\rho)$. For $\delta/\rho > 1$, $(2 - \rho/\delta)/\rho^2 > 1$ and hence the supplier would invest more than the investments made in case A and case C. Once again the result for the buyer is a straightforward substitution of $\delta/\rho > 1$ in $\lim_{\eta+\to 0} u_B^* = \theta_B/\sigma_B\,(\delta/\rho)$. For $0 < \delta/\rho < ½$, the numerator of the expression for $\lim_{\eta+\to 0} u_S^* < 0$ hence the supplier should set the control to zero. The corresponding proposition for the buyer firm is a straightforward result of substituting $0 < \delta/\rho < ½$ in the expression for $\lim_{\eta+\to 0} u_B^*$. Finally, for $1/2 < \delta/\rho < 1$, with perfect correlation ($\rho = 1$) the value of $\delta < 1$. In such a case $2 - \rho/\delta < \rho^2$ and therefore the investment made by the supplier in case B would be lower than that in case a and case C. Alternatively, when ($0 < \rho < 1$), we will have $2 - \rho/\delta > \rho^2$ and accordingly the investments made by the supplier in this case would be higher.

Proposition 5. In a discounted payoff game, investments in case A and case C would be identical when

$$\delta = -\rho + \sqrt{}\,\rho^2 + [2\,\lambda(1 - \rho^2) + 1] \qquad \text{(A23)}$$

Proof: Qualitatively, case A and case C are equivalent. The only difference in the two cases is the value of η^+ as a result of different values of the discriminant D. Therefore, for the investments to be equal we require the discriminant for Case A,

$$[\theta_B^2 (1 - \delta^2)]^2 + 8 \lambda [\theta_B^2 (1 + \delta^2 - 2 \rho \delta) - 2\lambda (1 - \delta^2)]$$

to be equal to that in case C,

$$D = [\theta_B^2 (1 - \delta^2)]^2 + 4 (2\lambda - 1) [\theta_B^2 (1 - \delta^2 - 2 \rho \delta) - 2\lambda (1 - \delta^2)]$$

With some algebraic manipulations we can obtain the desired result , that is, (A23)

Chapter 4

4. COOPERATIVE R&D, COLLUSION AND HIGH TECH COMPETITION

4.1. INTRODUCTION

Inter-firm relationships in the R & D first stage are often assumed to be either cooperative or non-cooperative, while a second stage product market is usually characterized by a non-cooperative Cournot competition. Most of the present R & D literature concentrates on the comparison of the pure cooperative case to the pure non-cooperative first stage, given Cournot competition in the product stage. Such frameworks may not be applicable to situations where either: (a) the firms' technology is determined by a mixture of independent R & D and cooperative research joint ventures (RJV), or (b) product market competition is not Cournot. A model of joint research venture operating competitively in a differentiated product market would allow participating firms to engage in independent R & D in addition to that performed jointly, and you see evidence of that, across the board, in a number of Japanese high tech industries (Suzumura, 1998).

After Schumpeter (1942) emphasized the importance of technological progress for economic growth, much attention has centered on the relationships between product market structure and technological progress. However, the relationship between market structure and technological progress is still an open question. The ambiguity regarding this relationship also results in difficulties in analyzing the benefits and costs of R & D competition. It is difficult to determine whether cooperation in R & D will result in collusion (and anti-competitive behavior) in the production stage or how the concentration ratio will affect R & D investment. Instead of analyzing a complete set of interactions, economists have tackled the issues related to cooperative R & D by adopting a two stage model and concentrating their attention on the effects of R & D competition before considering the competitive interactions of firms in the product market. They explicitly or implicitly assume that symmetric firms are effectively prohibited from collusion. Grossman and Shapiro (1986) and Katz (1986) first used this approach to analyze the effects of cooperative R & D.

Grossman and Shapiro adopt the upstream and downstream perspective and describe the possible benefits and costs of a research joint venture. Katz proposes a four stage model in which R & D activities are specified by three stages. Using this model, he discusses the general effects of cooperative R & D. Both approaches emphasize the possibility that cooperation produces greater total R & D because it can internalize the spillover externality, thereby avoiding duplication of R & D efforts and thus decreasing each firm's R & D expenditure. They also note the possibility that a RJV may have an anti-competitive effect when product market competition is intensive and suggest that the negative effect of a RJV may be prevented by allowing the participating firms to engage in independent R & D.

D'Aspremont and Jaquemin (1988) develop a constructive model and prove that cooperative R & D produces greater R & D effort in equilibrium than non-cooperative R & D when the spillover rate is relatively high and the product market is modeled as a homogeneous goods Cournot competition. In this model, both firms in the cooperative R & D venture coordinate their R & D expenditure to maximize joint profits. D'Aspremont and Jacquemin show that while one might expect cooperation to lead to a reduction of R & D expenditure by avoiding wasteful duplication, in fact cooperation actually produces greater R & D when the spillover rate is relatively high. A limitation in their model is that the firms participating in the RJV do not share their R & D outcomes but rather simply coordinate their R & D spending. This naturally leads to the question of why the firms want to coordinate their R & D expenditure. Moreover, the coordination of R & D expenditure will not necessarily avoid duplication of R & D since the participants do not share the results. Kamien, Muller and Zang (1992) extend d'Aspremont and Jacquemin's model to the case when the R & D outcome is fully shared and still conclude that a RJV results in greater R & D output than noncooperative R & D competition. Choi (1993) generalizes the model to the case where the R & D outcome is uncertain and finds the same outcome.

Although d'Aspremont and Jacquemin, Kamien et al and Choi succeed in showing the desirability of cooperative R & D, their work does not take into account some of the negative effects of cooperative R & D which were emphasized by Grossman and Shapiro and Katz. They fail to show the anti-competitive danger of cooperative R & D and the role of independent R & D (see also Jacquemin and Slade,1989, p.440).Additionally, Grossman and Shapiro and Katz emphasize the usefulness of working with differentiated goods markets and the possibility that product market competition may affect incentives to participate in cooperative R & D. To address these issues, Kamien et al adopt a horizontally differentiated goods market. But, in their analysis, it is difficult to determine how the degree of product differentiation affects the incentives to conduct R & D. Kamien et al build on the model introduced by Dixit (1979) and apply their analysis to the case in which the R & D outcome is fully shared among the participants. By assuming Cournot competition and concavity of the objective function, they show that full cooperation produces more R & D than non-cooperation. However, their specification of the R & D production function makes it difficult to compute the effect of product differentiation on R & D outcomes in that it does not allow for an analysis of the effect of changes in the parameters on R & D activity. Moreover, their model can explain neither the anti-competitive effect of cooperative R & D nor the role of independent R & D.

A distinctive characteristic of R & D is the spillover externality effect. If R & D for the single firm is not appropriable, the incentives at the industry level to do R & D are reduced. On the other hand, restoring appropriability by licensing, also incorrectly prices the good that R & D has created and may result in redundant and excessive levels of R & D. A solution to the appropriability problem can be found by cooperation in R & D. By working together, the firms under the cooperative agreement can internalize the spillover externality. Moreover, cooperation makes it possible to share the burden of R & D cost, avoid duplicated R & D efforts and save transfer costs. D'Aspremont and Jacquemin, Kamien, Muller and Zang and Choi emphasize all of these advantages in their constructive models. In addition, by assuming Cournot competition, they emphasize that cooperative R & D produces more output than noncooperative R & D competition if the internal spillover rate increases under cooperation. That is, they show not only the advantages of cooperative R & D but also the desirability of it. However, as Grossman and Shapiro and Katz previously pointed out , there exists the risk that the firms engaging in cooperation may use a RJV as a vehicle to jointly slow the pace of technological innovation. This paper proves that those risks can arise. By assuming Bertrand competition in the product market, we show that cooperation in R & D does not always produce more output than non-cooperative competition in R & D.

Suppose that cooperative R & D activity is solely determined by a research joint venture, as assumed in most of the literature. Then, if product market competition is intense, the cooperative agreement will be used to restrict the level of R & D since most of the potential gains from innovation will be dissipated to consumers. That is, when firms price compete , cooperation in R & D can be used to avoid the difficulty of a Prisoner's Dilemma, whereas firms in the non-cooperative R & D game are unable to avoid such situation. Unlike the Cournot model, the anti-competitive effect of RJV may be shown in this situation. However, the danger of anti-competitive effect may be reduced or may disappear altogether if the participating firms can also engage in independent R & D. Suppose that the member firms can continue their independent R & D even after agreeing to a cooperative agreement. If the research joint venture sets investment on R & D to zero, the member firms will return to the same non-cooperative levels of investment undertaken prior to the agreement. Total R & D output in this market will not be the same as was made when the RJV solely determined R & D expenditure. The different structure of the RJV may result in different outcomes and have different implications for R & D activity. For example, one could envisage a scheme of cooperative R & D in which the member firms in the RJV can choose their R & D effort levels independently after the joint venture's decision is made; we then examine its implications on total industry R & D activity to show how different outcomes are possible.

Extending the cooperative model to allow for independent R & D requires specification of both the parents' and the joint venture's incentive structures. We consider the case in which the research joint venture moves first and then the parent firms choose their independent R & D effort given the RJV's decision. Then it is assumed that each member of the RJV has access to information on the joint activity level. Moreover, the manager of the RJV is given incentives by the parent firms, who subsequently decide their own responses to the decision of the RJV. This suggest a three stage model of RJV / product market competition..

In the first stage, firms have an opportunity to join a cooperative R & D venture in which the cost and output of R & D are fully shared. At the second stage, each parent firm chooses its own R & D effort level. R & D efforts are assumed to reduce unit production costs; i.e., attention is confined to process innovation. During the third stage firms compete in the product market with collusion in the product market prohibited.

The analysis first asks how the cooperative R & D level depends on the degree of product differentiation when independent R & D is not allowed. When two goods are close substitutes, and so product competition is intense, most of the potential gains from R & D are dissipated to consumers. It is determined that the cooperative agreement may act as a vehicle to avoid such unprofitable results. When two goods are poor substitutes this result may be reversed, and cooperation may result in greater R & D output than non-cooperation. The result would be similar in the initial case using the Cournot model except that the analysis here reveals that the degree of product differentiation has an important impact on the RJV's incentives to innovate.

Alternative schemes of cooperative R & D can change R & D incentives and its social implications. Specifically, firms may spend at least as much in the cooperative stage as they would under the non-cooperative competition when RJV allows the participants to continue independent R & D. When independent R & D is allowed, both firms know that if cooperative R & D by RJV is not large enough, they will increase their R & D investment.

But, mostly, independent R & D is less efficient than cooperative R & D because it is not shared and does not avoid the duplication on R & D investment. When cooperative R & D allows room for independent R & D, firms can save R & D by agreeing to increase their cooperative investment on R & D. Given the importance of governmental policy with respect to RJVs, understanding the implications of alternative RJV schemes seems to be a valuable one to explore. A scheme that includes research joint venture plays an important role in investment in process innovation. In fact, this analysis shows that when independent R & D is allowed, the level of R & D in the RJV is not lower than in the purely non-cooperative equilibrium. That is, if the RJV allows the parent firms to continue their independent R & D, the danger of the collusive reduction in R & D is unlikely to be serious. Even if member firms' products are close substitutes, an antitrust authority need not worry about the anti-competitive risk of RJVs as long as the RJVs allow participants to continue independent R&D.

Lastly, we examine how changes in the model's parameters affect R&D effort levels in Each scheme. Specifically, a comparative static analysis is performed to determine the effect of the spillover rate ,the internal spillover rate and the cost of R&D on innovative activities. Most writers acknowledge the possibility that the intensity of competition in product markets, the rate of spillover, the efficiency of sharing cooperative R&D and the expensiveness of R&D costs play important roles with respect to R&D investment decisions. Since the framework of this paper allows one to analyze these relationships, it is possible to provide clues to addressing these questions.

4.2. MODEL

This section introduces a three stage model of R & D as an extension of the conventional two-stage model which allows for independent R & D. In the three-stage model, firms have the opportunity to conduct cooperative R & D at the first stage. In the second stage, each firm chooses its own level of R & D, given the cooperative decisions made in the first stage. In the last stage, each firm produces its own product, using the technologies developed in the previous stages, and plays a noncooperative price-setting game. This differs from the two-stage model, where firms cannot conduct independent R & D once they have agreed to participate in cooperative R & D. In this model, the firms choose either to participate in the cooperative agreement or to perform their own R & D non-cooperatively. In the second stage, they produce and compete in the product market, based on the technologies developed in the first stage.

We consider an economy with an oligopolistic sector, consisting of two firms each producing a single good. The price firm i sets and the quantity it realizes are denoted p and q, respectively, where i = 1 or 2. Following Dixit (1979), we specify the representative consumer's preferences regarding q_1 and q_2 as follows:

$$U(q_1,q_2) = a(q_1+q_2) - (q_1^2+2cq_1q_2+q_2^2)/2$$

Firms' products are substitutes, independent, or complements according to whether c>0, =0, or <0. Here, we assume that $0 \leq c < 1$. The representative consumer maximizes by

$$q_i = \text{Max}\left\{\frac{(1-c)a - p_i + cp_j}{1-c^2}, 0\right\}, \text{ where } i = 1, 2, i \neq j.$$

Initially, each firm operates under the same constant returns to scale technology. We denote the unit production cost before innovation by s. For an active market, we assume that (1-c)a>s. Firms can reduce this unit production cost by investing in R & D. In the first stage of the three stage game, firms decide whether or not to participate in the research joint venture and, if both agree, determine their effort levels in cooperative R & D. The output of the RJV is fully shared by both firms. In the second stage, after observing the first-stage decisions, the firms choose their independent R & D effort levels. When the cooperative agreement on R & D is reached, the manager of the joint venture decides its R & D level given later-stage reactions. Specifically, the research joint venture determines its R & D level to maximize the joint profits of the participants while the firms are interested in their own independent profit maximization. If a firm decides not to join the RJV, it then chooses its own R & D effort level noncooperatively and expends resources to develop its own technology. Finally, in the third stage, the previous stages and compete for their own profits in a Bertrand way. Consider the impact of R & D under noncooperative R & D development of a new process. Then both firms simultaneously choose their independent R & D effort level. Let x_i and x_j denote the amount of R & D for firms i and j, respectively. Then, unit production costs are given by $s_i(x_i, x_j) = s - x_i - \beta x_j$, where $0<s<(1-c)a$, $0<\beta<1$ and β represents the spillover parameter. Thus, the analysis allows the spillover externality to affect each firm's R & D production. However, technological improvement is limited, so that unit production cost can never be non-positive. The cost of R & D is assumed to be quadratic, to reflect diminishing returns to R & D expenditures. The usual specification of the R & D cost function is adopted:

$$R_i(x_i) = (\gamma x_i^2)/2$$

Now suppose that both firms agree to participate in the joint venture. Then the RJV and the individual firms determine R & D levels sequentially. Let x, x and x denote the amount of R & D undertaken by the research joint venture, firm i and firm j, respectively. Then, each firm's production cost after innovation is assumed to be $s_i(x_i, x_j) = s - x_i - \beta x_j - \theta x$ where

$0 \leq \beta < \theta \leq 1$.

The parameter θ represents the efficiency of internal technology transfer; i.e., θ measures the ease with which the common technology can be applied to the firms' output production. While the spillover rate of independent R & D may depend on the extent of involvement in the RJV, for simplicity, we assume that it is equal to β.

Under cooperation, the cost of R & D to each firm is assumed to be:

$$R_i (x_i , x) = (\gamma x_i + x/2)^2/2 \quad (1)$$

where x represents the R & D level of the RJV. This cost function represents a situation where the R & D process involves several activities and each firm has its own laboratory in which to conduct R & D. The cooperative RJV contract specifies the amount each participating firm will spend on shared R & D. If neither firm is undertaking independent R & D, the cost function of the RJV reduces to the cost function of a firm owning two identical production facilities. In this case, the total cost of producing cooperative R & D, x, will be

$$\text{Min}_{xi} (\gamma x_i^2)/2 + (\gamma x + x_i)^2/2$$

Assuming symmetry, this indicates that the optimal amount of R & D will be shared. When participants are allowed to continue independent R & D, their total R & D cost is assumed to be as in (1).

Certainly, this scenario is most applicable to R & D processes involving multidimensional components or several feasible paths to a discovery. For example, an automobile manufacturer may have many options for technological development, each of which would be composed of several different sectors of engineering. Moreover, the paths to the development of any given innovation may not be unique and even if the path were unique, there may be uncertainty about which path would bring the desired results. Thus, the individual firms' R & D activity need not follow identical paths. The case considered is one in which the joint venture can allocate two different projects of process innovation to each laboratory. After meeting the requirements of the cooperative R & D agreement, each participant can pursue the given project further so as to increase its own competitiveness. Cooperative agreements between firms with complementary R & D assets are often observed. Alternatively, this model can also represent the case where the total cost of improving a technology is expensive, but can be separated into several sub-projects. In this case, the two firms may agree on ex-ante cross licensing and concentrate their R & D efforts on improving a specific part of the given technology. An example of this type of RJV is found in the automobile industry's attempt to develop a car charged by electric power. In this case, one firm in the joint venture may concentrate on increasing the efficiency of the electric charging system, while another firm concentrates on reducing the cost of producing the electrically adapted engine system. The technologies developed by each firm are then subject to cross licensing. However, each firm may undertake additional R & D beyond that specified in the RJV contract to increase its own competitiveness. The cost function developed above can be applied to either of these examples. Here, the cost function (1) indicates that when each parent firm decides to produce additional information, the marginal cost of independent R & D is continuous and monotonically increasing in the level of R & D output allocated by the RJV.

In the third stage, both firms engage in Bertrand competition, with any collusion, implicit or explicit, in this stage assumed to be effectively prevented. Firms' payoffs consist of profits in the production stage less any R & D expenditure incurred in the previous stages. In addition, it is assumed that R & D cannot drive the marginal production cost to zero. Hence, the unit cost of R & D, y, is assumed to be large enough to guarantee that $s_i(x_i, x_j, x) > 0$. Furthermore, an interior solution to this R & D game is assumed to exist, so that both producers are active even after innovations. Thus, this model is primarily concerned with non-drastic innovation.

4.3. Two Stage Model

This section analyzes a variant of the traditional two stage R & D model. Since the production stage involves Bertrand competition given the technologies developed in the first stage, firm i's overall profit in the noncooperative competition is given by

$$\pi_i = (p_i - s + x_i + \beta x_j)^2 / (1 - c^2) - (\gamma x_i^2)/2 \qquad (2)$$

where

$$p_i = [(2 + c)(1 - c)a + 2s_i + cs_i\,] / (4 - c^2) \qquad (3)$$

Equations (2) and (3) are derived from the conditions for profit maximization given in the Appendix. In the first stage of this noncooperative R & D competition, each firm simultaneously chooses its level of R & D to maximize its own production profit net of R & D expenditure; that is, it solves

$$\text{Max}_{\,xi}\ (p_i - s + x_i - \beta x_j)^2 / (1 - c^2) - (\gamma x_i^2)/2 \text{ with } p_i \text{ given in} \qquad (3)$$

The first order conditions from it are derived as follows:

$$\partial \pi_i / \partial x_i = 2\{(2 + c)(1 - c)a - (2 - c^2)(\, s - x_i - \beta x_j\,)$$
$$+ c(s - x_j - \beta x_i\,)\}(2 - c^2 - \beta c)/(1-c^2)(4-c^2) - \gamma x_i = 0\ ,\ i,j = 1,2,\ i{\neq}j \qquad (4)$$

As was stated in the previous section, one needs to assume that -y is large enough to satisfy the second order sufficiency condition and to keep the production cost from being non-positive. There are two possible cases in which the second order condition is not satisfied. In the first case, both firms continue R & D until unit production cost is driven to zero because γ, the unit cost of R & D, is very low. The other possibility is that no symmetric equilibrium exists. When competition in the product market is intense, both firms have an incentive to overinvest in R & D to increase their competitiveness. But, if neither firm backs down from their competitive positions, both firms' profits may end up negative, which will force one firm to back down. Thus, when the rate of product substitutability is very high, an asymmetric equilibrium is expected. However, the asymmetric equilibrium does not establish which firm will remain active in the market. Because the two firms in this model are assumed to be symmetric, the symmetric result seems to be more appealing since there is no a priori reason to differentiate one firm from the other. In light of this observation, this paper restricts attention to the situation where the second order condition is satisfied. In section 4.2, it was also assumed that cost reduction from R & D cannot exceed current production cost; the possibility of zero marginal cost is excluded. The unit cost of R & D, γ is assumed to be great enough to guarantee that, in equilibrium, $x_i + \beta x_j < s$ or, equivalently, $a/s < \gamma(1+c)(2+c)(2-c)^2/2(1+\beta)(2-c^2 - \beta c)$.

Since we assume $a/s < \gamma(1+c)(2+c)(2-c)^2/2(1+\beta)(2-c^2 - \beta c)$, the second order conditions, $\gamma > 2\ (2-c^2 - \beta c)^2 / (1 - c)^2 (4 - c^2)^2$, are satisfied. Therefore, one obtains the unique following symmetric solution by solving the equations in (4):

$$x\hat{} = 2\ (2 - c^2 - \beta)\ (a - s\ ) / [\gamma(1+c)(2+c)(2-c)^2 - 2(1+\beta)(2-c^2 - \beta c)], \qquad (5)$$

where $(1-c)a>s$,

$$\gamma > 2(1+\beta)\ (2-c^2 - \beta c)a / (1+c)(2+c)(2-c)^2 s\ ,\ 0 \le c < 1\ ,\ 0 \le \beta < 1$$

The next result shows the existence and uniqueness of equilibrium.

Theorem 1. Suppose that $(1-c)\ a>s$, $0 \le c < 1$ and $0 \le \beta < 1$ Then, $x\hat{}$ is the unique interior solution if

$$\gamma > 2(1+\beta)\ (2-c^2 - \beta c)a / (1+c)(2+c)(2-c)^2 s$$

Using equation (5), one can analyze the effect that each parameter has on the equilibrium level of R & D. The spillover effect of R & D, the intensity of product market competition and the cost of R & D seem to play important roles in R & D activities. Until now, the literature has not systematically or formally analyzed the impact of these elements.

Theorem 2. Suppose that the parameters satisfy the constraints given in (5). Then:

(1) $\partial x\hat{}/ \partial\gamma < 0$ and $\partial x\hat{}/ \partial c < 0$.
(2) Define

$$c_o \equiv \{c: 2\ (2 - c^2 - \beta) = \gamma c(1+c)(2+c)(2-c)^2 \text{ and } 0 \le c < 1\}.$$

Then, c_o is unique and $\partial x\hat{}/ \partial\beta \ge 0$ if $0 < c \le c_o$ and $\partial x\hat{}/ \partial\beta < 0$ if $c_o < c < 1$

The first result in Theorem 2 states that the equilibrium level of R & D under non-cooperative competition decreases as either the cost of R & D or the rate of product substitutability increases. Because decreasing returns to R & D expenditure was assumed, it seems natural to expect a firm to decrease its effort level when the cost of R & D increases. As the products become closer substitutes, firms realize that they have little room to profit from R & D competition because product market competition is so intense. Accordingly, they choose to conduct less R & Dactivity in equilibrium.

The second result in Theorem 2 shows that the effect of the spillover externality differs as the rate of product substitutability varies. When each firm is close to being a local monopoly (that is, c is close to zero), an increase in the spillover rate encourages greater R & D. When competition in the product market is not so severe, the gain from cost reduction is exploited by both firms because total industry profit and the innovating firm's profit can increase together. A greater spillover rate increases the marginal profitability of the other firm's R & D, which in turn increases the first firm's profitability, too. Hence, both firms' R &D expands as β increases. When the rate of product substitutability increases, a higher spillover rate decreases the innovating firm's potential gain from its R & D spending, because it also strengthens the rival firm's competitiveness. The profitability of R & D decreases as β increases, and the incentive to conduct R & D is also reduced. Lastly; when the degree of product differentiation is in an intermediate range, the above proposition shows that the spillover rate has a positive effect on R &D until it reaches some critical value, when its effect is reversed. When the spillover rate is relatively low, there exists the possibility that R & D increases both total industry profit and the innovating firm's profit. In this instance, it is true that a larger spillover rate increases the marginal profitability of R & D. As the spillover rate exceeds some critical point, the damage from increasing the rival firm's competitiveness becomes dominant. The marginal profitability of R & D spending decreases and its effect on R & D is reversed.

Given the solution in (5), each product's equilibrium price can be rewritten as follows:

$$p_i = [(1 - c)a + s - (1+\beta)\, \hat{x}\,]/\,(2 - c) \tag{6}$$

where $\hat{x}$ is given in (5). Each firm's net profit is:

$$\pi_i = (1 - c)\, \{a - s + (1+\beta)\, \hat{x}\, \}^2/\,(1+c)(2 - c)^2 - (\gamma \hat{x}^2)/2 \tag{7}$$

when firms agree to cooperate on their R & D activity in the first stage, they form an RJV and the spillover parameter β is set to θ internally, where $\theta \geq \beta$. Since the level of R & D is determined so as to maximize combined profits, the problem solved by the RJV is equivalent to:

$$\text{Max}_x\ 2(p_i - s + \theta x)q_i(p_i) - (\gamma x_i^2)/4 \tag{8}$$

where

$$p_i = (1 - c)a + s - \theta\, x\, /\, (2 - c) \tag{9}$$

The first order condition for (8) is shown in the following equation:

$$8(1 - c)\theta(a - s + \theta x)\, /\, (1 + c)(2 - c)^2 - \gamma x = 0 \tag{10}$$

Again, assuming that the second order condition and the constraints for the positive production costs are satisfied, the following solution optimal level of cooperative R & D is obtained:

$$\bar{x} = 8\theta(1 - c)(a - s) / [\gamma(1 + c)(2 - c)^2 - 8\theta^2(1 - c)] \qquad (11)$$

where

$$(1\text{-}c)a>s,\ 0\leq c<1,\ 0\leq\theta\leq 1 \text{ and } a/s < \gamma(1+c)(2+c)(2\text{-}c)^2 / 8\theta^2(1 - c)$$

When two goods are close to perfect substitutes (that is, c is close to one), the solution in (11) indicates that the research joint venture will produce almost zero R& D investment. This is consistent with the findings of Grossman and Shapiro (1986), and more so in oligopolistic settings by Shapiro (1989), where firms find it in their collective interest to use a cooperative agreement to restrict their R & D when two goods are close substitutes. When the firms are Bertrand competitors with almost homogeneous products, constant returns to scale technology, and equal unit costs of production, any cost reduction brought about by shared R & D causes the equilibrium price to fall by almost the full amount of the cost reduction. Consequently, firms have no incentive to incur any R & D under a cooperative agreement. By assuming Bertrand competition in the product market, one obtains a result that differs from the one that occurs under Cournot competition; noncooperative competition may result in more R & D spending than does the cooperative agreement when two goods are close to perfect substitutes. The implication from Bertrand competition is that cooperation in the R & D stage may not always be better than the noncooperative scheme in terms of improving dynamic efficiency.

Before comparing the two schemes of R& D competition, we consider how each parameter affects the effort level of cooperative R & D.

Theorem 3. Suppose that the parameters satisfy the constraints given in (11). Then:

$$\partial \bar{x} / \partial\gamma < 0\ ,\ \partial \bar{x} / \partial c < 0 \text{ and } \partial \bar{x} / \partial\theta > 0\ .$$

Since the R& D cost function is assumed to be quadratic, it seems natural that the equilibrium level of R & D decreases as the coefficient of the R & D cost function increases. The level of cooperative R & D will also decrease as the rate of product substitutability increases. Since the member firms involved in cooperative R & D share R & D outcomes equally, any increase in competition in the product market squeezes out any potential gains; the incentive to invest in cooperative R & D decreases as the rate of substitution between products increases. On the other hand, the level of cooperative R & D increases as the internal transfer rate of R & D outcomes to participating firms increases. As the efficiency of new technology adoption increases, marginal revenue from R & D activity increases, promoting investment in R & D, ceteris paribus.

Assuming cooperative R & D, each product's market price is given by (9) and each firm's profit can be written as:

$$\pi_i = (1 - c)\ \{a - s + \theta\ \bar{x}\ \}^2 / (1+c)(2 - c)^2 - (\gamma\ \bar{x}^2)/8 \qquad (12)$$

By comparing the results from two schemes of R & D, we obtain the following proposition.

Theorem 4. Suppose that $\theta \geq (1+\beta)/2$. Then, the equilibrium level of R &D , $\bar{x}$ and $\hat{x}$, satisfies: $\bar{x} \geq 2\hat{x}$ if $0 \leq c \leq \bar{c}(\gamma,\theta,\beta)$ and $\bar{x} < 2\hat{x}$ if $\bar{c}(\gamma,\theta,\beta) < c < 1$ where $\bar{c}(\gamma,\theta,\beta)$ is the solution to $(2 - c^2 - c)/(2 - c^2 - \beta c) = 1/2\theta - 2(1 - c)\{2\theta - (1+\beta)\}/\gamma(1+c)(2-c)^2$ and $0 \leq \bar{c}(\gamma,\theta,\beta) < 1$.

Further, if $\theta \leq 1/2$, then $\bar{x} < 2\hat{x}$ unless $\beta = c = 0$ and $\theta = 1/2$

For $\theta \geq (1+\beta)/2$, Theorem 4 implies that the research joint venture results in greater R & D substitutability, c, is relatively low. Not surprisingly, this result coincides with the predictions made by most of the existing literature. When competition is not intense, cooperative R & D results in a greater level of R & D than noncooperative competition, irrespective of whether the product market is Bertrand or Cournot competitive. This result is cited in many contexts to emphasize that a cooperative scheme of R & D has advantages for promoting innovation. But, as the competition in product market is increased, most of the potential profits from the innovation will be dissipated by lower product prices. The research joint venture will attempt to use the cooperative arrangement to limit their R & D, thus retarding the level of innovation. This result suggests that cooperation in R & D should not universally be sanctioned. When $\theta \leq 1/2$, RJV has to spend more to get the same level of cost reduction than noncooperative R & D competition. This is due to the difference between the efficiencies of two schemes on reducing production costs. Since technology transfer under RJV is very costly and so less effective on cost reduction than noncooperative competition, cooperative R & D results in less output than noncooperative R & D. In fact, this conclusion is very obvious and simple. So, in this paper, we largely restrict our attention to the case that $\theta \geq (1+\beta)/2$. If there is not any other statement, here after it is assumed that $\theta \geq (1+\beta)/2$.

This section investigated whether cooperative agreements in R & D produce greater R& D output than noncooperative competition. The results of this analysis show that cooperative R & D schemes do not always yield greater technological improvement, especially when competition in the production stage is intense. When the product market is characterized by price competition and the products in the market are close substitutes, it is shown that cooperative R & D schemes retard technological improvement.

4.4. Three Stage Model

In this section, a three stage game is developed in which a cooperative R & D agreement allows participants to continue independent R& D. The section begins by considering how independent R & D activity is affected by the level of the joint venture's R & D efforts. The analysis determines the level of independent R & D effort that occurs, given the RJV's effort level.

By assuming that the effort level of RJV, x_r, is given, each firm's reaction function can be obtained from the first order condition of its profit maximization problem. Since each firm's price in the production stage is determined in the same way as in the previous section when the unit production cost is given, each firm's maximization problem can be written as:

$$\text{Max}_{x_i}\ (p_i - s + \theta\, x_r + x_r - \beta x_j)^2 / (1 - c^2) - \gamma/2\, (x_i + x_r/2)^2 \qquad (13)$$

where p_i is the same as in (3). By differentiating the above objective function (13) with respect to x_i , setting it equal to zero and solving for x_i one obtains the following reaction function for firm i:

$$x_i\ (x_j) = 2[(2 - c - c^2)(a - s + \theta x_r)\{\beta(2 - c^2)-c\}x_j](2 - c^2 -\beta c) - (1/2)\gamma(1-c^2)(4-c^2)^2 x_r /\gamma(1-c^2)(4-c^2)^2 - 2((2 - c^2 -\beta c)^2 \quad (14)$$

Since the second-order condition is satisfied by the conditions given in (5), each reaction function in (14) can be solved for equilibrium level which will be written in terms of x.. Let's denote those solutions by $x_i^*(x_r)$, i=1 or 2. Then, the conditions necessary for positive levels of independent R & D can be stated.

Theorem 5. Suppose that the conditions given in (5) and (11) are satisfied. Then,. $x_i^*(x_r) > 0$ for every $x_r < x_c$ and $x_i^*(x_r) = 0$ for every $x_r \geq x_c$ where

$$x_c = 4(2-c^2-\beta c)(a-s)/\ [\gamma(1 + c)(2+c)(2 - c)^2 - 4\theta(2-c^2-\beta c)]\ .$$

Furthermore, $\partial x_i^*(x_r)/\partial x_r < 0$ when $x_r < x_c$.

This result states that each participant will continue its own independent R & D if the level of cooperative R & D is not sufficiently large, while its incentive to undertake independent R & D disappears when cooperative R & D reaches some threshold level. In addition, it is shown that each participant's independent R & D decreases as the level of cooperative R & D increases up to that threshold level. When independent R & D is allowed, each member firm has private incentives to strengthen its own competitiveness. If the level of cooperative R & D is less than some critical value, the member firms may find it optimal to conduct noncooperative R & D in addition to the cooperative R & D outcome of the first stage of the game. The first result in Theorem 5 proves the existence of the critical level of cooperative R & D in which each participating firm in the RJV does not have the incentive to surpass the other by continuing independent R & D. It shows that when the level of cooperative R & D effort is high enough, the marginal cost of conducting independent R& D is so high that the participant refrains from independently strengthening its own competitiveness. The existence of the lower bound x,: can be thought of as a simple case of decreasing returns to scale in R & D. These properties on the participants' behavior are later shown to play an important role in the pattern of R & D in equilibrium. Once a firm agrees to any positive level of cooperative R & D, it can be shown that it will have no incentive to conduct any independent R & D in equilibrium. On the other hand, the second result demonstrates that, when the level of cooperative R & D is relatively small, independent R & D increases monotonically as the cooperative R & D level decreases. It states that as the level of the cooperative R & D increases, the incentive to conduct the independent R & D decreases.

We now consider the equilibrium level of cooperative R & D and the participants' responses to it. Because each firm participating in thecooperation in R & D cannot be used to avoid unprofitable investment when its level is not exogenously restricted. However, once each participant realizes that cooperative R& D is less costly than independent R & D, one can show that both participants prefer to conduct all of their R & D exclusively in the joint venture. That is, cooperative R & D is an all or nothing proposition. As shown in (16), each participant's independent R & D, x_i is dependent on the level of cooperative R & D, x_r. The best response of x_i, x_i^*, to x_r can be represented as a function of x_r. We define x* to be the equilibrium level of cooperative R & D which solves the following profit maximization problem.

$$x^* \equiv \{x_r: \text{Max}_{xr}\ \{p_i - s + \theta\, x_r + (1+\beta)\, x_i^*(x_r)\}^2 / (1 - c^2) - \gamma/2\, (x_i^*(x_r) + x_r/2)^2$$

where p_i is given in (3) (15)

Theorem 6. $x^* = \text{Max}\{x_c, \bar{x}\}$ and $x^* > 2\hat{x}$, where $\bar{x}$ and $\hat{x}$ are given in (11) and (5), respectively, and $x_c \equiv 4(2-c^2-\beta c)(a-s)/ [\gamma(1 + c)(2+c)(2 - c)^2 - 4\theta(2-c^2-\beta c)]$. Furthermore, $x_i^*(x^*) = 0$

When the level of cooperative R & D is not restricted and the joint venture permits the participants to continue independent R & D, the incentives for independent R & D become zero if cooperative R & D is sufficiently productive. When firms consider cooperation in R & D to be a less expensive way of conducting R & D, cooperative R & D maintains its cost saving superiority until all incentives to conduct independent R & D disappear. Moreover, the output under cooperative R & D is at least as much as that cooperation in R & D cannot prevent competition when each member retains the right to pursue R & D independently. In the following corollary, conditions are established under which cooperative R & D output is the same as that when independent R & D is not allowed.

Corollary 7. Assume that all of the parameter restrictions given in Theorem 4.6 are satisfied.

Then, $x^* = \bar{x}$ if $(2\theta-1)/(2\theta-\beta) \geq c/(2-c^2)$ where $\bar{x}$ is given in (11). Otherwise, $x^* = x^c$ where x^c is given in Theorem 6

Given the above claim, it is clear that allowing independent R & D affects the results from cooperative R & D when: (1) the rate of product substitutability, c, is relatively high; and (2) the spillover rate of independent R & D, β, and the efficiency of the internal technology transfer of the RJV, θ, are small. When independent R & D is not allowed, it was shown that cooperation in R & D can be used to avoid unprofitable R & D competition. The above analysis determines when anti-competitive behavior is mostly like to arise. When two goods are close substitutes R & D competition will not be profitable, because intensive competition in the product market dissipates potential gains from lower cost. In addition, as the efficiency of internal technology transfer or the spillover rate decreases, cooperative R & D that does not admit independent R & D reduces R & D expenditure more than the alternative of permitting independent activity, as the former scheme is free from the pressure of private interests.

This section introduced a cooperative RJV whilst permitting independent research and development. The analysis found that R & D output under this latter cooperative scheme is always greater than in the case where non-cooperative R& D competition prevails. In addition, even though the given scheme of cooperative R & D permits the member firms to continue independent R& D, the results in our analysis show that no member firms make use of this option in equilibrium.

4.5. Conclusions

Cooperative R & D is known to have several advantages over non-cooperative R & D. A cooperative R & D agreement makes it possible to internalize the spillover externality, share the burden of R & D cost and avoid duplicative efforts.D'Aspremont and Jacquemin, Kamien, Muller and Zang and Choi show that these advantages of cooperative R& D induce greater R& D output than non-cooperative R & D competition. But, when product market competition is intense, the potential gain from innovative activity may be dissipated to customers and a RJV may be used as an instrument to avoid unprofitable competition rather than encouraging R & D. This possibility was analyzed here and it was shown that a RJV may reduce technological improvements when the goods are close substitutes.

This paper also examined the case when an agreement on cooperative R & D does not interfere with the participating firm's ability to continue with independent R & D. It was found that R & D output under a RJV is greater than when there is noncooperative R & D competition. Furthermore, no firms under the cooperative agreement conduct independent R & D in equilibrium, even though the scheme permits such an option.

References

Choi,J.P (1993), 'Cooperative R&D with Product Market Competition', *International Journal of Industrial Organization*, 11, 553-571

D'Aspremont,C. and A. Jacquemin (1988), 'Cooperative and Noncooperative R&D in Duopoly with Spillover', *American Economic Review*, 78, 1133-37

Dixit, Avinash (1979), 'A Model of Duopoly Suggesting A Theory of Entry Barriers', *Bell Journal of Economics,* 1979, 20-32.

Grossman,G.M. and Shapiro,C. (1986),'Research Joint Venture: An Antitrust Analysis', *Journal of Law, Economics and Organization*,2,315-337

Jacquemin, A. and Slade, M.E. (1989), 'Cartels, Collusion and Horizontal Merger', in *Handbook of Industrial Organization* Vol. I, Schmalensee, R. and R.D. Willig, eds., New York: Elsevier Science Publ., 415-473

Kamien,M.I. , Muller,E. and Zang,I. (1992), 'Research Joint Ventures and R&D Cartels', *American Economic Review* 82, 1293-1306

Katz, M.L.. (1986),"An Analysis of Cooperative Research and Development", *Rand Journal of Economics* 17, 527-543

Shapiro, C. (1989), "Theories of Oligopoly Behavior", in *Handbook of Industrial Organization* Vol. I, R. Schmalensee and R.D. Willig, eds., New York: Elsevier Science Publ., 329-414

Schumpeter, J. A. (1942), *Capitalism, Socialism and Democracy,* New York: Harper & Row.

Suzumura, K (1995), *Competition, Commitment and Welfare*, Oxford; Clarendon Press

APPENDIX

DERIVATION of (2) and (3)

Each firm's profit function after innovations is given by

$$\pi_i = (p_i - s + x_i + \beta x_j)\, q_i(p_i) - (\gamma x_i^2)/2 \quad \text{(A1)}$$

By differentiating (A1) with respect to p_i one obtains

$$(1\text{-}c)a\text{-}2p_i + cp_j + s_i = 0 \quad \text{(A2)}$$

where $s_i = s - x_i - \beta x_j$, $i,j = 1,2$ and $i \# j$

From (A2), one gets (2) since $(1\text{-}c)a - 2p_i + cp_j + s_i = 0$

It is easily shown that the second-order derivative from (2.20) with respect to $p_.$, which is -2, is negative. Therefore, the reaction function for $p_.$ is given by

$p_i = \{(1\text{-}c)a + s\text{-}xi\text{-}\beta xj + cp_j\}/2$ (A3) where i, j= 1,2 and $i \neq j$

Solving the equations given in (A3) simultaneously, we get the result given in (3).

Proof of Theorem 1:

By using the equation (3), the objective function in (2) can be written as follows:

$$\pi_i(x_i) = [(2 + c)(1 - c)(a - S) + (2 - c^2 - \beta c\}\, x_i + \{\beta(2 - c^2 - c\}x_j]^2 / (1 - c)^2 (4 - c^2)^2 - \gamma/2\, x_i^2 \quad \text{(A4)}$$

Since the profit function π_i is quadratic in x_i and the second-order condition is satisfied by the given assumption, a unique local maximum coincides with the global maximum.

First, it is proved that the second order conditions for the existence of the equilibrium are satisfied from the given assumption in this proposition. The given assumption is

$$\gamma > 2(1+\beta)(2\text{-}c^2 - \beta c)a / (1+c)(2+c)(2\text{-}c)^2 s$$

Since $(1\text{-}c)a > s$ and $c < 1$,

$$2(1+\beta)(2\text{-}c^2 - \beta c)a / (1+c)(2+c)(2\text{-}c)^2 s > 2(1+\beta)(2\text{-}c^2 - \beta c) / (1 - c^2)(2+c)(2 - c)^2$$

Moreover, $2+c > 2 - c^2 - \beta c$ because $0 \leq \beta < 1$ and $0 \leq c < 1$. So, it can be concluded that

$$\gamma > 2\,(2\text{-}c^2 - \beta c)^2 / (1 - c^2)((4 - c^2)^2$$

That is, the second order condition for the interior solution is satisfied.

Let $\hat{x_i}$ be the maximum point in the above profit function (A4) when firm i takes x_j as given. Then, from the first-order condition, it can be written as follows:

$$x_i^\wedge = -2\,[\{\beta(2-c)^2 - c\}x_j + (2+c)(1-c)(a-s)](2-c^2-\beta c)/(1-c)^2(4-c^2)^2 / $$
$$/\,2[(2\text{-}c^2-\beta c)^2/(1-c^2)((4-c^2)^2-\gamma/2] \quad \text{(A5)}$$

Since the denominator is negative by the second-order condition and $0 \le c < 1$, $x_i^\wedge$ will be positive if

$$\{\beta(2-c)^2 - c\}x_j + (2+c)(1-c)(a-s) > 0 \quad \text{(A6)}$$

For the notational convenience, let's define

$$Q(c) \equiv \{\beta(2-c)^2 - c\}x_j + (2+c)(1-c)(a-s)$$

If $\beta(2-c)^2 - c > 0$, $Q(c) > 0$ since $0 \le c < 1$, $x_j > 0$ and $a > s$. Therefore, $x_i^\wedge$ will be positive. If $\beta(2-c)^2 - c < 0$, we need the following condition for the positive $x_i^\wedge$ from the inequality (A6):

$$xj < (2+c)(1-c)(a-s)/\,c - \beta(2-c)^2 \quad \text{(A7)}$$

Now, under the assumption of symmetry,

$$x_i^\wedge = x_j^\wedge \equiv x^\wedge$$

Since we restrict our attention to a symmetric equilibrium, the inequality (A7) is equivalent to

$$x^\wedge < (2+c)(1-c)(a-s)/\,c - \beta(2-c)^2 \quad \text{(A8)}$$

where $x^\wedge$ solves (A5) when $x_i = x_j$

Note that $x^\wedge$ was also given in (5). By substituting it into (A8), we get the condition that

$$2(2\text{-}c^2\text{-}\beta c) < (1-c)^2(4-c^2)^2 \quad \text{(A9)}$$

If the inequality (A9) is satisfied, the symmetric solution $x^\wedge$ will be always positive. But, note that it was already shown that (A9) is satisfied in the beginning of this proof. Lastly, $x^\wedge$ in (5) satisfies the condition that $(1+\beta)x^\wedge < s$ since it is assumed that

$$\gamma > 2(1+\beta)(2\text{-}c^2 - \beta c)a/(1+c)(2+c)(2\text{-}c)^2 s \text{ Q.E.D.}$$

Proof of Theorem 2:

(1) It is trivial to find that $\partial x^\wedge/\partial\gamma < 0$ because γ appears only in the denominator in the equation (5). By taking the first-order derivative of (5) with respect to y, one can easily verify that $\partial x^\wedge/\partial\gamma < 0$.

To prove that $\partial x^\wedge/\partial c < 0$, one can differentiate $x^\wedge$ given in equation (5) with respect to c. This gives us

$$\partial \hat{x}/\partial c = [-2\gamma(a\text{-}s)(2\text{-}c)\{\text{-}y(1\text{+}c)]\ (8 - 6c^2 + c^3 + 2c^4) + \beta(4 - 4c + 3c^2 + 5c^3)\ /$$
$$\{\gamma(1 + c)\ (2 + c)\ (2 - c)(2 - c)^2 - 2(1 + \beta)(2 - c^2 - \beta c)\}^2$$

Since $0< c < 1$ and $\beta\geq 0$, we can conclude that $\partial \hat{x}/\partial c < 0$. From equation (5), one can obtain

$$\partial \hat{x}/\partial \beta = 2(a - s)[2(2\text{-}\ c^2\ \beta c)^2 - \gamma c(1\text{+}c)(2\text{+}c)(2\text{-}c)^2\ /\ \{\gamma(1 + c)$$
$$(2 + c)\ (2 - c)(2 - c)^2 - 2(1 + \beta)(2 - c^2 - \beta c)\}^2$$

Define $h(c) \equiv 2(2\text{-}c^2\text{-}\ \beta c)^2$ and $g(c) \equiv \gamma c(1\text{+}c)(2\text{+}c)(2\text{-}c)^2$.

Then, the sign of $\partial \hat{x}/\partial \beta$ will depend on the difference between h(c) and g(c). That is,

$$\partial \hat{x}/\partial \beta \geq(<) 0 \text{ if } h(c) \geq(<) g(c).$$

Note that $h'(c) = -4(2c+\beta)(2\text{-}c^2\text{-}\beta c) < 0$ for $c\in(0,1)$. When $0<c<1$, h(c) is monotonically decreasing to c. It is also found that $h(0)>g(0)$ and $h(1)<g(1)$. Since both h(c) and g(c) are continuous to c, it can be said that there exist c_o such that

$$h(c_o) = g(c) \text{ and } 0<c_o< 1.$$

To show the uniqueness of c_o, note that $g''(c) < 0$ when $0<c_o< 1$.. By examining the first and second order derivatives, it can be shown that g(c) has only one maximum when $0<c_o< 1$.. So, there will exist at most two different values for c_o such that $h(c_o) = g(c_o)$. Let's denote them by c_{o1} and c_{o2} and assume, without loss of generality, $co_1<co_2$. Since h(c) is monotonically decreasing and $h(0)>g(0)$, it can be said that

$$h(c)>g(c) \text{ for every } c\in(c_{o2},1).$$

But, $h(1)<g(1)$. Therefore, there exist another c_o, in the interval that $c_{o2}<c_o< 1$, such that h(c) = g(c). But, it contradicts the result that there are at most two values for co and that c_{o2} is the greater one. Hence, c_o is unique.

Proof of Theorem 3:

It is easy to establish from equation (11) that $\bar{x}$ is inversely related to γ. Therefore, $\partial \bar{x}/\partial\gamma < 0$. To show that $\partial \bar{x}/\partial\gamma < 0$, we take the first order derivative of $\bar{x}$ with respect to c to get:

$$\partial \bar{x}/\partial c = [16\gamma\theta(2\text{-}c)\{a\text{-}s)\ (-1 + c - c^2)\ /\ \{\gamma(1 + c)\ (2 - c)^2 - 8\theta(1 - c\}$$

Therefore, $\partial \bar{x}/\partial c < 0$ when $c < 0$.

By taking the first order derivative of equation (11) with respect to θ, we obtain

$$\partial \bar{x}/\partial\theta = 8(1\text{-}c)(a\text{-}s)\ \gamma(1 + c)\ (2 - c)^2 - 8\theta^2(1 - c\}/\{\gamma(1 + c)\ (2 - c)^2 - 8\theta^2(1 - c\}^2$$

Therefore, we can conclude that $\partial \bar{x}/\partial\theta > 0$.

Proof of Theorem 4:

From (5) and (11) ,

$$\bar{x} - 2\hat{x} = 8\theta(1-c)(a-s) / [\gamma(1+c)(2-c)^2 - 8\theta^2(1-c)] - 4(2-c^2-\beta c)(a-s)/ [\gamma(1+c)(2+c)(2-c)^2 - 2(1+\beta)(2-c^2-\beta c)] \quad \text{(A10)}$$

Given $\bar{x} - 2\hat{x}$, by some algebraic operations, one can get

$$\bar{x} \geq (<) 2\hat{x} \text{ if } (2-c^2-c)/(2-c^2-\beta c) \geq(<) 1/2\theta - 2(1-c)\{2\theta - (1+\beta)\}/\gamma(1+c)(2-c)^2$$

Define $m(c) \equiv (2-c^2-c)/(2-c^2-\beta c)$ and $n(c) \equiv 1/2\theta - 2(1-c)\{2\theta - (1+\beta)\}/\gamma(1+c)(2-c)^2$

Now suppose that $\theta \geq (1+\beta)/2$. Then, $m'(c) = (\beta-1)(2+c^2)/(2-c^2-\beta c) < 0$ and $n'(c) = 4(2\theta-1-\beta)(1+c+c^2) / \gamma(1+c)^2(2-c)^3 \geq 0$.

Further, $m(0) > n(0)$ and $m(1) < n(1)$. Therefore, there exists a unique $c \in (0,1)$ such that $m(c) = n(c)$. Denote it by $\bar{c}(\gamma,\theta,\beta)$. That is,

$\bar{c}(\gamma,\theta,\beta) \equiv \{c: (2-c^2-c)/(2-c^2-\beta c) = 1/2\theta - 2(1-c)\{2\theta-(1+\beta)\}/\gamma(1+c)(2-c)^2 \text{ and } c \in (0,1)\}$.

Therefore, we obtain, $\bar{x} \geq 2\hat{x}$ if $0 \leq c \leq \bar{c}(\gamma,\theta,\beta)$ and $\bar{x} < 2\hat{x}$ if $\bar{c}(\gamma,\theta,\beta) < c < 1$. Now suppose that $\theta \leq 1/2$. From (A10) it is derived that $\bar{x} < 2\hat{x}$ if $4\theta(1-c)(2\theta-1-\beta)/\gamma(1+c)(2-c)^2 < 1-2\theta[(2-c-c^2)/(2-\beta c-c^2)]$.

Since $0 \leq c < 1$, $0 \leq 2\theta \leq 1$ and $0 \leq \beta < 1$,

$$4\theta(1-c)(2\theta-1-\beta)/\gamma(1+c)(2-c)^2 \leq 0 \text{ and}$$

$$1-2\theta[(2-c-c^2)/(2-\beta c-c^2)] \geq 0,$$

where the equalities hold only when $\beta = c = 0$ and $\theta = 1/2$

Therefore, the result that $\bar{x}/2 \leq \hat{x}$ when $\theta \leq 1/2$ is obtained unless $\beta = c = 0$ and $\theta = 1/2$.

Proof of Theorem 5:

Since the denominator in (14) is the same as the second order condition for the noncooperative equilibrium, we know that it is positive. One can also claim that the slope of the reaction function in (14) is less than one. To prove it, suppose not. Then, the slope will satisfy that

$$2\{\beta(2-c^2) - c\}(2-c^2-\beta c) / \gamma(1-c^2)(4-c^2) - 2(2-c^2-\beta c)^2 > 1$$

Since the denominator was shown to be positive in the proof of Proposition 1, the above inequality can be rewritten

$$2\,(1+\beta)(2-c^2-\beta c) > \gamma(1+c)\,(2+c)\,(2-c)^2$$

But, remember that it was assumed, for the positive production cost after innovation, in (5) that $\gamma(1+c)\,(2+c)\,(2-c)^2 > 2(1+\beta)\,(2-c^2-\beta c)$, a contradiction.

Since the slopes of the reaction functions are less than one, the conditions for the interior solution is

$$2[(2-c-c^2)(a-s+\theta x_r)(2-c^2-\beta c) - (1/2)\gamma(1-c^2)(4-c^2)^2 x_r > 0\,.$$

Since x_i^* (x_r) should be non-negative , from the above inequality, the following result is obtained:

$$x_i^*\,(x_j) > 0 \text{ if } x_r < 4(2-c^2-\beta c)(a-s)/\,[\gamma(1+c)(2+c)(2-c)^2 - 4\theta(2-c^2-\beta c)]$$

$$x_i^*\,(x_j) = 0 \text{ if } x_r \geq 4(2-c^2-\beta c)(a-s)/\,[\gamma(1+c)(2+c)(2-c)^2 - 4\theta(2-c^2-\beta c)]\,.$$

By solving the reaction functions in (14) simultaneously, it is obtained that

$x_i^*(x_r) = 2(2-c^2-\beta c)(a-s) + \{2\theta(2-c^2-\beta c) - (\gamma/2)\gamma(1+c)(2+c)(2-c^2)\}\,x_r/\,[\gamma(1+c)(2+c)(2-c)^2 - 2(1+\beta)(2-c^2-\beta c)]$ where i = 1 or 2.

Taking the derivative of $x_i^*(x_r)$ with respect to x_r when $x_i^*(x_r) > 0$ gives

$\partial\, x_i^*(x_r)/\partial\, x_r = 2\theta\,(2-c^2-\beta c) - (\gamma/2)\gamma(1+c)(2+c)(2-c^2)\}\,x_r/[\gamma(1+c)(2+c)(2-c)^2 - 2(1+\beta)(2-c^2-\beta c)]$

The denominator is positive by the given assumption in (5). It was also assumed in(11) that

$$\gamma > 8\theta^2(1-c)a\,/\,(1+c)(2-c)^2\,s$$

Since $(1-c)a > s$, $2+c > 2-c^2-\beta c$ and $2\theta > 1$, we derive from the inequality

$\gamma > 8\theta^2(1-c)a\,/\,(1+c)(2-c)^2\,s > [4\theta(2-c^2-\beta c)/\,[(1+c)(2+c)(2-c)^2\,]$. Therefore, the nominator is negative and $\partial\, x_i^*(x_r)/\partial\, x_r < 0$.

Proof of Theorem 6

By assuming that x is given, one can solve for each firm's independent R& D from the reaction function given in (14) as follows:

$$x_i^*\,(x_r) = 2(2-c^2-\beta c)\,(a-s) + \{2\theta(2-c^2-\beta c) - (\gamma/2)(1+c)(2+c)(2-c)^2\}x_r\,/\,\{\gamma(1+c)(2+c)\,(2-c)^2 - 2(1+\beta)\,(2-c^2-\beta c)\}$$

By substituting $x_i^*(x_r)$ into the objective function in (15), joint profits can be written in terms of the level of cooperative R & D. The second order derivative of the above function with respect to x_r can be shown to be:

$$\gamma(1-c)^2(4-c^2)^2 - 2(2 - c^2 - \beta c)^2 > 0$$

This inequality is derived from the assumption of the existence of the solution given in (5). Hence, the joint profit function is convex in the level cooperative R & D, x_r, which implies that as the greater x_r, the greater is the joint profit .

By Theorem 4, it is known that the solution for independent R & D given in (15) will only hold for $x_r \leq x_c$. If $x_r > x_c$, then $x_i^*(x_r) = 0$ by Theorem 4.4. For $x_r > x_c$, the objective function is the same as the function given in (12), which is maximized at $\bar{x}$.

Therefore, it is clear that the joint profit function is maximized at 0, x_c or $\bar{x}$. It was assumed that $2\theta > 1+\beta$, so it is easily shown that, since $x_c > 0$ from Theorem 4, joint profits are always greater at x_c than at $x = 0$. Since $\bar{x}$ is a local maximum, considering the results in Theorem 4 and defining x_c, the optimal level of cooperative R & D is $x^* = \text{Max}\{x_c, \bar{x}\}$. For either of these values $x_i^*(x^*)$ will be zero. Lastly, by comparing x_c and $\hat{x}$, it is straightforward to establish that $x_c > 2\hat{x}$, because $2\theta > 1+\beta$, and therefore $x^* \geq x_c > 2\hat{x}$.

Proof of Corollary 7:

From Theorem 6 we get that $x^* = \text{Max}\ [x^c, \bar{x}]$. By substituting the solution of each variable into the above equation, we have $\bar{x} > x^c$

If $8\theta(1 - c)(a-s) / (1 + c)(2 - c)^2 - 8(1 - c)\theta^2 > [4(2-c^2-\beta c)(a - s)/ [\gamma(1 + c)(2+c)(2 - c)^2 - 4\theta(2-c^2-\beta c)]$

or, equivalently, if $(2 - c^2)(2\theta - 1) - c(2\theta - \beta) > 0$.

Therefore, the results in Corollary 1 follow.

Chapter 5

5. TECHNOLOGICAL COMPETITION AND R&D COOPERATION WITH PRODUCT DIFFERENTIATION

5.1. INTRODUCTION

Asymmetries between firms are frequently observed in market competition as for example in the case that one firm has a more advanced technology. If there exists some difference between firms, it will certainly affect the incentives to engage in innovative activity. The asymmetries between those firms will generate different incentives to introduce new technology. Since the outcome of technological competition has an obvious effect upon the firms' market positions, firms need to take account not only of the immediate profits that it brings but also the advantage that it may confer in subsequent competition when later innovations are expected. To explore this we first construct a two period model and ask how the existence of such subsequent innovative opportunities affects the outcome of technological competition.

The analysis uncovers two different forces on determining the incentives to innovate. The competitive incentive is defined as the difference between a firm's profits if it innovates and the profits it would make if its rival innovated instead. The profit incentive is determined by calculating the increase in a firm's 'profits if it alone were investing in R & D. Given those forces, we explore how the incentives to innovate depend on the degree of product differentiation or niche building in product markets. If the products are less substitutable, the profit incentive dominates each firm's willingness to invest in R & D and it leads to the result that the currently less advanced firm engages in more R & D. If the products are very substitutable, then the competitive incentive determines the outcome of technological competition so that the currently more advanced firm increases its superiority in technology. Hence, the rate of product differentiation is shown to be an important determinant predicting the outcome of technological competition. The existence of a second period of competition largely reinforces the outcome from a single period race.

An alternative outcome could be expected with technological competition when firms can share both the cost and the outcome of innovative activity. The majority of models consider the case that there is only one winner in the technological competition. But alternative models develop technological competition in which each firm engaging in R & D can obtain a patent on a cost reducing technology. Since innovative investments are often very expensive and knowledge has a tendency to leak to others, firms may have an incentive to conduct their innovative activities cooperatively.

Cooperation in R & D among competing firms can produce more rapid technological progress. Since the new technology is shared among competitors through cooperative R & D, firms can avoid the duplication of R & D. The cooperation in R & D can also be a solution to the leakage of information. Since knowledge is inherently a public good, the research done by one firm can be used by another firm even though the latter does not have permission to use the inventive output. Cooperation in R & D is a solution to this problem because cooperative research agreements can internalize spillover externalities. But cooperation between firms' R & D activities may not always produce a better social outcome. The potential gain from R & D will be dissipated to consumers if price competition in the product market is intense. This creates the potential collusive reduction in R & D. That means, firms could use a cooperative agreement in R & D as a vehicle to slow the pace of technological innovation.

In exploring the relationship between technological competition and product differentiation we ask how the rate of product substitutability influences technological progress. The number of firms in the market determines the intensity of price competition. But market competition is also affected by the degree of product differentiation. When the products in the market are less substitutable, the participants in the market will experience less competition. Instead of asking how the incentive to innovate is affected by the increase in the number of firms in the market, which is a common theory in analyzing the relation between R&D and product differentiation (Suzumura, Chapt.4), we consider the question of how the incentive to innovate is related to the degree of product differentiation.

When two products are close substitutes, technological competition is intensified and it drives the market 'to be monopolized' by a firm. If two products are less substitutable, the firms have greater monopolistic power over customers. This discourages a firm from stealing its rival firm's customers through innovation and the market keeps its competitive structure unchanged. It also turns out that the effect of a spillover externality on technological progress is dependent on the closeness of the two products. Knowledge is inherently a public good and it is difficult to prevent its use by others. The analysis shows that the incentives to innovate are generally reduced as the rate of such leakage of knowledge increases. However, when products are very different, the firm that has less of an incentive to innovate has a tendency to raise its R & D effort as the spillover rate increases. The increase in the spillover rate helps the firm that has less of an incentive to improve its marginal contribution of technological progress and compensates for the reduction in its own competence.

Before reviewing previous lines of thought on the interaction between technological competition and market structure in the next section, we present a model of a horizontally differentiated product market in Section 5.3. Section 5.4 examines the conditions that influence the pattern of market evolution. It shows that the pattern of market evolution depends on the rate of product differentiation. In section 5.5 we suggest how the dynamic effect of technological competition on market evolution will be different from the static one. Section 5.6 contains some observations on Cooperative R&D features in otherwise competitive markets.

5.2. A REVIEW OF TECHNOLOGICAL COMPETITION AND MARKET STRUCTURE

When firms are not identical, there is no reason to suppose that their incentives to innovate will be same. We first note the role of each individual firm's market position on the incentive to innovate. The question about the advantage or disadvantage of current market dominance on technological competition has been one of main themes in empirical industrial economics. We ask if the firm which is already a leader has a greater incentive to perform R & D than its rival. We analyze it in the context of an oligopolistic market and explore the role of product differentiation on the development of market structure.

Although market structure may influence innovative activity, it is itself influenced by technological progress. The outcome of one patent race will change each firm's market position and affect the incentives in the next race. When a sequence of innovations is expected, the existence of such reciprocal effects requires a firm to take account not only of the immediate profits that an innovation brings, but also the strategic advantage or disadvantage it may confer in subsequent races. Hence, it is worthwhile to analyze the strategic incentives to innovate in the context of a series of innovative opportunities. For this purpose, we extend the static analysis to a two period model.

After Schumpeter (1942) emphasized the role of technology on economic growth and addressed the importance in driving the economic progress of large, oligopolistic firms, a traditional line of reasoning has been that monopoly power is a stimulus to R & D. Gilbert and Newberry (1982), see also Dasgupta (1986), proved that, when an incumbent monopolist is faced with potential entrants, the monopolist's incentive to remain a monopolist is greater than the entrant's incentive to become a duopolist. However, Arrow (1962) sought to establish the reverse proposition that more competitive environments would give a greater incentive. He considers the gains to the originator of an innovation, in monopoly and competition. For a drastic innovation, which leaves the inventor a monopolist, an incumbent monopolist would have less of an incentive than would a competitive firm who currently has no share in the market because the competitive firm becomes a monopoly whereas the monopolist only replaces itself. An opposite implication comes from two different forces that determine the economic profit through innovation. The firm in Gilbert and Newberry recognizes that it is in a race against its rival to be the first to innovate and so the incentive for R & D reflects the difference between the firm's profits if it innovates and the profits it would make if its rival innovated first. Because there is some dissipation of rents when the market is shared rather than monopolized, the incumbent monopolist has a greater incentive than a potential entrant. The incentive on which Arrow focuses is determined by calculating the increase in a firm's profits if it alone were investing in R & D. The incentive to innovate is independent of any strategic considerations of preemptive innovation. This leads to the conclusion that a competitive market structure is more conducive to innovation than a monopolistic one because the superior position from a competitive market position provides a higher return from owning the exclusive right to a new technology. The first incentive, which we owe to Beath, Katsoulacos and Ulph (1989), is called the competitive incentive and the latter the profit incentive. Most technological competition will need to take account of those two forces on the incentive to innovate. But, both Gilbert and Newberry and Arrow show very extreme cases of those two incentives by limiting their analysis to either a monopolistic or perfectly competitive market. By introducing a differentiated products market, it appears that the results from Gilbert and Newberry and Arrow are really extreme cases rather than a mainstream result of technological competition.

Empirical studies have also investigated the relationship between technological change and market structure. They examine how a technological improvement influences market concentration. The studies have presented mixed results. In some industries, the large institutions are the major innovators. Phillips (1966, 1971) examined his theory with data on eleven industry groups and later on the aircraft industry. He found that the relative success in innovation was an important determinant of the growth of firms and of growing concentration. Mansfield (1984) on the steel and petroleum industries and Grabowski and Mueller (1978) lend support to the results of Phillips. But, there is also considerable evidence that dominant companies are slow innovators. Blair (1972), Geroski and Pomroy (1990), and Carlsson (1984) provide evidence in support of this perspective. There is no absolutely unambiguous answer. These results require theoretical models to aid in studying patterns of market evolution. Our analysis shows that the rate of product differentiation plays an important role.

We construct an oligopolistic model in which a differentiated product market is assumed. We start our analysis by drawing upon Vickers (1986). He considers a dynamic model in which two firms compete for a series of non-drastic innovations. Since his approach for computing the incentive for R & D is defined in terms of value functions, we can apply it in our analysis to predict which firm will win a patent. Our analysis first explains two patterns of market evolution. It reveals that each firm's desire for R & D is largely determined by the profit incentive when the rate of product substitutability is low, while technological competition is influenced by the competitive incentive when two products are close to perfect substitutes. The rate of product differentiation plays an important role in determining the relative magnitude of those two forces and the opposite conclusion in technological competition is derived by varying the rate of product differentiation. We also compare the static analysis to the results of a two period model. It shows the difference which can arise between them and improves our understandings of the effect of continuous innovations on market evolution.

5.3. A SIMPLE MODEL

We assume an economy with two firms, each one producing a differentiated good. There are two firms, h and w. Their initial technologies are represented by constant marginal production costs s_h and s_w. The first period innovation provides the cost-cutting technology s_l. If allowed, the second period innovation offers the cost-cutting technology s. Here, technological progress is limited to be the cost-cutting technology, so called the process innovation. The firm that acquires new technology s_l or s can use it exclusively and produces its output at the cost of s_l or s, respectively. It is assumed, without loss of generality, that $s_h>s_w>s_l>s$. At the beginning of each period, they compete for new technology s_l or s. Their competition for new technology is like a simple auction in which each firm proposes a bid which represents the maximum amount that firm will pay for the patent of the new technology and the highest bidder wins it. The winner pays -- as expense for buying the new technology --the maximum that the other firm would have paid in order to have the patent rather than not to have it. The loser does not owe anything.

The product market is specified by a differentiated duopoly of the Dixit (1979) type with linearity in demands assumed as follows:

$$q_h = a - bp_h + cp_w$$

$$q_w = a - bp_w + cp_h$$

where q_i represents the demand for firm i and p_i its price.

It is further assumed that

$$a > 0 \, , \, b > c \geq 0 \qquad (1)$$

and

$$q_h = a - bs_h + cs \geq 0 \qquad (2)$$

The goods are independent when c=0, while they are substitutes when c>0. When b=c, the goods are perfect substitutes. The assumption (2) implies that both firms are guaranteed to be active even after innovation.

After the race for new technology s_l or s, the firms compete in product market where the Bertrand competition is assumed. They set prices and the non-cooperative Nash equilibrium concept is adopted as the equilibrium in the product market.

5.4. First Period Competition

At the beginning of the first period, there is a competition for the patent that gives the exclusive right to employ the cost level s_l in the given period. Each firm's initial unit cost is denoted by s_h and s_w , respectively. They are myopic and do not form expectations for the next period. Each firm competes for the patent and proposes a bid for it. Then, we ask who is willing to bid more and examine how the rate of product differentiation influences the market development.

In the product market, firm i chooses its price level p_i to maximize its profit, taking p_j as given, where $i \neq j$ and i, j = h, w, respectively. Let π_h (s_h ,s_w) denote firm h's profit level, ignoring R & D expenses, when it has the cost level s_h and its rival has the cost level s_w. Similarly, π_w (s_w ,s_h) is defined for firm w when it has the cost level s_w and its rival has the cost level s_h .Then it is easily seen that provided that q_j is positive, the reaction function for firm i is

$$p_i\,(p_j) = (a + bs_i + cp_i\,)/2b \text{ , where i,j= h or w and } i \neq j \qquad (3)$$

It is straightforward to compute the equilibrium price from the reaction function. Since the slope of the reaction function is positive but less than one, the unique interior solution can be derived as

$$p_i^*(s_i, s_j) = (a(2b+c)+2b^2 s_i + bc\, s_j)/(4b^2 - c^2), \text{ where } i,j= h \text{ or } w \text{ and } i\neq j \quad (4)$$

Let g_h and g_w denote firm h's and w's incentive to win the new technology s_l, respectively. Then, firm h's incentive is given by

$$g_h(s_h, s_w, s_l) = \pi_h(s_l, s_w) - \pi_h(s_h, s_l).$$

The first term on the right hand side is firm h's payoff after it wins the race and the second term is its payoff when it loses the race. Similarly, firm w's incentive to win the new technology s_l is given by

$$g_w(s_w, s_h, s_l) = \pi_w(s_l, s_h) - \pi_w(s_w, s_l)$$

From the assumption that the competition for the new technology s_l is like a bidding game, firm h wins if and only if $g_h(s_h, s_w, s_l) > g_w(s_w, s_h, s_l)$. Let $\rho(s_h, s_w, s_l)$ denote the difference between two firm's incentives. That is,

$$\rho(s_h, s_w, s_l) \equiv g_h(s_h, s_w, s_l) - g_w(s_w, s_h, s_l)$$

Following the definition of each term on the rhs we get

$$\rho(s_h, s_w, s_l) = \pi_h(s_l, s_w) - \pi_h(s_h, s_l) - \pi_w(s_l, s_h) + \pi_w(s_w, s_l)$$

Define $\sigma(s_h, s_w) \equiv \pi_h(s_h, s_w) + \pi_w(s_w, s_h)$

Then, the function $\rho(s_h, s_w, s_l)$ can be rewritten

$$\rho(s_h, s_w, s_l) = \sigma(s_l, s_w) - \sigma(s_h, s_l) \quad (5)$$

By substituting the solution in (4) into each firm's profit function, the difference between two firms' incentives can be calculated as following:

$$\rho(s_h, s_w, s_l) = b(s_w - s_h)/(4b^2 - c^2)^2 R(s_h, s_w, s_l) \quad (6)$$

where

$$R(s_h, s_w, s_l) \equiv (s_h + s_w)\{(2b^2 - c^2)^2 + b^2c^2\} - 4bc(2b^2 - c^2)s_l - 2a(b-c)(2b+c)^2$$

From the relation in (6), we can find the answers to the question of how the market will evolve. If $\rho(s_h, s_w, s_l) > 0$, firm h will have a greater incentive to win the race for s_l.

Proposition 1. Suppose that $s_h > s_w > s_l$ *. Then, there exists a unique*

$c^*(s_h, s_w, s_l)$ *such that*
$\rho(s_h, s_w, s_l) > 0$ if $c \in [0, c^*(s_h, s_w, s_l))$ and
$\rho(s_h, s_w, s_l) \le 0$ if $c \in [c^*(s_h, s_w, s_l), b)$

Proof given in the Appendix

This proposition shows the effect of product differentiation on market development. It implies that the current low cost firm will have a greater incentive to innovate than its rival firm if the rate of product differentiation is high, while the current high cost firm will win the new technology race when the rate is low. When the products are close substitutes, the competition in the product market is so intense that the willingness to buy a new patent is determined by competitive incentive. Since a low cost firm's profit is greater as the difference between the production costs increases, the current low cost firm has a greater incentive to innovate. When c=0, each firm is a local monopoly and its desire for R & D is determined by the profit incentive. If the high cost firm wins the new patent, this will bring a larger cost cut and so a greater incentive to innovate. Proposition 5.1 shows that the force determining the incentive to innovate gradually moves from the profit incentive to the competitive incentive as the rate of product differentiation increases.

Interpretation of Proposition 1 helps us understand the debate regarding the better market structure for technological progress. The Schumpeterian hypothesis can be interpreted as a case that the two products are close substitutes, while Arrow's conclusion can be applied to the case when the two products are close to being monopolies.

From the given proposition, we can infer the effect on technological competition. We ask how the race will be dependent on the value of s_l.

Proposition 2. Suppose that $s_h > s_w > s_l$.

Then, $\partial c^*(s_h, s_w, s_l)/\partial s_l > 0$ and $\partial \rho(s_h, s_w, s_l)/\partial s_l > 0$.

Proof given in the Appendix

The comparative statics in this proposition indicates that the critical rate of product differentiation, $c^*(s_h, s_w, s_l)$, decreases as the size of the innovation increases. This result comes from the fact that the current low cost firm's incentive to innovate increases more rapidly than its rival firm's incentive as the technological improvement becomes larger. For example, suppose the new technology provides only a small cost reduction. Then, the improvement of the low cost firm's profit may be trivial while the high cost firm will still get a considerable reward from it. But, suppose that technological progress is quite significant. Then, the reward to the low cost firm will not be trivial and the increase of its incentive will be relatively greater than the current high cost firm. Therefore, as technological improvement is greater, the firm that is currently ahead in technology becomes more active in technological competition.

5.5. INTERPERIOD COMPETITION

The asymmetry between firms' market positions generates the difference between their incentives to innovate. Through a patent race, the firm that is already ahead may become increasingly dominant or its rival may acquire the superiority. Technological competition will affect each firm's market position. The relationship between market structure and innovation is not one directional. Therefore, it will be more desirable to analyze the relationship between market structure and innovation in a dynamic context. Here, we examine how far the results in the previous section carry over when the analysis is extended to a two period model.

At the beginning of each period, two firms compete for the new technology. The first period innovation provides the cost-cutting technology s_l Its winner will produce its output at the cost of s_l. The second period innovation offers the cost-cutting technology s. Its holder can produce its output at the cost of s. Those technologies are put up for auction. We assume symmetric demand functions for firms h and w, and make the same assumptions about the parameters as in the previous section. Again, the equilibrium concept in the product market is the non-cooperative Nash equilibrium.

To examine the magnitude of each firm's bids and the sequence of technology allocations, we need to understand how profits are determined in each period. Since two firms compete over two periods, each firm will consider not only the current profit but also the next period's profit at the time of the first round patent race. We start by calculating each firm's profit in the second period.

There are two possible outcomes in the first period; firm w won the patent of s_l or firm h won it. Depending on these two outcomes, the second period profit will be determined as a result of the second period race. As we proved in the previous section, the winner of the new technology in one period competition is characterized in Proposition 1. When firm h wins the first period race, the critical rate of product differentiation is $c^*(s_w, s_l, s)$ in the second period race, while it is replaced by $c^*(s_h, s_l, s)$ when firm w wins the new patent s_l. Since $s_w < s_h$, $c^*(s_w, s_l, s) > c^*(s_h, s_l, s)$.

Then, we consider the following three cases:

i. $0 \le c \le c^*(s_h, s_l, s)$
ii. $c^*(s_h, s_l, s) < c \le c^*(s_w, s_l, s)$
iii. $c^*(s_w, s_l, s) < c < b$

Depending on the degree of product differentiation, the following three patterns are expected in the second period: the winner of s_l loses the second period race as in case (i), the winner in the second period is conditional on who won the first period race as in case (ii) or the winner in the first period gets the new patent in the second period as in case (iii).

Now, each firm's incentive in the first period can be calculated by counting those results. Let $g_h^o(s_h, s_w, s_l, s)$ and $g_w^o(s_w, s_h, s_l, s)$ represent firm h's and firm w's incentive for the new technology s_l, respectively. In case (i), the incentive to innovate in the first period can be calculated as follows:

$$g_h^o(s_h, s_w, s_l, s) = \pi_h(s_l, s_w) + \pi_h(s_l, s) - \pi_h(s_h, s_l) - \pi_h(s, s_l) + \pi_w(s, s_h) - \pi_w(s_l, s).$$

The first two terms on the rhs are firm h's payoff over two periods after it wins the race s_l and the other terms are its profits over two period minus its rival's bid for the race s when it loses the first period race. Similarly, firm w's incentive can be computed. Then, they can be written:

$$g_h^o(s_h, s_w, s_l, s) = \pi_h(s_l, s_w) + \pi_w(s, s_h) - \pi_h(s_h, s_l) - \pi_h(s, s_l)$$

and

$$g_w^o(s_w, s_h, s_l, s) = \pi_w(s_l, s_h) + \pi_h(s, s_w) - \pi_w(s_w, s_l) - \pi_w(s, s_l)$$

Each function is computed as the difference between each firm's profit when it wins the race s_l and the profit when it loses the first period race. If a firm wins the race s_l, it will lose the second period race, while it can buy the patent s by paying its rival's bid when it loses the first period race. Define

$$\phi(s_h, s_w, s_l, s) \equiv g_h^o(s_h, s_w, s_l, s) - g_w^o(s_w, s_h, s_l, s)$$

Then, $\phi(s_h, s_w, s_l, s)$ can be written:

$$\phi(s_h, s_w, s_l, s) = \sigma(s_l, s_w) - \sigma(s_l, s_h) + \pi_w(s, s_h) - \pi_h(s, s_w)$$

where $\sigma(s_h, s_w) \equiv \pi_h(s_h, s_w) + \pi_w(s_w, s_h)$

Note that the first two terms on the rhs coincide with $\rho(s_h, s_w, s_l)$ in (5). They are exactly the same as the difference between two firms' incentives for the race s_l when they are myopic. The other two terms are the difference of payments for the new patent s.

In case (ii), firm w always wins the second period race because $c^*(s_h, s_l, s) < c \le c^*(s_w, s_l, s)$. In the second period, it can produce its product at the unit cost of s by paying $\pi_h(s, s_l) - \pi_h(s_h, s)$ if it won the race s_l or paying $\pi_h(s, s_w) - \pi_h(s_l, s)$ if it lost the race s_l. Therefore, we get

$$g_h^o(s_h, s_w, s_l, s) = \pi_h(s_l, s_w) + \pi_h(s_l, s) - \pi_h(s_h, s_l) - \pi_h(s_h, s) \text{ and}$$

$$g_w^o(s_w, s_h, s_l, s) = \pi_w(s_l, s_h) + \sigma(s_h, s) + \pi_h(s, s_w) - \pi_h(s, s_l) - \pi_w(s_w, s_l) - \pi_w(s, s_l) - \pi_h(s_l, s).$$

Therefore,

$$\phi(s_h, s_w, s_l, s) = \sigma(s_l, s_w) - \sigma(s_l, s_h) + \sigma(s, s_l) - \sigma(s, s_h) + \sigma(s_l, s) - \pi_h(s_h, s) - \pi_h(s, s_w).$$

The first two terms on the right hand side coincide with $\rho(s_h, s_w, s_l)$ in (5) and the next two terms represent the difference of the incentives for the race s when the firms are myopic. The last two terms are the difference of firm w's payments for the second period race s.

Similarly, the difference of two firms' incentives in case (iii) is calculated as follows:

$$g_h^{o}(s_h, s_w, s_l, s) = \pi_h(s_l, s_w) + \pi_h(s, s_w) - \pi_w(s, s_l) + \pi_w(s_w, s) - \pi_h(s_h, s_l) - \pi_h(s_h, s),$$

$$g_w^{o}(s_w, s_h, s_l, s) = \pi_w(s_l, s_h) + \pi_w(s, s_h) - \pi_h(s, s_l) + \pi_h(s_h, s) - \pi_w(s_w, s_l) - \pi_w(s_w, s)$$

and

$$\phi(s_h, s_w, s_l, s) = \sigma(s_l, s_w) - \sigma(s_l, s_h) + \sigma(s, s_w) - \sigma(s, s_h) - \pi_h(s_h, s) + \pi_w(s_w, s).$$

In each case, firm h wins the race s_l when $\phi(s_h, s_w, s_l, s) > 0$, while firm w wins when $\phi(s_h, s_w, s_l, s) \leq 0$.

By substituting the profit function in (7) into $\phi(s_h, s_w, s_l, s)$, we can figure out the condition for the pattern of market development.

Proposition 3. Suppose that $s_h > s_w > s_l > s$. Then

If $0 \leq c < c^*(s_h, s_l, s)$, $\phi(s_h, s_w, s_l, s) > 0$.
If $c^*(s_w, s_l, s) \leq c < b$ and s_h and s_w *satisfy*

$$s_h + s_w \geq \{2a(2b+c)[3(2b^2 - c^2) - 2bc] + 2bc(2b^2 - c^2)(2s_l + 3s)\} / 3(2b^2 - c^2)^2 + 2(bc)^2,$$

then $\phi(s_h, s_w, s_l, s) \leq 0$.

Proof given in the Appendix

This proposition first shows that the existence of a subsequent race strengthens each pattern of market development when the products are close to the extreme case. Suppose that the rate of product differentiation is less than $c^*(s_h, s_l, s)$ and $\sigma(s_l, s_w) - \sigma(s_l, s_h) < 0$. Unless there exists a race in the second period, Proposition 1 predicts that the low cost firm increases its dominance since $\sigma(s_l, s_w) - \sigma(s_l, s_h) < 0$. But, in the two period competition, it is possible to observe the pattern of alternating winners in those cases because the existence of the second period race boosts the high cost firm's incentive. When the market products are close substitutes, we can also expect similar results. But, when the rate of product differentiation is moderate, it is ambiguous.

Unlike the one period model, the technological competition in this section deals with two new technologies. We consider how the change in the improvement of each technology will affect the race.

Proposition 4. Suppose that $s_h > s_w > s_l > s$.

If $0 < c < c^*(s_h, s_l, s)$, $\partial\phi(s_h, s_w, s_l, s)/\partial s_l > 0$ and $\partial\phi(s_h, s_w, s_l, s)/\partial s < 0$.
If $c^*(s_w, s_l, s) < c < b$, $\partial\phi(s_h, s_w, s_l, s)/\partial s_l > 0$ and $\partial\phi(s_h, s_w, s_l, s)/\partial s > 0$

Proof given in the Appendix

Proposition 4 shows that the effect of increasing s_l is to encourage innovation by firm h, which is the same as found in Proposition 2. As the improvement of the immediate innovation is smaller, the low cost firm is less attracted to it. But, the effect of s is shown to be dependent on the pattern of market evolution. When firm w knows that it will win only s, a small improvement by s will lead firm w to be more attracted to buying s_l, which will decrease $\phi(s_h, s_w, s_l, s)$. But, when firm w knows that it will win both s_l and s, a smaller improvement on the new technologies will provide relatively less interest to firm w because firm w's expected gain will be less significant than firm h's expected gain from them.

5.6. Notes on Cooperative R&D in a Competitive Market

Inter-firm relationships in the R & D first stage are often assumed to be either cooperative or non-cooperative, while a second stage product market is usually characterized by a non-cooperative Cournot competition. Most of the present R & D literature concentrates on the comparison of the pure cooperative case to the pure non-cooperative first stage, given Cournot competition in the product stage. Such frameworks may not be applicable to situations where either: (a) the firms' technology is determined by a mixture of independent R & D and cooperative research joint ventures (RJV), or (b) product market competition is not Cournot. A model of joint research venture operating competitively in a differentiated product market would allow participating firms to engage in independent R & D in addition to that performed jointly.

After Schumpeter (1942) emphasized the importance of technological progress for economic growth, much attention has centered on the relationships between product market structure and technological progress. However, the relationship between market structure and technological progress is still an open question. The ambiguity regarding this relationship also results in difficulties in analyzing the benefits and costs of R & D competition. It is difficult to determine whether cooperation in R & D will result in collusion in the -production stage or how the concentration ratio will affect R & D investment. Instead of analyzing a complete set of interactions, economists have tackled the issues related to cooperative R & D by adopting a two stage model and concentrating their attention on the effects of R & D competition before considering the competitive interactions of firms in the product market. They explicitly or implicitly assume that symmetric firms are effectively prohibited from collusion. Grossman and Shapiro (1986) and Katz (1986) first used this approach to analyze the effects of cooperative R & D.

Grossman and Shapiro adopt the upstream and downstream perspective and describe the possible benefits and costs of a research joint venture. Katz proposes a four stage model in which R & D activities are specified by three stages. Using this model, he discusses the general effects of cooperative R & D. Both approaches emphasize the possibility that cooperation produces greater total R & D because it can internalize the spillover externality, thereby avoiding duplication of R & D efforts and thus decreasing each firm's R & D expenditure. They also note the possibility that a RJV may have an anti-competitive effect when product market competition is intensive and suggest that the negative effect of a RJV may be prevented by allowing the participating firms to engage in independent R & D.

D'Aspremont and Jaquemin (1988) develop a constructive model and prove that cooperative R & D produces greater R & D effort in equilibrium than non-cooperative R & D when the spillover rate is relatively high and the product market is modeled as a homogeneous goods Cournot competition. In this model, both firms in the cooperative R & D venture coordinate their R & D expenditure to maximize joint profits. d'Aspremont and Jacquemin show that while one might expect cooperation to lead to a reduction of R & D expenditure by avoiding wasteful duplication, in fact cooperation actually produces greater R & D when the spillover rate is relatively high. A limitation in their model is that the firms participating in the RJV do not share their R & D outcomes but rather simply coordinate their R & D spending. This naturally leads to the question of why the firms want to coordinate their R & D expenditure. Moreover, the coordination of R & D expenditure will not necessarily avoid duplication of R & D since the participants do not share the results. Kamien, Muller and Zang (1992) extend d'Aspremont and Jacquemin's model to the case when the R & D outcome is fully shared and still conclude that a RJV results in greater R & D output than noncooperative R & D competition. Choi (1993) generalizes the model to the case where the R & D outcome is uncertain and finds the same outcome.

Although d'Aspremont and Jacquemin, Kamien et al and Choi succeed in showing the desirability of cooperative R & D, their work does not take into account some of the negative effects of cooperative R & D which were emphasized by Grossman and Shapiro and Katz. They fail to show the anti-competitive danger of cooperative R & D and the role of independent R & D. Additionally, Grossman and Shapiro and Katz emphasize the usefulness of working with differentiated goods markets and the possibility that product market competition may affect incentives to participate in cooperative R & D. To address these issues, Kamien et al adopt a horizontally differentiated goods market. But, in their analysis, it is difficult to determine how the degree of product differentiation affects the incentives to conduct R & D. Kamien et al build on the model introduced by Dixit (1979) and apply their analysis to the case in which the R & D outcome is fully shared among the participants. By assuming Cournot competition and concavity of the objective function, they show that full cooperation produces more R & D than non-cooperation. However, their specification of the R & D production function makes it difficult to compute the effect of product differentiation on R & D outcomes in that it does not allow for an analysis of the effect of changes in the parameters on R & D activity. Moreover, their model can explain neither the anti-competitive effect of cooperative R & D nor the role of independent R & D.

A distinctive characteristic of R & D is the spillover externality effect. If R & D for the single firm is not appropriable, the incentives at the industry level to do R & D are reduced. On the other hand, restoring appropriability by licensing, also incorrectly prices the good that R & D has created and may result in redundant and excessive levels of R & D. A solution to the appropriability problem can be found by cooperation in R & D. By working together, the firms under the cooperative agreement can internalize the spillover externality. Moreover, cooperation makes it possible to share the burden of R & D cost, avoid duplicated R & D efforts and save transfer costs. d'Aspremont and Jacquemin, Kamien, Muller and Zang and Choi emphasize all of these advantages in their constructive models. In addition, by assuming Cournot competition, they emphasize that cooperative R & D produces more output than noncooperative R & D competition if the internal spillover rate increases under cooperation. That is, they show not only the advantages of cooperative R & D but also the desirability of it. However, as Grossman and Shapiro and Katz previously pointed out , there exists the risk that the firms engaging in cooperation may use a RJV as a vehicle to jointly slow the pace of technological innovation. This paper proves that those risks can arise. By assuming Bertrand competition in the product market, we show that cooperation in R & D does not always produce more output than non-cooperative competition in R & D.

Suppose that cooperative R & D activity is solely determined by a research joint venture, as assumed in most of the literature. Then, if product market competition is intense, the cooperative agreement will be used to restrict the level of R & D since most of the potential gains from innovation will be dissipated to consumers. That is, when firms price compete , cooperation in R & D can be used to avoid the difficulty of a Prisoner's Dilemma, whereas firms in the non-cooperative R & D game are unable to avoid such situation. Unlike the Cournot model, the anti-competitive effect of RJV may be shown in this situation. However, the danger of anti-competitive effect may be reduced or may disappear altogether if the participating firms can also engage in independent R & D. Suppose that the member firms can continue their independent R & D even after agreeing to a cooperative agreement. If the research joint venture sets investment on R & D to zero, the member firms will return to the same non-cooperative levels of investment undertaken prior to the agreement. Total R & D output in this market will not be the same as was made when the RJV solely determined R & D expenditure. The different structure of the RJV may result in different outcomes and have different implications for R & D activity. For example, one could envisage a scheme of cooperative R & D in which the member firms in the RJV can choose their R & D effort levels independently after the joint venture's decision is made; we then examine its implications on total industry R & D activity to show how different outcomes are possible.

Extending the cooperative model to allow for independent R & D requires specification of both the parents' and the joint venture's incentive structures. We consider the case in which the research joint venture moves first and then the parent firms choose their independent R & D effort given the RJV's decision. Then it is assumed that each member of the RJV has access to information on the joint activity level. Moreover, the manager of the RJV is given incentives by the parent firms, who subsequently decide their own responses to the decision of the RJV. This suggest a three stage model of RJV / product market competition.. In the first stage, firms have an opportunity to join a cooperative R & D venture in which the cost and output of R & D are fully shared. At the second stage, each parent firm chooses its own R & D effort level. R & D efforts are assumed to reduce unit production costs; i.e., attention is confined to process innovation. During the third stage firms compete in the product market with collusion in the product market prohibited.

The analysis first asks how the cooperative R & D level depends on the degree of product differentiation when independent R & D is not allowed. When two goods are close substitutes, and so product competition is intense, most of the potential gains from R & D are dissipated to consumers. It is determined that the cooperative agreement may act as a vehicle to avoid such unprofitable results. When two goods are poor substitutes this result may be reversed, and cooperation may result in greater R & D output than non-cooperation. The result would be similar in the initial case using the Cournot model except that the analysis here reveals that the degree of product differentiation has an important impact on the RJV's incentives to innovate.

Alternative schemes of cooperative R & D can change R & D incentives and its social implications. Specifically, firms may spend at least as much in the cooperative stage as they would under the non-cooperative competition when RJV allows the participants to continue independent R & D. When independent R & D is allowed, both firms know that if cooperative R & D by RJV is not large enough, they will increase their R & D investment. But, mostly, independent R & D is less efficient than cooperative R & D because it is not shared and does not avoid the duplication on R & D investment. When cooperative R & D allows room for independent R & D, firms can save R & D by agreeing to increase their cooperative investment on R & D. Given the importance of governmental policy with respect to RJVs, understanding the implications of alternative RJV schemes seems to be a valuable one to explore. A scheme that includes research joint venture plays an important role in investment in process innovation. In fact, this analysis shows that when independent R & D is allowed, the level of R & D in the RJV is not lower than in the purely non-cooperative equilibrium. That is, if the RJV allows the parent firms to continue their independent R & D, the danger of the collusive reduction in R & D is unlikely to be serious. Even if member firms' products are close substitutes, an antitrust authority need not worry about the anti-competitive risk of RJVs as long as the RJVs allow participants to continue independent R & D.

5.7. Conclusions

In this paper, we analyzed the effect of different time periods on R & D competition. In this context the positioning of rival firms was assumed to come from initial technologies and firms' products. Our analysis first showed the relationship between the pattern of market evolution and the degree of product differentiation through 'niche formation'.. When two products are not very substitutable, the profit incentive dominates the race for the new technology, which results in alternating winners in both one period and inter- period competition. It would suggest that firms who are ahead would reinforce their advantage through branding for which they could enjoy temporary monopoly profits. But, as two products become close substitutes, the competitive incentive dominates the pattern of market evolution. In the process of examining those relations, it is also shown that current technologies and the magnitude of technological progress are important determinants.

From a different angle, as outlined in Sec.5.6, when products in a market are close substitutes and price competition is intense, cooperative R&D can be used as a 'hidden tool' for avoiding unprofitable competition. But if firms are allowed to engage in a mix of independent and cooperative R&D, then innovative output under cooperation is not less than under non-cooperative technological competition.

References

Arrow, K. J. *(1962),* 'Economic Welfare and-The Allocation of Resources for Invention', *The Rate and Direction of Inventive Activity: Economic and Social Factors,* Princeton: Princeton University Press.

Beath, J. Y. Katsoulacos and D. Ulph (1987), 'Sequential Product Innovation and Industry Evolution', *Economic .Journal 97,* 32-43.

Beath, J. ,Y. Katsoulacos and D. Ulph (1989), 'Strategic R & D *Policy', Economic Journal, 99, 74-83.*

Blair, J. *(1972), Economic Concentration,* New York: Harcourt, Brace and Jovanovich.

Carlsson, B. (1984), 'The Development and Use of Machine Tools in Historical Perspective', *Journal of Economic Behaviour and Organization, 5, 91-114.*

Choi,J.P (1993), 'Cooperative R&D with Product Market Competition', *International Journal of Industrial Organization*, 11, 553-571

D'Aspremont,C. and A. Jacquemin (1988), 'Cooperative and Noncooperative R&D in Duopoly with Spillover', *American Economic Review*, 78, 1133-37

Dasgupta, P. (1986), 'The Theory of Technological Competition', in K. Binmore and P. Dasgupta (eds.), *Economic Organizations as Games,* Basil Blackwell: Oxford, 139-164

Dixit, Avinash (1979), 'A Model of Duopoly Suggesting A Theory of Entry Barriers', *Bell Journal of Economics*, 20-32.

Geroski, P. A. and Pomroy, R. (1990), 'Innovation and The Evolution of Market Structure', *Journal of Industrial Economics,* 38, 299-314.

Grabowski, H. G. and Mueller, D. C. (1978), 'Industrial Research and Development, Intangible Capital Stocks, and Firm Profit Rates', *Bell Journal of Economics,* 9, 328-43.

Gilbert, R. and Newberry, D. (1982), 'Pre-emptive Patenting and The Persistence of Monopoly', *American Economic Review, 74,* 514-26.

Grossman,G.M. and Shapiro,C. (1986),'Research Joint Venture: An Antitrust Analysis', *Journal of Law, Economics and Organization*,2,315-337

Kamien,M.I. , Muller,E. and Zang,I. (1992), 'Research Joint Ventures and R&D Cartels', American Economic Review 82, 1293-1306

Katz,M.L.. (1986),'An Analysis of Cooperative Research and Development', *Rand Journal of Economics* 17, 527-543

Mansfield, E.(1984), 'R & D and Innovation: Some Empirical Findings', in *R & D, Patents and Productivity, Z.* Griliches (ed.), Chicago: University of Chicago Press.

Phillips, A. (1966), 'Patents, Potential Competition, and Technical Progress', *American Economic Review,* 56, 301-10.

Phillips, A. (1971), *Technology and Market Structure: A Study of The Aircraft Industry,* Lexington, Mass: Lexington Books.

Schumpeter, J. A. (1942), *Capitalism, Socialism and Democracy,* New York: Harper & Row.

Suzumura, K (1995), *Competition, Commitment and Welfare*, Oxford; Clarendon Press

Vickers, J. (1986), 'The Evolution of Market Structure When There is A Sequence of Innovations', *Journal of Industrial Economics,* 35, 1-12.

APPENDIX

Proof of Proposition 1

Proof: Under the given demand functions, each firm's price is determined to satisfy

$$\text{Max}_{p_h}\ \pi_h(s_h, s_w) = (p_h - s_h)q_h \text{ and } \text{Max}_{p_w}\ \pi_w(s_w, s_h) = (p_w - s_w)q_w$$

Since the second order conditions are satisfied, the reaction functions can be derived from the first order conditions as follows:

$$p_h(p_w) = (a + bs_h + cp_w)/2b$$

and

$$p_w(p_h) = (a + bs_w + cp_h)/2b$$

The interior solution from those two reaction functions is computed as follows:

$$p_h(s_h, s_w) = (a(2b+c)+2b^2 s_h + bc\, s_w)/(4b^2 - c^2)$$

and

$$p_w(s_w, s_h) = (a(2b+c)+2b^2 s_w + bc\, s_h)/(4b^2 - c^2)$$

By substituting these two arguments into each firm's profit function, we get

$$\pi_h(s_h, s_w) = b\{ (a(2b+c) - (2b^2 - c^2)\, s_h + bc\, s_w) \}/(4b^2 - c^2)^2$$

and

$$\pi_w(s_w, s_h) = b\{ (a(2b+c) - (2b^2 - c^2)\, s_w + bc\, s_h) \}/(4b^2 - c^2)^2$$

Therefore, the difference between two firms' incentives to innovate can be written as

$$\rho(s_h, s_w, s_l) = b(s_w - s_h)/(4b^2 - c^2)^2\, R(s_h, s_w, s_l)$$

where

$$R(s_h, s_w, s_l) \equiv (s_h + s_w)\{(2b^2 - c^2)^2 + b^2c^2\} - 4bc(2b^2 - c^2)s_l - 2a(b-c)(2b+c)^2\}.$$

Since $s_h > s_w$ and $b>0$ by the given assumption, firm w will have a greater incentive to innovate if R(.) is positive and firm h will take over the advantage on costs if R(.) is negative.

In order to prove the existence of $c^*(s_h, s_w, s_l)$, it will be enough to show that

$$R(s_h, s_w, s_l) < 0 \text{ when } c = 0$$

and

$$R(s_h, s_w, s_l) > 0 \text{ when } c = b.$$

when c=0, $R(s_h, s_w, s_l) = 4b^3[b(s_h + s_w) - 2a] < 0$ since it was assumed that

$a - bs_h + cs \geq 0$. If c=b, $R(s_h, s_w, s_l) = 2b^4(sh+s_w-2s) > 0$ because it was assumed that $s_h > s_w > s_l$. Since the function R(.) is continuous to c, by the Intermediate Value Theorem, there exists $c^*(s_h, s_w, s_l)$ such that

$R(s_h, s_w, s_l)\big|_{c=c^*} = 0$

The uniqueness of $c^*(s_h, s_w, s_l)$ can be shown by examining the second and the third derivatives of the function R(.). Suppose that there exist at least two non-negative $c^*(s_h, s_w, s_l)$ such that $R(s_h, s_w, s_l)\big|_{c=c^*} = 0$ Let's define c_l and c_2 to be these values and $c_l < c_2$. Since $a - bs_h + cs \geq 0$, $R(s_h, s_w, s_l)\big|_{c=0} = 4b^3[b(s_h + s_w) - 2a] < 0$.

Since $R(s_h, s_w, s_l)\big|_{c=0} < 0$ and c_l is inf $c^*(s_h, s_w, s_l)$ such that $R(s_h, s_w, s_l)\big|_{c=c^*} = 0$ there must exist at least one local maximum in the interval between c_l and c_2. For a local maximum, the first order derivative of R(.) with respect to c must be decreasing around that local maximum. From the function R(.), we can compute the third derivative of it as follows:

$$\partial^3 R(s_h, s_w, s_l)/\partial c^3 = 6\{4c(s_h + s_w) + 4bs_l + 4a\}$$

Since all parameters are assumed to be non-negative, the third derivative of R(.) is always positive for every non-negative c. The second derivative of R(.) is as follows:

$$\partial^2 R(s_h, s_w, s_l)/\partial c^2 = 6\{2(c^2 - b^2)(s_h + s_w) + 4bcs_l + 2a(b+c)\}$$

At c=0, it will be $\partial^2 R(s_h, s_w, s_l)/\partial c^2\big|_{c=0} = 6b\{2a - b)(s_h + s_w)\} > 0$.

From the result that $\partial^3 R(s_h, s_w, s_l)/\partial c^3 > 0$. and $\partial^2 R(s_h, s_w, s_l)/\partial c^2\big|_{c=0} > 0$,

It can be inferred that $\partial^2 R(s_h, s_w, s_l)/\partial c^2 > 0$ for every non-negative c.

Therefore, the first derivative of R(.) will monotonically increase which contradicts the existence of a local maximum

Proof of Proposition 2

Proof. From the proof of Proposition 9.1 , $c^*(s_h, s_w, s_l)$ satisfies $R(s_h, s_w, s_l)\big|_{c=c^*} = 0$. Therefore, by the Implicit Function Theorem, we get $\partial c^*(s_h, s_w, s_l)/\partial s_l = -[\partial R(s_h, s_w, s_l)/\partial s_l]/[\partial R(s_h, s_w, s_l)/\partial c]\big|_{c=c^*(\ldots)}$

Since $c^*(s_h, s_w, s_l)$ is the unique solution such that $R(s_h, s_w, s_l)\big|_{c=c^*} = 0$ and $\partial^2 R(s_h, s_w, s_l)/\partial c^2 > 0$, there must exist a unique c' such that $\partial R(s_h, s_w, s_l)/\partial c\big|_{c=c'} = 0$ and $c' < c^*(s_h, s_w, s_l)$. If not, there will be another c such that $R(s_h, s_w, s_l) = 0$ which contradicts Proposition 9.2 .

Since $\partial^2 R(s_h, s_w, s_l)/\partial c^2 > 0$ and $c' < c^*(s_h, s_w, s_l)$, it must be that $\partial R(s_h, s_w, s_l)/\partial c\big|_{c=c^*(.)} > 0$. From that $R(s_h, s_w, s_l) = 0$, we can also show that $\partial R(s_h, s_w, s_l)/\partial s_l = \partial R(s_h, s_w, s_l)/\partial s_l = 4bc(c^2 - 2b^2) < 0$.

Therefore, $\partial c^*(s_h, s_w, s_l)/\partial s_l > 0$.

By differentiating $\rho(s_h, s_w, s_l)$ with respect to s_l we get

$$\partial \rho(s_h, s_w, s_l)/\partial s_l = 4b^2c(2b^2 - c^2)(s_h - s_w)/4b^2c(2b^2 - c^2)^2.$$

Since $b > c$ and $s_h > s_w$, we get the result that $\partial \rho(s_h, s_w, s_l)/\partial s_l > 0$.

Proof of Proposition 3

Proof. (1) If $0 \leq c < c^*(s_h, s_l, s)$, then $\phi(s_h, s_w, s_l, s) = \sigma(s_l, s_w) - \sigma(s_h, s_l) + \pi_w(s, s_h) - \pi_h(s, s_w)$ By applying the relation in (9.6), it can be written

$$\phi(s_h,s_w,s_l,s)=\{b(s_h-s_w)(2b^2-c^2)[2a(2b+c)-(2b^2-c^2)(s_h+s_w)+2bc(2s_l-s)]\}/(4b^2-c^2)^2$$

Since $a - bs_h + cs > 0$ by assumption (9.2) and $s_h > s_w > s_l > s$,

$$2a - b(s_h + s_w) + 2cs_l > 0 \text{ and } 2a - 2bs + c(s_h + s_w) > 0.$$

Therefore, we can derive

$$2a(2b+c)-(2b^2-c^2)(s_h+s_w)+2bc(2s_l-s) =$$
$$2b[2a-b(s_h+s_w)+2cs_l]+c[2a-2bs+c(s_h+s_w)] > 0$$

Since each term on the rhs of the function $\phi(s_h, s_w, s_l, s)$ is positive, we can conclude that $\phi(s_h, s_w, s_l, s) > 0$.

(2)When $c \geq c^*(s_w, s_l, s)$, the winner in the first period race will have a greater incentive in the second period race s than its rival firm. Then, as in case (iii),

$$\phi(s_h, s_w, s_l, s) = \sigma(s_l, s_w) - \sigma(s_l, s_h) + \sigma(s, s_w) - \sigma(s, s_h) - \pi_h(s_h, s) + \pi_w(s_w, s).$$

By substituting the results in (9.7) directly into the above function and rearranging terms, it is derived that $\phi(s_h, s_w, s_l, s) \leq 0$, if

$$s_h + s_w \geq \{2a(2b+c)[3(2b^2 - c^2)-2bc] + 2bc(2b^2-c^2)(2s_l+3s)\}/\ 3(2b^2-c^2)^2 + 2(bc)^2 > 0$$

Now we need to show that there exist s_h and s_w such that the given assumptions and the related conditions are met. Suppose that $s_h = s + (a/b) - \varepsilon$, $s_h - \varepsilon = s_w$, $c = b - \varepsilon$, where ε is infinitesimal. Then the assumptions in (9.1) and (9.2) are met. Further, $\lim_{\varepsilon\to 0} \rho(s_w,s_l,s) < 0$. It implies that $c \geq c^*(s_h, s_l, s)$. Now we need to show only that

$$s_h + s_w \geq \{2a(2b+c)[3(2b^2 - c^2)-2bc] + 2bc(2b^2-c^2)(2s_l+3s)\}/\ 3(2b^2-c^2)^2 + 2(bc)^2$$

When ε approaches zero, the left-hand side of the above inequality is close to $4(a-bs_l+bs)/5b$, which is greater than zero because $a - bs_l + bs > a - bs_h + cs > 0$. Therefore, the conclusion of the proposition (2) is established.

Proof of Proposition 4

Proof. (1) If If $0 \leq c < c^*(s_h', s_l, s)$, from the proof of Proposition 9.3, we directly get $\partial\phi(s_h, s_w, s_l, s)/\partial s_l = 4b^2c(2b^2 - c^2)(s_h - s_w)/(4b^2 - c^2)^2 > 0$

and

$$\partial\phi(s_h, s_w, s_l, s)/\partial s = -2b^2c(s_h - s_w)(2b^2 - c^2)/(4b^2 - c^2)^2 < 0.$$

If $c^*(s_w, s_l, s) < c < b$, we can similarly get

$$\partial\phi(s_h, s_w, s_l, s)/\partial s_l = 4b^2c(2b^2 - c^2)(s_h - s_w)/(4b^2 - c^2)^2 > 0 \text{ and}$$

$$\partial\phi(s_h, s_w, s_l, s)/\partial s = 6b^2c(s_h - s_w)(2b^2 - c^2)/(4b^2 - c^2)^2 > 0.$$

Therefore, the results of the proposition hold.

Chapter 6

6. Innovation and Competition in Network Markets

6.1. Introduction

We look at a competitive situation in network markets where there is uncertain technological development in product/process technologies. Firms 'price' compete in those markets to gain market share before any of them succeeds in getting an innovation to move ahead of its rival(s). If the firms are in a technology race and the probability of innovation success is small, then a firm with a bigger network advantage is likely to attract more customers in the absence of innovation. If, however, any of those firms expect innovation with a high probability and none of them have a big advantage then they keep on sharing the market until the innovation occurs.

Many high technology industries are characterized by positive network externalities. Firms essentially compete against each other for goods that share a network.

A corresponding model of competition contains two special features that applies equally well to network markets. One is the uncertainty in technological development or uncertainty in the realization of a firm's R&D effort. The other is the dynamic nature of price competition between firms in the presence of network effects.

Firms compete with each other over an extended period of time and must therefore strategically choose prices as the market shares of the firms evolve.

Most existing models of network markets focus on only one of the two features. Further, almost all the models have the commonality that one firm captures the market instantaneously and sells to all consumers from then on (the 'winner-takes-all' market) . However, the history of high technology industry abounds with instances where rival firms (and technologies) have had extended battles for providing the industry standard (Uttenback, 1994).

In network markets evolution of market share is a very interesting phenomenon especially in the face of uncertainty about future product quality. This chapter also attempts to provide a framework that could capture the richness of market share evolution in the presence of network externalities.

We rely on a stochastic racing model in Gottinger (2002)and also take some cues from Schumpeterian racing in the seminal contribution by C. Futia (1980).

In order to motivate the setup we start from some unconventional ideas on antitrust analysis in dynamically competitive industries (Evans and Schmalensee,2001):

> "Firms that are not leaders in network industries generally have little hope of reaching that status unless they come up with a major innovation – one that can defeat the natural advantage that network effects bestow on the industry leaders. Incremental innovation – making slight improvements in the leaders' products – will not enable a small firm to overtake a leader that enjoys the benefits of network economies. Similarly, the possibility of being displaced by a major innovation will shape leaders' research agendas. If there is a chance that today's products will be replaced by a major innovation, a leader's survival depends on bringing this innovation to market and thereby replacing itself before others do. As a result, competition in network industries often involves intense R&D efforts aimed at capturing or retaining market leadership. It is not atypical for a fringe firm that invests heavily to displace the leader by leapfrogging the leader's technology ..." (Evans and Schmalensee, 2001,pp. 10-12)

This situation described may also be encountered in 'dynamic oligopoly' where exogeneously emerging new technologies are rapidly eroding costs or where market structure responds endogeneously to intense racing behaviour (Shapiro,1989,Sec.5; Baumol,2002,Chapt. 1).

We are exploring the problem of tradeoff between 'network dominance' and 'radical innovation' that could tip the market the other way, with a significant caveat added that breakthrough R&D is highly uncertain. From a strategic perspective, in this environment, for any two firms of asymmetric size, both compete dynamically over prices to win market share. In this dynamic process there are two ways to achieve (temporary) monopolistic status. The 'smaller' firm can use dynamic pricing competition to delay the time in which the 'larger' firm wins a critical market share in the hope to hit the innovation first and displace it. If the probability of innovation and the discount factor are sufficiently high, there is an equilibrium in which duopoly persists (no firm achieves a critical market share) until one of the two firms wins the race for innovation.

We briefly summarize a historical example from markets for IT products. In the personal computer (PC) operating system market. Microsoft products (MS DOS and Windows) have been dominating the market since the mid 1980s. An operating system is the fundamental program that controls the allocation and use of computer resources. Thus, the utility that operating systems provide to consumers depends on the number of compatible applications. As a general rule an application that relies on a specific operating system will not function on another operating system unless it is ported to that specific operating system. Therefore, because of its dominance, the majority of applications have been written to run on Microsoft operating systems (MS DOS). The domination of MS DOS has become even stronger since the arrival of Windows 95 in the PC operating system market. This, in turn, has provided a great indirect positive network externality to PC owners who adopted Windows 95 as an operating system. Many other firms, such as IBM and BEA Systems, Inc., introduced their own operating systems and tried to compete with Windows. These products, however, lacked sufficient compatible applications to efficiently compete with Microsoft products. The lack of compatible applications prevented enough application developers and consumers from regarding OS/2 Warp or BeOS as a viable alternative to the dominant incumbent, Windows. This obstacle prevented these potential entrants from obtaining a sizable market share. Their failure to enter the market successfully, however, was not due to the inferior quality of their operating systems. In fact, OS/2 Warp was reported to be at least as good as Windows, and BeOS offers superior support for multimedia applications. If consumers who use multimedia applications frequently adopt Windows at the expense of BeOS, they have to give up the convenience that is provided by BeOS. Thus, for multimedia specific users, adopting BeOS as their operating system at the expense of another operating system might provide the highest utility. Nevertheless, the lack of compatible applications, which in turn implies the lack of positive network externality, has prevented consumers from adopting OS/2 Warp or BeOS. As a conclusion, the positive network externality for the dominant incumbent (Windows) has worked as an entry barrier against entrants (OS/2 Warp or BeOS) which do not have network externality. Such an entry barrier could only be overcome by a radical innovation, virtually leapfrogging the dominant incumbent.

In Section 6.2 we provide paradigmatic cases from ICT industries that indicate restrictions to overcome technological barriers. Section 6.3 presents the context of technological competition in network industries. Section 6.4 outlines the equilibrium conditions attainable for multi-state Markov games resulting in Markov equilibria.

Section 6.5 addresses some extensions of the framework and draws conclusions .

6.2. Market Histories

We substantiate our claim on a natural tradeoff between network size and quality change (through significant technological change) by looking independently on four market histories for the IT industry.

A. Internet Explorer

The first version of Internet Explorer was introduced in the web browser market in July 1995. This version of Internet Explorer was reportedly inferior to Netscape's Navigator. Microsoft made many improvements in its next version, Internet Explorer 3.0, in August 1996. Internet Explorer 3.0 matched nearly all the features in Navigator. However, Microsoft was not able to draw significant market share at the expense of Navigator with this enhanced version. Internet Explorer 4.0, released in late 1997, finally managed to obtain roughly the same number of reviewers who preferred it to Navigator as the number of those who preferred Navigator. In 1996, most consumers were much more familiar with Navigator, the dominant web browser than with Internet Explorer. Thus although the quality of Internet Explorer was much improved since its release into the market, more than eighty percent of consumers were still using Navigator until late 1996. It was evident that Internet Explorer could not draw a significant percentage of consumers away from Navigator by simply improving the quality of its web browser. Senior executives within Microsoft concluded that Internet Explorer could not catch up with Navigator's market share by itself. J Allchin, senior executive within Microsoft, wrote to P. Martiz, in late December 1996:

> "I don't understand how IE (Internet Explorer) is going to win. The current path is simply to copy everything that Netscape does, packaging and product wise. Let's

{suppose} IE is as good as Navigator/Communicator . Who wins? The one with 80 percent market share. Maybe being free helps us, but once people are used to a product it is hard to change them. Consider Office. We are most expensive today, but we're still winning…"

From 1996 to 1998, Internet Explorer's market share increased dramatically. The estimated market share of Navigator fell from eighty percent in January 1996 to fifty five percent in November 1997, while that of Internet Explorer increased from five percent to thirty six percent over the same period. These changes in market shares, however, were mainly due to the fact that Microsoft leveraged Windows to increase the usage of Internet Explorer, rather than constantly improving the quality of its browser.

B. Server Operating System

The environment of the server operating system market is different from that of the PC operating system in the sense that a server is maintained by a group of computer experts (not by novices as in the case of a PC) and is intended for specific purposes , rather than for general uses. Moreover, a choice of server operating systems requires many technical features, such as functionality, system management, performance, reliability (stability) and security. Functionality and performance are important technical features for both PCs and servers, but other aspects are not very important for PCs. This difference comes from the fact that while a PC is designed for use by one person at a time , a server is designed to provide data, services, and functionality through a digital network to multiple users. Most individual PC owners do not have an incentive to buy a server operating system, since server operating systems generally cannot function efficiently on PC hardware. In other words, the consumers in the two markets are basically separated. According to Data Quest, the Unix System is currently the most widely used operating system platform. It expanded its market share from thirty six percent in 1996 to fourty three percent in 1998. The new comer in the server operating system market, Windows NT, also achieved great success during that period; its market share rose from ten percent in 1996 to sixteen percent in 1998. Linux license shipments in this year grew at a rate of 212.5 percent, accounting for more than seventeen percent of all server operating system units shipped. Other than Unix servers and Windows NT, Open VMS, Novel NetWare and OS/2 are the major competitors in the server operating system market. A small product differentiation in a server operating system enables it to create and to maintain its own demand. In sum, a dominant product cannot eliminate other products with its prevailing positive network externalities when substitutability for products are low.

C. OS/2 Warp

In late 1994, IBM introduced its Intel-only-compatible operating system, OS/2 Warp, as an alternative to Windows. OS/2 was originally designed to be optimized for Intel microprocessors. This resulted in a lack of portability. Because the Intel compatible PC dominated the PC market, the lack of portability did not prevent consumers from adopting

OS/2 as an operating system. Furthermore, OS/2 was not reported to be inferior to Windows. . The greatest disadvantage of adopting OS/2 as an operating sytem was the lack of compatible software, approximately 2,500 applications were available. In 1995, IBM still attempted to compete with Windows 95 in the PC operating system market with its release of OS/2 2.0. However, IBM figured that it would lose between seventy and ninety percent of its sales volume if it installed OS/2 to the exclusion of Windows 95. In 1996, IBM withdrew from the PC operating system market and, instead, has been repositioning OS/2 for the server operating system market. The failure of OS/2 Warp to gain enough market share to survive is due mainly to its lack of applications rather than inferiority to Windows. By the time OS/2 Warp was released, Windows was already the predominant operating system and ran an overwhelming number of applications. Most consumers used Windows not because it was superior in quality to its competitors, but rather because it provided the greatest positive network externality among the available PC operating systems.

In other words, Microsoft successfully deterred entry into the PC operating system market by using its predominating network externality.

D. BeOS

BEA Systems, Inc.(BEAS), founded in 1990 by a former executive of Apple's product division, released its cross-platform operating system, BeOS. BeOS functions virtually identically on both Intel-compatible PCs and Macintosh systems. In addition, BeOS is optimized for multiprocessor media-based systems. These two features provide great convenience for multimedia-specific users. BEA has stated from the beginning that it intends to coexist within the Windows and Apple World as a specialized operating system. Even taking this specific purpose into account , the market share of BeOS is too small compared to the number of Windows users. The most outstanding disadvantage is the lack of compatible applications (approx. 1,000). Be, Inc. tried to overcome this problem by maintaining a website which provided a list of freeware and shareware applications. Be, Inc. failed to gain sizable market share, and was eventually sold to Palm. However, Palm continues to produce BeOS and to maintain its BeWare website. BeOS still exists as a niche operating system, in spite of its superior support for multimedia applications. The failure of BeOS to obtain a significant market share is evidence in support of the proposition that the incumbent can deter entry by using its network externality.

6.3. Asymmetry of Market Evolution

For network economies, Katz and Shapiro (1992) look at situations whether there is too much or too little technological innovation in a market with network externalities, compared to the social optimum. In particular, they explore whether a new product which embodies technological progress is introduced too early or too late compared to the social optimum. In their model, technological progress is deterministic. Only the entrant gets the benefit of improving technology, but once it enters the market its product is fixed. Therefore, in any equilibrium of their model , either the new firm captures the market as soon as it enters or it doesn't enter at all. Their model is thus not able to capture the richness of pricing strategies and market evolution as a function of market shares. For instance, it is unable to explain the phenomenon of two competing technologies fighting for superiority in a market when both are making sales until one firm finally leaves the market.

Earlier Harris and Vickers (1987) presented two models of races in which there is both technological uncertainty and strategic interaction between competitors as the race unfolds.

Their aim is to see how the equilibrium effort levels of competitors vary with the intensity of rivalry between them. They show that under certain conditions the leader in the race makes greater efforts than the follower, and efforts increase as the gap between competitors in their progress decreases. The model presented here can be seen along similar lines to that of Harris and Vickers, but more realistically, with the network advantage as the state variable instead of progress, and prices providing strategic interaction between firms instead of the amount of effort put into R&D. While there is one ultimate goal for each firm in the multistage race of Harris and Vickers to reach the finishing line of the race first, we leave it open for firms which network they want to build. It is this feature that can lend profit maximization by firms to a complex network evolution pattern. Also the amount of effort put into R&D stochastically moves firms to a new stage in the race, whereas in our model prices -- the variables of strategic interaction – deterministically move firms to a new market share.

While a lot of work has been done in the area of R&D, very little of it specifically addresses markets with network externalities. Katz and Shapiro look at the choice of product compatibility in a market with technological progress. They look at both the cases of deterministic and uncertain technological progress. However, technological progress in their model is exogeneous and they look at a two-period game which does not provide a very suitable framework for looking at the dynamic pricing strategy of firms and the resulting evolution of market shares. Choi (1994) looks at a two-period model of a monopoly in a market with network externalities.. He studies the incentive of the monopolist to introduce an incompatible improved product in the presence of network externalities. Kristiansen (1998) studies the consequences of network externalities on the riskiness of R&D projects chosen by an entrant and an incumbent. He shows that the incumbent chooses a too risky project that too often lets a new firm with an incompatible technology enter. In addition, the entrant has an incentive to choose more certain projects than are socially optimal and these strengthen the possibility of adoption of an incompatible technology.

This chapter develops and analyses a model of technological uncertainty where firms compete strategically in prices in the presence of network externalities. Technological uncertainty is modelled as an improvement in the quality of the firm's product.

Whether the firm gets the innovation, however, is uncertain. In the simplest model, once a firm gets the innovation, the race ends and there is no further innovation.

Once the innovation occurs, when there is no uncertainty, the model looks like that of Katz and Shapiro—the firm with the quality plus network advantage sells to all the consumers subsequently. We attempt to analyze how firms share the market by strategically choosing their prices before a firm succeeds in getting an innovation.

The advantage of a firm is measured by the sum of its network size and the quality of its product as a 'proxy' of its innovation intensity. If the firms are in a technological race but the probability of innovation is small then again the firm with the bigger advantage sells to all the consumers in the absence of innovation. If however those firms expect innovation with a high probability then so long as neither firm has a very big advantage both firms take turns in selling to the consumers in the absence of innovation. Thus if the firms are on an equal base neither firm gets pushed out unless one of the firms gets an insurmountable advantage in the process. That is, because with firms that are sufficiently close in terms of their advantage, neither firm finds it worthwhile to push the other firm out of the market since the 'losing' firm prices more aggressively than the 'leader' as it has more to gain by staying in the market.

We provide some anecdotal observations across various industries that show a strong rivalry on the technological front to gain market share between a leader in the field and its approaching rival(s).

Clearly those interactive patterns reveal technological races. We can even extend those observations to megamergers and alliances as products of network economies that didn't protect those networks from relentless technological attacks by upstarts, new entrants or Schumpeterian entrepreneurs hailing 'creative destruction' . This asymmetric view reflects the match between the 'Old Guard vs. the Vanguard' (Hamel and Switzer, 2004) in the sense that an incumbent's position endows her with a natural network advantage which could only be overcome by a breakthrough innovation of a new entrant depending on some probability of innovation success. We have manifestations of intense rivalry and 'neck-and-neck' competition across industries .

6.4. Modeling Technology Racing in a Network

We start out with a simple model in which two firms , Y and Z, are producing a good using incompatible technologies, the good is infinitely durable. The firms have products of identical qualities which we normalize to zero. For simplicity the marginal cost of production is assumed to be zero for both firms.

We define: The network base of firm i at time t , b_{it} , is the total number of consumers it has sold to until time t, $i \in \{Y,Z\}$.

The network advantage of firm i at time t is $n_{it} \equiv b_{it} - b_{jt}$, $i , j \in \{Y,Z\}$.

A new consumer arrives in the market every period. Each consumer has an inelastic unit demand for the good and must decide at which firm to buy as soon as she enters the market. Consumers care about how many other consumers buy the same product as they do because of network externalities. That is, they are likely to choose products of the larger network over those of the smaller. They also care about the quality of the product and its price. For simplicity, all 'representative' consumers have identical preferences. We may state their utility functions as $u(n_t ,q_t, p_t)$ where q_t is the quality of the product as a perfect substitute for the network advantage and p_t is its price. Throughout the phase of adding uncertainty to the innovation process the consumers are expected to be risk-neutral. We assume that there is a threshold difference in network sizes of the two firms, D, such that if neither firm's network is D (critically) bigger than the other's then consumers get the same network benefits from the two firms. More realistically, one could think of D not just as a number but as an 'order of magnitude'. Therefore, if neither firm has a network advantage of D then consumers buy from the firm which charges a lower price if the quality is the same and are indifferent between the two firms if they charge the same price. Once a firm establishes a network advantage of D over the other firm , consumers get a much bigger benefit from it. Thus, if both firms charge the same price then consumers prefer the firm which has the network advantage of D (or more). It follows that once a firm gets a network advantage of D it becomes a (temporary) monopolist of the market.

If both firms did not have identical qualities to start out with, then we could think of the network advantage as comprising of the network difference plus the quality difference, i.e., treat network and quality as perfect substitutes in the consumer's utility.

The proposed rule for consumer decisions implies that consumers are myopic , i.e., the current base of consumers with the firms is what matters to them. While in practice we would expect consumers to form expectations about the future networks of firms, and thus introduce the possibility of multiple fulfilled-expectations equilibria, our assumption of myopic consumers would help select the most efficient equilibrium outcome among them. Both assumptions – -of myopic consumers and consumers with fully rational expectations – are extreme ones, and what is more realistic is something in between the two. Having myopic consumers has the added advantage of making the analysis more tractable. We conceive the interactive decision process as multi-stae dynamic Markov game with its path ending in a Markov perfect equilibrium (Perloff, Karp and Golan, 2007, Chapt.6).

Let n_{Yt} represent the state of the system (we could equivalently choose n_{Zt} to be the state variable). Thus state 1 denotes the situation where firm Y has one (order of magnitude) more consumer than firm Z , state – 1 denotes the situation where firm Z has one (order of magnitude) more consumer than firm Y. We define 3 to be the absorbing state for firm Y and – 3 the absorbing state for firm Z, i.e. we let D equal 3. The net discounted payoff of a firm in its absorbing state is M , for the other firm likewise. The absorbing state can be thought of as the threshold advantage in quality or network which is big enough to deter the other firm from ever trying to catch up. Thus the firm that has this advantage becomes a monopolist in the market. It is the sole seller in the market making monopoly profits of M whereas the other firm leaves the market and thus gets zero profits.

The product is subject to technological innovation. We assume that an innovation pushes a firm to its absorbing state. Thus we assume that the innovation is equivalent to a big enough network advantage that gives a firm an insurmountable lead over the other firm, in many given cases of asymmetrical network advantage the innovations need to be 'radical'. The innovation, however, is uncertain, either a firm gets the required quality improvement or there is no improvement at all. The probability that a firm gets the innovation in any time period is $\alpha \in [0,1/2]$ which is the same for both firms. We could think of $\alpha > 0$ as representing the technological environment in which the firms operate. We assume that once one firm succeeds, there are no further innovations in the market. We also assume for notational simplicity that at most one firm gets the innovation. Thus the probability that neither firm gets the innovation in any one time is $1 - 2\alpha$. In this situation, we look at the innovation process as 'exogeneous' (though we could make it 'endogeneous' by letting the probability of innovation success depend on the network size as a proxy for the degree of accumulated knowledge (learning) in determining innovation success).

We could think of the technological innovation as a new feature that the firms try to introduce in their respective products. Once one firm gets its innovation it can get a patent even though the firms produce incompatible products. We assume that the new improved product that a firm might introduce is compatible with its older product. Compatibility, in this model, translates into network sharing – compatible products share a network.

Firms compete in prices and thus must decide what price to charge at each of the states in $S = \{-2,-1,0, 1,2\}$ in order to maximize their respective profits given by

$$\pi_Y(s_0,p) = \Sigma_t\, \delta^t\, (1 - 2\alpha)^{t-1}\, [(1 - 2\alpha)p_{Yt}x_{Yt} + \alpha M] + \delta^{\tau+1}I(s_{\tau+1} = 3)M, , t = 0,1,2, \ldots , \tau$$

$$\pi_Z(s_0,p) = \Sigma_t\, \delta^t\, (1 - 2\alpha)^{t-1}\, [(1 - 2\alpha)p_{Zt}x_{Zt} + \alpha M] + \delta^{\tau+1}I(s_{\tau+1} = 3)M, , t = 0,1,2, \ldots , \tau$$

$$s_{t+1} = s_t + x_{Yt},$$

with

$$x_{it} = \begin{cases} 1 \text{ if } p_{it} < p_{jt} \\ 0 \text{ if } p_{it} > p_{jt} \\ 0 \text{ or } 1 \text{ if } p_{it} = p_{jt} \end{cases}$$

where p_{it} is the price charged by firm i in period t, $x_{it} \in \{0, 1\}$ is the number of period t consumers that firm i sells to , $\tau + 1$ is the time period in which a firm reaches its absorbing state even without getting the innovation, $s_0 \in S$ is the initial state and $p = (p_1 , p_2)$ where

$$p_i = \{ p_{it} \}, t = 0,1,2,\ldots,\tau$$

We thus have a game where the firms are identical except in the sizes of their networks. There is uncertain technological innovation but the size of the innovation and the probability of innovation are again identical for both firms. Therefore, by comparing the solution of a game with no uncertainty with the solution of our game we should be able to gain valuable insights into the effects uncertainty has on competition between two firms in the presence of network externalities. The pertinent technical results are relegated to the Appendix.

The major results can be summarized as follows:

Propositions 2 and 3 illustrate the effect of uncertainty on equilibrium behaviour in a market with network externalities. In Proposition 1 we saw that when the only difference between two firms is in the sizes of their networks of consumers, the firm with the bigger network sells to all consumers that subsequently enter the market.

However, once we introduce uncertainty about the quality of a firm's product this no longer is true. Even if the uncertainty faced by the firms is fully symmetric and the only difference between the firms is in the size of their respective networks, the firm with the bigger network does not always sell in equilibrium. For a sufficiently high success rate in innovation, it is the firm with the smaller network that sells provided the network distance is not too large.

The reason for this strikingly different outcome compared to the situation without uncertainty is as follows: When there is no uncertainty , the only way either firm can realize positive profits is by reaching its absorbing state.Outside of their respective absorbing states both firms make the same profits, i.e. zero. Thus the way for either firm to make positive profits is to sell to all the consumers and reach its absorbing state. However, since the firm with the larger network needs a smaller addition to its network to reach its absorbing state, it needs a shorter time span to reach its absorbing state, hence its discounted profits from selling to all consumers is larger. Not selling to any consumers, on the other hand, gives both firms zero profits. Thus since the firm with the bigger network has more to gain from selling to all subsequent consumers while not selling gives it the same profits as the firm that is behind, it is willing to price more aggressively in order to lure the consumers. Thus in equilibrium the firm that is ahead always sells.

The introduction of uncertainty, even when it is uniform across the firms , alters the incentives of the firms to fight for the consumers. When the difference in network (size) between the two firms is sufficiently small and the probability of success is high the presence of uncertainty reduces the incentive of the firm that is ahead to fight for the current consumer relative to that of the firm with the network disadvantage. That is because with a high rate of innovation the leading firm has a high probability of getting its monopoly profits whether it sells to the current consumer or not. The firm with the network disadvantage, on the other hand, has a bigger stake in winning the current consumer since by not letting the other firm get close to its absorbing state, it keeps its own chances of getting the innovation and thus reaping the high monopoly profits alive. However, when the leading firm has a big network advantage, i.e., is close to its absorbing state, its incentive to sell is much higher since it can then guarantee itself the monopoly profits by selling to the current customer. (Thus as $\delta \to 1$ and $\alpha \to 1/2$, we see the firm with a network advantage of 2 selling and also the firm with a network disadvantage of 1.)

Until now all the discussion has been in terms of network advantage or disadvantage. We could equally well have had the discussion in terms of quality advantage or disadvantage since network and quality are perfect substitutes in a consumer's utility. Thus without uncertainty, in the presence of network externalities, if the only difference between two firms was in the quality of their products then the firm with the better quality product would sell to all the consumers. With uncertain quality improvement however, if the probability of quality improvement were high enough then the firm with the lower quality would sell to the consumer. Both firms would remain in the market until one of the firms got an innovation that gave it an insurmountable lead over the other.

6.5. Extensions and Conclusions

We have observed competitive situations in network markets where there is uncertain technological development in product/process technologies. Firms 'price' compete in those markets to gain market share before any of them succeeds in getting an innovation to move ahead of its rival(s). If the firms are in a technology race but the probability of innovation success is small then a firm with a bigger network advantage is likely to attract more customers in the absence of innovation. If however any of those firms expect innovation with a high probability, and none of them have a big advantage, then they keep on sharing the market until the innovation occurs.

We have looked at a simple model of a market with network externalities where there is technological innovation. It would be interesting to explore what kind of modifications to our basic model might change some of the results . The model is based on the assumption of symmetry in terms of the innovation that the firms expect.

If we introduce asymmetric innovation this would permit us to endogenize innovation to the extent that we could look at the decisions of firms how much to improve quality. If we look at a more dynamic model of having sequential innovation and multiple races we might be able to see whether there is a clustering of innovations , and by examing the size of innovations, whether firms would rather tend toward one big risky innovation or rather for a series of small ones which are less risky. Under welfare theoretic considerations there may be related questions on whether there is too much or too little innovation in view of a social optimum (Gottinger,2003).

Our simple model shows how competing firms behave in a market with network externalities before the resolution of technological uncertainty. If our firms are in waiting (for the breakthrough innovation to come true) but the probability of innovation is small, then the firm that has a network advantage makes all the sales. However, if the probability of innovation is large, then it is not always the firm with the bigger network that sells. While a firm with a network advantage of 2 would make the sale, it is the firm with a network disadvantage of 1 that makes the sale if she is lucky to catch this innovation.

Alternatively, it could also serve as an explanation for why a firm that is in the end driven out of the market may just hang on there for a while, with a network disadavantage, before she finally gives up and exits (or is exited from) the market.

Furthermore, as some sort of byproduct of this analysis, we could pursue the interaction between network effects and innovation for market structures. If network effects are 'competitive barriers' that could only be overcome by radical innovation then, by implication, the synergy of network effects and radical innovation through the incumbent would constitute a formidable powerhouse to consolidate monopolistic positions in dynamic product markets where 'winner-takes-all markets' are created .

REFERENCES

Choi,J.P. (1994)'Irreversible Choice of Uncertain Technologies with Network Externalities', *Rand Journal of Economics* 25, 382-401

Baumol, W.J.(2002), *The Free Market Innovation Machine*, Princeton, N.J.: Princeton Univ. Press

Evans,D.S. and R. Schmalensee (2001)'Some Economic Aspects of Antitrust Analysis in Dynamically Competitive Industries', National Bureau of Economic Research, Cambridge, MA. Working Paper 8268, http://www.nber.org/papers/w8268

Fudenberg ,D. And J. Tirole (1993), *Game Theory*, Cambridge, Ma: MIT Press

Futia,C. (1980),'Schumpeterian Competition', *Quarterly Journal of Economics 94*, 675-695

Gottinger,H.W.(2002)' Modeling Stochastic Innovation Races', *Technological Forecasting and Social Change* 69, 607-624 (2003) *Economies of Network Industries* , London: Routledge

Hamel, G. and L. Switzer (2004), 'The Old Guard vs. the Vanguard', *The Wall Street Journal* (Online Edition), Feb. 23

Harris,C. and J. Vickers (1987)'Racing with Uncertainty', *Review of Economic Studies* 54, 1-21

Katz,M. And C. Shapiro (1992)'Product Introduction with Network Externalities', *The Journal of Industrial Economics* 40, 55-83

Kristiansen,E.G. (1998)'R&D in the Presence of Network Externalities: Timing and Compatibility', *Rand Journal of Economics* 29,531-547

Perloff, J.M., Karp, L.S. and A. Golan (2007), *Estimating Market Power and Strategies*, Cambridge: Cambridge Univ. Press

Shapiro, C. (1989) ,'Theories of Oligopoly Behavior', in *Handbook of Industrial Organization*, Vol. 1,

R. Schmalensee and R.D. Willig, eds., Amsterdam: North Holland, 329-414

Uttenback,J.M. (1994) *Mastering the Dynamics of Innovation* , Boston: Harvard Business School Press

APPENDIX

We look for Markov equilibria, Fudenberg and Tirole (1993), which are non-collusive and symmetric. In such an equilibrium we look for a firm that if it does not sell to the consumer it is indifferent between selling or not selling. Thus if firm Y is the firm not selling at state s

$$p_Y(s) + \delta \prod_Y(s+1) = \delta \prod_Y(s-1)$$

where $\prod(s)$ represents the continuation payoff starting from state s. If Z is the firm not selling at state s then

$$p_Z(s) + \delta \prod_Z(s-1) = \delta \prod_Z(s+1)$$

In such an equilibrium the non-selling firm ensures that even if against all expectations the consumer buys its product then it will not make negative profits in equilibrium.

Definition 1. An equilibrium is non-collusive if neither firm charges a positive price at a non-absorbing state. Alternatively, if either firm charges a positive price at a non-absorbing state, equilibrium is collusive.

Definition 2. The equilibrium is symmetric if $p_Y(s) = p_Z(-s)$ for all permissible s and $x_Y(s) = x_Z(-s)$ for all permissible $s \neq 0$.

If instead of having an infinite horizon game we look at a game with a long but finite horizon, the non-collusive equilibria are the ones we expect would most likely be sustainable.

We first consider the case in absence of uncertainty, i.e. $\alpha = 0$.

Proposition 1. For $\alpha = 0$, the symmetric non-collusive Markov equilibrium prices are unique: the firm with a positive network advantage makes all the sales in equilibrium.

Proof. Suppose firm Z sells at s = 2. If firm Y were to sell to the consumer at s = 2 , then in the next period it would get a profit of M. Therefore, if in a non-collusive equilibrium firm Y does not sell at s = 2 as we have assumed, it must be getting a continuation payoff at least as big as M next period. There are two possibilities for s = 1 -- either firm Y sells or firm Z does.

Suppose firm Y sells at s = 1. Then once the state reaches 1 it must alternate between 1 and 2 forever more from then on. The continuation payoff to firm Y at state 1 then is just the discounted sum of the price it charges to the consumer at s = 1 every other period. For this to be at least M the price at s = 1 must be positive and equilibrium is then collusive. Suppose firm Z sells at s = 1 also. Then once s = 1 is reached it must remain within the states -1, 0,1 forever more. But then again for firm Y's continuation payoff at s = 1 to be at least M , it must get a positive payoff at s = 0 or - 1 , a contradiction. Thus Y must sell at s = 2. Suppose firm Z sells at s = 1 and Y sells at s = 2. Then once state 1 is reached the state must remain within the states -1,0,1. In a non-collusive equilibrium where neither firm charges a positive price Y's continuation payoff at s = 0 cannot be positive. Z's continuation payoff at s = 2 is zero. Similarly, the smallest price Z is willing to charge at s = 1 cannot be less than zero. However, firm Y's continuation payoff at s = 2 is then positive and at most zero at s = 0, it is therefore willing to charge a negative price at s = 1 in order to lure the consumer into buying its product. But that means the consumer should buy from firm Y at s = 1 since its price is lower than Z's , a contradiction. Thus firm Y must sell at s = 1 also.

We have so far shown that if a symmetric , non-collusive Markov equilibrium exists then it must have the firm with the network advantage selling. We now show that such an equilibrium does indeed exist and that it is (almost) unique.

If in equilibrium the firm with the network advantage wins always then the continuation payoffs of both firms at s = 0 must be zero in a symmetric equilibrium since both firms are willing to give up exactly the same surplus in order to win the consumer. This surplus is equal to the continuation payoff from winning the current which has to be at least zero.

At s = 1, the lowest firm Z is willing to charge is zero since whether it sells to the current consumer or not it is going to get a payoff of zero from then on. But that means it must charge a price of zero at s = 2 also. The continuation payoff at s = 0 from winning is then $\delta^2 M$.

Thus both firms charge $-\delta^3 M$ at s = 0 and get zero discounted payoffs. It can be checked that these are equilibrium prices.

Thus the unique equilibrium prices are as follows:

$$p(2) = p(-2) = 0$$

$$p(1) = p(-1) = 0$$

$$p(0) = -\delta^3 M$$

Both firms charge the same prices. Firm Y sells to the consumer at s = 1,2 ,... firm Z sells to the consumer at s = -1,-2 either firm could sell at s = 0.

Thus we see that in the absence of uncertainty the firm that is already ahead in terms of network size is the 'winning' firm. The other firm that has a network disadvantage is unable to overtake the firm that is ahead. This result is similar to that obtained by Katz and Shapiro

(1992). Once a firm acquires a bigger network the other firm is unable to overcome its disadvantage. Since in our model quality and network are perfect substitutes in the consumer's utility , we could replace network by quality to get the same result. The firm with the higher quality sells to all consumers, the lower quality firm is unable to push out the better quality firm from the market given that both firms start out with the same network size.

We now introduce uncertainty into the game and see how firms behave. As in the previous case, the only difference between the firms is in their networks. The uncertainty faced by firms is symmetric: both firms have the same probability of getting an innovation and the effect of an innovation is symmetric for both firms.

Proposition 2. There exist δ_* and α^* such that for $\delta_* < \delta < 1$ and $0 < \alpha < \alpha^*$ the non-collusive symmetric equilibrium prices are unique. The firm with the bigger network sells to the consumer, either firm could sell when s = 0.

Proof. The proof proceeds along a sequence of lemmas.

Since we are looking for symmetric equilibria, at s = 0 the lowest price both firms are willing to charge must be the same. Thus in equilibrium both firms must be indifferent between selling or not at s = 0, i.e. at s = 0 both firms have the expected payoffs. Again, since we are looking at symmetric equilibria we need only focus on behaviour at s = 0,1,2. The different possibilities at s = 1 and s = 2 determine the different candidates for equilibrium outcomes. There are four possible candidates for equilibrium network advantage evolution given that no innovation occurs in the meantime.

$x_Y(1) = 1 , x_Y(2) = 1 ,$

$x_Z(1) = 1 , x_Y(2) = 1 ,$

$x_Z(1) = 1 , x_Z(2) = 1 ,$

$x_Y(1) = 1 , x_Z(2) = 1,$

where $x_i(s) = 1$ means that at state s firm i sells to one consumer (and thus $j \neq i$ sells to no one since there is only one consumer in the market at any time period) in the absence of innovation having taken place.

Define $p_i^*(s)$ be the lowest price firm i is willing to charge and p(s) to be the equilibrium price at s. The lowest a firm is willing to charge at any state is just the difference between its profits if it lost the current consumer and if it won it. In other words, the maximum a firm is willing to give up in order to attract a consumer is exactly the amount of extra profit the firm can expect to make by selling to that consumer. Define $\pi_i^W(s)$, $\pi_i^L(s)$ to be the expected profits of firm i next period onwards from respectively winning and losing the current consumer at state s , let $\pi_i(s)$ be the ex ante expected payoff of i at state s.

We prove the proposition using the following lemmas:

Lemma 1. Case (iii) cannot occur in equilibrium.

Proof. Suppose (iii) described the equilibrium network evolution.

Then $p_Y^*(1) = p(1) = \delta(1 - 2\alpha)p(0)$ (1)

This is just the difference in payoffs to firm Y from losing versus winning the current consumer.

$$\pi_Y^W(1) = 0 + \delta\alpha M + \delta\,(1 - 2\alpha)\,\pi_Y(1)$$

$$\pi_Y^L(1) = (1 - 2\alpha)p(0) + \delta\alpha M + \delta\,(1 - 2\alpha)\,\pi_Y(1)$$

$$p_Y^*(1) = \pi_Y^L(1) - \pi_Y^W(1).$$

Similarly,

$$p_Z^*(0) = p(0) = \delta(1 - 2\alpha)p(1) \qquad (2)$$

Equations 1 and 2 together imply that

$$p(1) = \delta^2(1 - 2\alpha)^2 p(1).$$

But that in turn implies that either $p(1) = 0$ or $\delta = 1$ and $\alpha = 0$. Since we are looking at the case where $\alpha \neq 0$, $p(1)$ must be zero, which means from (2), $p(0) = 0$. Thus

$$\pi_Y(0) = \pi_Z(0) = \frac{\alpha M}{1-\delta(1 - 2\alpha)} \equiv \pi(0)$$

We can calculate $p_Z^*(2)$ and $p_Y^*(2)$ (=$p(2)$ since Y is the losing firm at $s = 2$)

$$p_Z^*(2) = -\,\delta\alpha M - \delta^2(1 - 2\alpha)\pi(0)$$

$$p_Y^*(2) = \delta\alpha M + \delta^2(1 - 2\alpha)\pi(0) - \delta M$$

But for $\delta < 1$, $p_Y^*(2) < p_Z^*(2)$ which means firm Y must be the one selling to the consumer at $s = 2$, a contradiction.

Lemma 2. Case (iv) describes the network evolution in equilibrium only when $\delta^2(1 - 2\alpha)^2 > 1/2$.

Proof. $\pi_Z^W(1) = 0 + \delta\alpha M + \delta\,(1 - 2\alpha)\,\pi_Z(1)$

$$\pi_Z^L(1) = (1 - 2\alpha)p(2) + \delta\alpha M + \delta\,(1 - 2\alpha)\,\pi_Z(1)$$

$$p_Z^*(1) = p(1) = \pi_Z^L(1) - \pi_Z^W(1)$$

$$\Rightarrow p(1) = \delta(1 - 2\alpha)p(2) \tag{3}$$

We can calculate $p(2) = p_Y^*(2)$ using the same method:

$$p(2) = \frac{\delta\alpha M}{1 - \delta(1 - 2\alpha)} + \frac{\delta(1 - 2\alpha)}{1 - \delta^2(1 - 2\alpha)^2} p(1) - \delta M$$

$$p_Z^*(2) = \frac{\delta\alpha M}{1 - \delta(1 - 2\alpha)} - \frac{\delta^2(1 - 2\alpha)^2}{1 - \delta^2(1 - 2\alpha)^2} p(2) \tag{4}$$

Substituting the expression for p(2) in (3) we get

$$p(1) = \frac{\delta^2(1 - 2\alpha)^2 \alpha M}{1 - \delta(1 - 2\alpha)} + \frac{\delta^2(1 - 2\alpha)^2}{1 - \delta^2(1 - 2\alpha)^2} p(1) - \delta^2(1 - 2\alpha) M \tag{5}$$

We similarly calculate p(0) using the relation of (3) to get p(0) = 0 since

$$p(0) = \frac{\delta^2(1 - 2\alpha)^2}{1 - \delta^2(1 - 2\alpha)^2} p(2) - \frac{\delta(1 - 2\alpha)}{1 - \delta^2(1 - 2\alpha)^2} p(1)$$

This in turn implies that $p_Y^*(1) = 0$.

For case (iv) to occur in equilibrium therefore p(1) must be non-negative. That leads to $p_Y^*(1) \le p(1)$; it also implies that p(2) is non-negative, therefore

$p_Z^*(2) \le 0 \le p(2)$ from equation (4). From (5) we see that p(1) is non-negative only if $\delta^2 (1 - 2\alpha)^2 \ge 1/2$.

Lemma 3. As $\delta \to 1$ and $\alpha \to 0$, the pattern of network evolution described in (iv) can only occur in a collusive equilibrium.

Proof. As $\delta \to 1$, $\alpha \to 0$, $\delta^2 (1 - 2\alpha)^2 \ge 1/2$. Thus from lemma 2 case (iv) can occur in an equilibrium. But when $\delta^2 (1 - 2\alpha)^2 \ge 1/2$, we see from (5) that $p(1) > 0$, i.e., the equilibrium is collusive.

Lemma 4. Case (i) describes the pre-innovation network evolution in a non-collusive equilibrium only when $3\alpha [1 + \delta(1 - 2\alpha)] \le 1$.

Proof. We calculate the lowest prices firms are willing to charge as described earlier on

$p_Y^*(2) = \delta\alpha M + \delta^2(1 - 2\alpha)\,\alpha M + \delta^3(1 - 2\alpha)^2 M - \delta M + \delta(1 - 2\alpha)\,p(1) + \delta^2(1 - 2\alpha)^2\,p(2)$

$p_Z^*(2) = p(2) = -\delta\,\alpha\,M - \delta^2(1 - 2\alpha)\,\alpha\,M$

$p_Y^*(1) = \delta^2(1 - 2\alpha)\,\alpha M + \delta^3(1 - 2\alpha)^2\,\alpha M - \delta^2(1 - 2\alpha)\,M - \delta(1 - 2\alpha)\,p(2)$

$p_Z^*(1) = p(1) = -\delta^2(1 - 2\alpha)\,\alpha M - \delta^3(1 - 2\alpha)^2\,\alpha M$

$p(0) = -\delta(1 - 2\alpha)\,p(1) - \delta^2(1 - 2\alpha)^2\,p(2) - \delta^3(1 - 2\alpha)^2 M$
$= \delta^3(1 - 2\alpha)^2 M\,[2\alpha + 2\delta\alpha(1 - 2\alpha) - 1]$

We can use the above equations to solve for p(0) , p (1), and p(2) simultaneously. It can be checked that $p_Y^*(2) \le p(2)$ always holds, but that $p_Y^*(1) \le p(1)$ holds only if

$$3\alpha\,[1 + \delta(1 - 2\alpha)\,] \le 1 \tag{6}$$

It can be checked that when inequality (6) is satisfied then p(0) , p(1), and p(2) are all negative. Note that (6) holds when $\delta \to 1$ and $\alpha \to 0$. Thus when inequality (6) is satisfied the network evolution described in case (i) occurs as a result of the non-collusive equilibrium described by the prices given above. Both firms charge p(s) , $s \in \{-2, -1, 0, 1, 2\}$, where p(0), p(1), and p(2) are as given above and $p(-2) = p(2)$, $p(-1) = p(1)$. At s = 1,2 firm Y sells to the consumer in the market, at s = – 1, – 2 firm Z sells to the consumer , and at s = 0 either firm could sell.

We see that the equilibrium when there is no uncertainty is just the limit of the above equilibrium as $\alpha \to 0$.

Lemma 5. Case (ii) describes the pre-innovation network evolution in a non-collusive equilibrium only when

$1 - 3\delta^2(1 - 2\alpha)^2 \le 0$ or when
$\delta^4(1 - 2\alpha)^4 + 4\,\delta^2(1 - 2\alpha)^2 - 1 \le 0$ and $\alpha - 3\delta^2(1 - 2\alpha)^2 - (1 - 2\alpha)(1 - \delta) \ge 0$.

Proof. Suppose (ii) describes the pattern of equilibrium network evolution in the absence of innovation. Then , $p_Z^*(2) = p(2)$ and $p_Y^*(1) = p(1)$:

$$p_Z^*(2) = \frac{\delta\alpha M}{1 - \delta(1 - 2\alpha)} - \frac{\delta(1 - 2\alpha)}{1 - \delta^2(1 - 2\alpha)^2}\,p(1) \tag{7}$$

$$p_Y^*(2) = \frac{\delta\alpha M}{1 - \delta(1 - 2\alpha)} + \frac{\delta^2(1 - 2\alpha)^2}{1 - \delta^2(1 - 2\alpha)^2} p(0) - \delta M \tag{8}$$

$$p_Y^*(1) = \frac{\delta\alpha M}{1 - \delta(1 - 2\alpha)} + \frac{\delta(1 - 2\alpha)^2}{1 - \delta^2(1 - 2\alpha)^2} p(0) - \delta\alpha M - \delta(1 - 2\alpha)\, p(2)\, \delta^2(1 - 2\alpha)M \tag{9}$$

$$p_Z^*(1) = \frac{\delta\alpha M}{1 - \delta(1 - 2\alpha)} - \frac{\delta^2(1 - 2\alpha)^2}{1 - \delta^2(1 - 2\alpha)^2} p(1) + \delta\alpha M \tag{10}$$

$$p(0) = \delta(1 - 2\alpha)\, p(1) \tag{11}$$

Using equations (7) and (11) to substitute in the values of p(2)and p(0) in equation (9) we get

$$p(1) = -\frac{[1 - \delta^2(1 - 2\alpha)^2]\, \delta^2(1 - 2\alpha)^2(1 - \delta)M}{[1 - \delta(1 - 2\alpha)][1 - 3\delta^2(1 - 2\alpha)^2]} \tag{12}$$

For (ii) to occur in equilibrium it must be true that $p_Z^*(1) \le p(1)$ and $p_Y^*(2) \le p(2)$. It can be checked that $p_Y^*(2) \le p(2)$ iff $1 - 3\delta^2(1 - 2\alpha)^2 \le 0$ or

$\delta^4(1 - 2\alpha)^4 + 4\delta^2(1 - 2\alpha)^2 - 1 \le 0$. It can also be checked that $p_Z^*(1) \le p(1)$ iff $1 - 3\delta^2(1 - 2\alpha)^2 \le 0$ or $\alpha - 3\delta^2\alpha(1 - 2\alpha)^2 - (1 - 2\alpha)(1 - \delta) \ge 0$, thus proving the lemma.

Lemma 6. For $\delta \to 1$ and $\alpha \to 0$ the equilibrium described in lemma 5 is collusive.

Proof. For $\delta \to 1$ and $\alpha \to 0$, $1 - 3\delta^2(1 - 2\alpha)^2 < 0$, thus case (ii) can occur in equilibrium from lemma 5. But it can be checked from (12) that for $1 - 3\delta^2(1 - 2\alpha)^2 \le 0$ and $\delta < 1$, p(1) is positive.

Thus from lemmas 1 to 6 we can infer that as $\delta \to 1$ and $\alpha \to 0$, the (almost) unique non-collusive equilibrium shows the following properties. In the absence of innovation both firms charge the prices as below: As $\delta \to 1$ and $\alpha \to 0$, the equilibrium prices in the absence of innovation are:

$$p(2) = p(-2) = -\delta\alpha M - \delta^2(1 - 2\alpha)\alpha M$$

$$p(1) = p(-1) = -\delta^2(1 - 2\alpha)\alpha M - \delta^3(1 - 2\alpha)^2\alpha M$$

$$p(0) = \delta^3 (1 - 2\alpha)^2 M [2\alpha + 2\delta\alpha (1 - 2\alpha) - 1]$$

As $\alpha \to 0$, the equilibrium prices in the absence of innovation are:

$$p(2) = p(-2) \to 0$$

$$p(1) = p(-1) \to 0$$

$$p(0) \to -\delta^3 M$$

Firm Y sells to the consumer in the market at s = 1, 2 and firm Z sells when s = – 1, – 2. When s = 0 , either firm could sell but both earn the same expected profits when s = 0 , i.e., $x_Y(1) = x_Y(2) = x_Z(-1) = x_Z(-2) = 1$ and $x_Y(0) = 1$ or $x_Z(0) = 1$.

Proposition 3. There exist δ_* and α_* such that for $\delta_* < \delta < 1$ and $\alpha_* < \alpha < 1/2$, the non-collusive symmetric equilibrium prices are unique. The firm with network advantage of 2 and the firm with network advantage of 1 sell.

Proof. For lemmas 1, 2, 4, and 5, we infer that the only possible outcome in equilibrium has the firm with the advantage of 2 and the firm with the disadvantage of 1 sell prior to an innovation occurring.From lemma 5 we see that for δ close to 1 and α close to 1/2 , the equilibrium prices are negative. The equilibrium is therefore non-collusive. As $\delta \to 1$ and $\alpha \to 1/2$, the equilibrium prices are as follows:

$$p(2) = p(-2) \to -M/2$$

$$p(1) = p(-1) \to 0$$

$$p(0) \to 0$$

Chapter 7

7. NETWORK ECONOMIES FOR OPEN SOURCE TECHNOLOGIES (OST)

7.1. INTRODUCTION

Research and Development (R&D) is a crucial phenomenon both from the point of view of the individual firm and the economy as a whole. Since innovation could be regarded as a public good, society as a whole benefits from innovation. However, the private benefits to a firm from innovating are likely to be different from the social benefits. In the absence of any mechanism preventing it, the benefits to an innovating firm are likely to be quickly dissipated by the entry of other imitating firms. In such a scenario, firms are unlikely to innovate. Thus according to conventional thinking, firms need to have some sort of reward for innovating. Intellectual property rights such as patents and copyrights provide this compensation. A big portion of the R&D literature has focused on the optimal patents' duration and breadth and the incentive of firms to innovate.

However, a different trend has emerged these days especially with the increasing proliferation of hi-tech (network) industries. Instead of trying to get exclusive ownership rights, an increasing number of firms are making their technology freely available i.e., their technology is no longer proprietary or 'open source' (Cane, 2004).

In the so-called browser war, in the 1990s, we have witnessed intense competition in the market for internet browsers between Microsoft and Netscape. Netscape had a major head start on Microsoft, controlling 90% of the browser market by 1996 before Microsoft started aggressively selling in the market. With the entry of Microsoft, both firms engaged in a race to have the best available product.

Given the intense competition between the two firms, by the end of 1997 Microsoft was pricing the Internet Explorer free. In contrast, Netscape was charging corporations licensing fees for using their browser. By the end of 1997, Microsoft had stolen a large chunk of Netscape's market share. Netscape eventually followed suit and started giving away its browser free.

The extended battle between Microsoft and Netscape had its toll on the profits of both companies. In 1998 Netscape came up with a new strategy and decided to release its source code, the actual line of programming language, for the Netscape Communicator. This allowed users and developers to look inside the workings of the browser, to modify the software and even to redistribute the new version under their own brand name, provided that the modified source code was also freely available. The whole idea is to turn the entire internet community into a vast research division for Netscape browser.

The term 'open source software' has been widely used in the popular and professional literature (Varian and Shapiro, 2003; Lerner and Tirole, 2004). Instead of keeping their technology proprietary, the firms will distribute it freely. It is this phenomenon that this chapter attempts to explore. We wish to study the decisions of firms whether to keep their technologies proprietary or not.

Even though the whole unorthodox open approach may seem counterintuitive, Netscape was not the only one who employed it. Apache, a program for serving world wide web sites, and Sendmail, a program that routes and delivers internet electronic mail, are examples of free open source programs that dominate the market. Open source approaches have been expanded to the biotechnology and health care industries, Economist (2004a). Linux, an increasingly popular operating system created in 1991 is another classic example of successful open source software. Many of the programmers and software designers advocating OSS may share a utopian vision of software development, or they may simply want to prove themselves to be better than software giant Microsoft. However, the whole idea of OSS may not be so anti-capitalistic as it seems. It is hard to believe that profit-aiming firms will employ the OSS strategy without considering more pragmatic matters. The emergence of OSS as an observable phenomenon may be because the markets under consideration are no longer conventional markets. These markets exhibit "network externalities"- a market has network externalities when buyers of a good exert positive benefits on the other users of the same good. For instance consumers are likely to value computer hardware more the more users of the hardware there are. This could be because there is likely to be a better support system the larger is the network of consumers buying the product. Similarly, it is more likely for improved software to get written for the computer hardware the bigger is the network of consumers buying it. But network externalities can be working both ways, positive or negative, for example, incompatibility with network systems on a rival operating system (such as MS Office) is a major obstacle in the OSS pursuit of the desktop though low prices for OSS products would be a strong incentive to switch and for new customers to enter.

In such a market time is of utmost importance in the race for product improvement. Firms cannot afford to let their competitors get ahead in the race for technological innovation since that would give them the added advantage of a bigger network. Also, consumers in these markets tend to exhibit a very high level of loyalty. That is because learning to use the product involves a cost. Once a consumer becomes familiar with particular software, she is unlikely to switch to a completely different brand performing the same tasks. Instead, she would rather purchase new releases of the same brand even though there can be various close substitutes with similar qualities available in the market. This enhances the effect of network externalities in the long run. Further, OSS *can* feasibly translate into better quality in markets such as those for computers.

The effect of OSS on product improvement is two-pronged. Making the technology freely available meansthat there can be more people directly working on improving the product. For example, ever since Linux went fully OSS, thousands of programmers have volunteered elaborate improvements of their own design for no more reward than the respect of the geek subculture. It is like expanding the R&D department, so larger improvements in quality can be realized. Secondly, there is likely to be a better supply of complementary goods. For instance giving out the source code for an operating system is likely to lead to more software being developed for it, which is in essence equivalent to having a better quality operating system i.e., consumers now find this OS more attractive.

On the other hand, making technology freely available means a loss in license fees. There is also the fear of technology being stolen. But in a market with network externalities, if the firm giving away its technology already has a sufficiently big network then it is more difficult for other firms just entering the market to steal the technology and get ahead since they would also have to overcome the network advantage of the existing firm (Gottinger, 2003). Besides in this digital era, the relative ease of creating software with similar functionalities using different programming codes has made the whole idea of keeping technology proprietary less relevant.

We can thus think of OSS as increasing the rate of product improvement or increasing the success rate of R&D. We model OSS via license fees and assume that OSS increases product development deterministically.

A lower license fee represents a less proprietary technology. A zero or negative license fee means that the technology is totally non-proprietary. Positive license fees represent a proprietary technology - the firm is not willing to freely distribute its technology. The more 'open' a firm is the higher is its rate of R&D - in our model R&D translates directly into the quality of the product. The greater the R&D, the higher is the quality of the product. OSS improves the quality of the product in our model by increasing the supply of people or firms working on improving the product.

We look at a market with network externalities with an incumbent and an entrant. The incumbent, unlike the entrant, already has an installed base of consumers. Our objective is to explore the decisions of the firms regarding how proprietary they want to make their technology, i.e., how copyright or 'open' to make their product. The decision of copyright or open mentioned above, is modelled via license fees. We wish to see whether the incumbent could use 'open' as an entry deterring strategy. We also compare the incumbent's decision with that of a monopoly's.

We explicitly model the direct and indirect effects of network externalities. As in most models, we have the network term showing up in the consumers' utility; the bigger the network, the better off the consumers are. Consumers prefer to use a popular word processor because they know the format of their work can be easily transported to other users' computers. This is the direct effect of network on consumers' utilities. In our model there is also an indirect effect of network externalities - a bigger network translates into better quality. For example, more software companies are willing to produce programs for an operating system if it has a larger consumer base. That is because the downstream software companies thus can tap into this larger network of customers. This improves the quality of the OS. This is the indirect effect of network on consumers' utilities.

Open source system approaches entail some transitional practicable disadvantages against the prevailing standard.

Because of building up a network there will be fewer applications which arise as roadblocks towards further dissemination, for example, as in the case of Linux, only a single digit percentage works for computer games (Economist, 2004b). Incompatibility issues with the dominant operating system are also one of the biggest obstacles for further dissemination, in particular, for large corporations who would face significant switching costs with possible operational disruptions. On the benefit side, however, open source systems may induce R&D

in complementary products and sectors because of lower license fees, thus lower costs of R&D, thee are more incentives to enlarge and expand product development and applications beyond core innovations. Because of its continuously ongoing character it is more likely to be incremental than seminal which poses questions of their own as to whether open source systems can genuinely foster innovation. For dedicated applications as initially built up from scratch such as search through Google it may yield some big advantages , not the least because of comparatively low implementation and operational costs.

This chapter is organized as follows: Section 7.2 looks at the literature related to this work. In Section 7.3. we present the model. In Section 7.4, we look at the equilibrium results and give interpretations. Section 7.5 draws conclusions on further use.

7.2. Patenting, Licensing and Open Source Technologies

The issues covered in this chapter relate to work on network externalities, R&D, entry deterrence and licensing.

R&D is an extensively researched area in industrial organization starting with Arrow's pioneering article where he asked: "What is the gain from innovation to a firm that is the only one to undertake R&D, given that its innovation is protected by a patent of unlimited duration?" (Arrow, 1962). Since then there has been a spate of research on R&D covering issues such as the incentives to innovate, patent races, welfare implications of R&D, choice and adoption of technologies. However, most of this work has focused on conventional markets rather than on markets with network externalities in which dynamic or 'Schumpeterian' competition evolves (Evans and Schmalensee, 2001). We explicitly look at the effect of network externalities on R&D competition and introduce the possibility of firms not wanting their technology to be proprietary which is not recognized by the traditional R&D literature.

Within the topic of R&D, there has been some work devoted to licensing. This literature takes as the starting point one or more firms having a patent. Licensing is then a means of disseminating an innovation. Among the incentives for licensing are product market competition which creates incentives for managers who would otherwise exploit their monopoly positions, cost savings to the licensees which could be appropriated by the licensing firm, and lowering rivals' incentives to invent around the innovation. Katz and Shapiro (1985) look at the incentives to engage in licensing once an innovation is developed in a world of perfect patents. They also look at the incentives to innovate, given the feasibility of licensing. Katz and Shapiro (1986) examine the optimal licensing strategy of a research lab selling to firms who are product market competitors. They show that the seller's incentives to develop an innovation may be excessive and the incentives to disseminate information may be too low. Kende (1998) explores the conditions under which a monopolist selling a system consisting of a main component and differentiated secondary components can increase profits by allowing competition in the market for the secondary components. Opening the system in this fashion can increase profits by giving consumers an added *incentive* to incur the setup cost of purchasing the main component.

The results show that an open system is likely to be more profitable than a closed one when it is more elastic, when secondary-component variety is more valued, and when the share of the main component in the total system budget of the consumer is high.

Licensing plays an important role in our model. However the relation between licensing and innovation has been reversed compared to the traditional licensing literature described above. Instead of licensing being used as a means of diffusing an innovation *after* it has occurred, in our model licensing actually leads to continuously higher innovation.

Farrell and Saloner (1985, 1986) and Katz and Shapiro (1985,1986) are the pioneering works exploring the implications of network externalities in industrial organization. Farrell and Saloner concentrate on the demand side and show that the existence of network externalities leads to coordination problems and thus to a multiplicity of equilibria. In a model where two conflicting technologies compete, they show that "excess inertia" might exist in equilibrium, i.e., the adoption of a new standard might be too slow compared to the social optimum.

Katz and Shapiro extend the scope of Farrell and Saloner's works by including the supply side. They look at the issues of compatibility and pricing in the presence of network externalities. The model of Katz and Shapiro (1985) will serve as a building block for our model. The issues we address, however, are different. They use their model to reinforce the importance of consumer expectations in markets with network externalities. They also show that the private decisions of firms regarding compatibility is greatly affected by whether firms can act unilaterally (or if a consensus is required) and whether side payments are feasible. Katz and Shapiro (1986) show that in the presence of network externalities the private and social incentives to achieve compatibility may diverge.

They show the conditions under which firms may use compatibility as a medium for reducing competition.

While a lot of work has been done in the area of network externalities, little of it specifically addresses R&D. Katz and Shapiro(1992) look at whether there is too much or too little technological innovation in a market with network externalities compared to the social optimum. In particular they look at whether a new product which embodies technological progress is introduced too early or too late compared to the social optimum. Their conclusion is that contrary to what was earlier believed to be true, there is *excess momentum* in equilibrium, i.e., a new product is introduced too soon compared to the social optimum. That happens because the sooner the product is introduced, the sooner the firm can start building up a network and reaping its benefits. Choi (1994) looks at a two-period model of a monopoly in a market with networkexternalities. He studies the incentive of the monopolist to introduce an incompatible improved product in the presence of network externalities. Kristiansen (1996) studies the consequences of network externalities on the riskiness of R&D projects chosen by an entrant and an incumbent. He shows that the incumbent chooses a too risky project that too often lets a new firm with an incompatible technology enter as compared to the social optimum. In addition, the entrant has an incentive to choose more certain projects than are socially optimal and these strengthen the possibility of adoption of an incompatible technology. Regibeau and Rockett (1998) analyze compatibility choices of two firms which must also decide when to introduce their goods in a market characterized by network externalities. They show that the firms' incentives to achieve compatibility depend crucially on the time at which the degree of compatibility must be chosen. The current paper is also related to the literature on investment as a means of entry deterrence. Firms compete not only with existing firms, as is transparent, but also with potential entrants. In an extension of the Spence model Dixit (1980) shows that an incumbent firm may make irrevocable commitment of investment in order to alter the initial conditions of the post-entry game to its own advantage. One of the questions we are interested in is whether the incumbent chooses its license fees so as to discourage entry. That is, the incumbent could be thought of as choosing investment in *quality* as a means of deterring entry.

7.3. NETWORK COMPETITION UNDER LICENSING

There are two firms, an incumbent, I. and an entrant, E. The incumbent has an installed base of consumers of $x_I > 0$ unlike the entrant ($x_E = 0$). We consider a two stage game in a market with network externalities. The products of the firms are incompatible (i.e., they have separate networks).

In the first stage, firms charge a license fee (f) to other downstream firms for use of their product (for example, Microsoft licenses their Windows operating system to other companies to develop applications software). The number of downstream firms willing to work on a firm's product (m_i) depends on the license fee charged and also the initial network of the firm (the consumer base x_i for firm i).

$$m_i = k + x_i - f_i,\ k > 0 \qquad (1)$$

k *is* a measure of the potential market size of downstream firms independent of the license fee and initial network.

The smaller the license fee charged, the more freely the firm distributes its technology and in our terminology, the more 'open' the firm is. We assume no competition in getting downstream firms to buy the firms' licenses. m_i decreases as f_i increases because as the licenses become more expensive fewer downstream firms buy them. This is just the standard argument fora downward sloping demand in price. As for the relationship between m_i and x_i, since the downstream firms are developing products that could be used in conjunction with the firm's product (like complements), the larger the installed base of customers that the firm has, the larger is the potential demand for the downstream firms' product. Thus, the more the downstream firms are willing to pay for the license.

Let us define: If $f_i < f_j$ then firm i chooses to be more open than firm j. (Alternatively firm j chooses to be less open than firm i).

In the second stage firms engage in Cournot competition to sell their products directly to the consumers. The inverse demands for the products of the two firms are given by

$$p_i = A + q_i + \gamma x_i - (x_I + x_E) \qquad (2)$$

where $i \in \{I.E\}$. p_i is the price charged by firm i. $x_i \geq 0$ is the amount of output firm i sells, x_i is the initial network of firm i. q_i is the quality of firm i's product.

Note that ideally we would want to include the *expected* network size in the demand functions instead of just the initial network size. . However, the implications of forming expectations for equilibria in games similar to ours have been extensively studied (see Katz &

Shapiro, Farrell & Saloner). Since we are not interested in analyzing the role of expectations and would like to keep our model simple we just include the initial network size in the consumer's utility function.

The more downstream firms (m_i) a firm licenses out to, the better the quality q_i of its product will be. We assume the following functional form for q_i:

$$q_i = m_i\,,\; i \in \{I,E\} \tag{3}$$

Firm *i's* profit is:

$$\Pi_i = x_i\,p_i + f_i\,m_i\,,\; i \in \{I,E\}$$

The first term represents the profits from direct sales and the second term represents the revenues from licensing. Both firms are assumed to have identical costs which we have normalized to zero. By staying out of the market the entrant makes zero profit.

As the profit function above shows, the license fees (and hence the decision about how closed or open a firm wants to be) affects a firm's profits through two avenues. The first is the direct effect on profits through the licensing revenues. Then there is also an indirect effect through the quality of the firm's product which affects the profits made from direct sales.

The timing of the game is as follows

1. Incumbent I sets its license fee f_I. This determines quality q_I.
2. Entrant E decides whether to enter.
3. If E enters, it chooses a license fee f_E from its set of acceptable license fees. This determines quality q_E.
4. Firm(s) play an output game (Cournot).

Firms choose their license fees and output levels to maximize their profits. However we do restrict the strategy set of the entrant. We do this in order to rule out situations where the entrant enters in order to make money solely out of licensing knowing that at the fee it charges or close to it, it could not sell any output in the second stage. Since the downstream firms could be thought of as producing complementary goods, it would be unreasonable to expect them to buy licenses knowing that the entrant has no *potential* to sell output. Hence we restrict the entrant to choosing a license fee from its set of "acceptable license fees". An acceptable license fee for the entrant, given that the incumbent charges a license fee f_I, is f_E such that for every $\varepsilon > 0$, $x_E\,(f_I\,,\, f_E - \varepsilon) > 0$ where $x_E\,(f_I\,,\, f_E\,)$ is the optimal output for the entrant in the ensuing Cournot game. Thus, the "downstream firms" are not willing to buy licenses unless the entrant has the potential to sell output by making an arbitrarily small reduction in its license fees.

As in other two-stage games, we will now proceed to solve the second stage output game first in order to determine the Subgame Perfect Equilibria.

7.4. Equilibrium Licensing

Given the results from the second stage output game, we will move on to solving the first stage.

Note that if q_i were independent of m_i, then the only component of the firm's profit that depends on f_i is the revenue from licensing which is maximized when firm i charges a license fee of $[k + x_i]/2$. This is our full 'closed' benchmark.

Before we go on to see how the two firms strategically choose their license fees we look at the decision of the incumbent if it were a monopolist in this market.

Case 1: Monopoly: No potential entrant

Theorem 1. The monopolist charges a license fee $f_I^M = [k + (1 - \gamma) x_I - A]/3$.

The proof follows the structure of a Stackelberg game, a complete proof is given in the Appendix.

We see in Proposition 1 that if $\gamma < 1$, the optimal license fee is *increasing* in x_I; if $\gamma > 1$. the optimal license fee is *decreasing* in x_I. To see why, note that the firm's profit has two components - the revenue from selling licenses and that from direct sales. As we saw above, the revenue from licenses is maximized when the license fee is $[k + x_I]/2$. However, by lowering its license fee the firm can improve its product's quality and thus make more profits from its direct sales. So the optimal license fee is less than $[k + x_I]/2$. Thus increasing the license fee by a small amount beyond the optimal one increases the revenue from licenses and decreases that from direct sales, and the two exactly balance at the optimal license fee. When $\gamma < 1$, the contribution of network size to consumer utility is small compared to its contribution to m. The result is that starting from an optimal f for a given x_I, a higher x_I means that increasing f_I will increase the revenues from licenses by dx_I but decrease the revenue from direct sales only by

$(1 + \gamma)dx_I/2 < dx_I$. Therefore at the higher x_I profits have to be increasing in f at the previously optimal f. Thus, given the concavity of the profit function in f, the optimal license fee must be *increasing* in x_I. Exactly the opposite argument holds when $\gamma > 1$. Thus the optimal license fee is *decreasing* in x_I when $\gamma > 1$.

Case 2. Duopoly: With Incumbent and Potential Entrant

We now look at a market that has an incumbent firm (I) with an installed consumer base of x_I and a potential entrant (E).

Once the firms have decided their license fees, they play a Cournot output game (Shapiro, 1989).

The result of the Cournot game is described by the intersection of the two reaction functions that gives the unique interior Cournot outputs, i.e.:

$$x_I = (A + 2q_I + 2\gamma x_I - q_E)/3\ ,\ x_E = (A + 2q_E - \gamma x_I - q_I)/3$$

Call these optimal output levels $x_i(f_I, f_E)$, $i \in \{I,E\}$.

First we make the following definitions.

If the incumbent charges its monopoly license fee f_I^M *, and the entrant stays out of the market, then we say that entry is blocked.*

If the incumbent charges a fee different from f_I^M *in equilibrium, and the entrant stays out of the market, then we say that entry is deterred.*

If the entrant enters but sells nothing in equilibrium then we say that entry is restricted.

If the entrant sells a positive amount in equilibrium, we say that entry is unrestricted.

We can now go on and characterize the entry decision of firm E and the equilibrium license fees for the two firms. But before we do that we briefly state the optimal response of the entrant, assuming that the firms produce optimally in the Cournot subgame, to the different license fees that the incumbent can charge. For proofs please refer to the appendix. We can show that there exists a license fee f_I^D for the incumbent such that for all $f_I < f_I^D$ the optimal response of the entrant is to stay out of the market and for $f_I > f_I^D$ it is to enter. There exists $f_I^R > f_I^D$ such that in the interval $[f_I^D, f_I^R]$ the best response of the entrant is to charge the largest acceptable license fee that makes optimal x_E exactly 0, and for $f_I > f_I^R$ it is optimal for the entrant to enter and charge its unconstrained optimal license fee resulting in a positive x_E

Theorem 2. The levels of x_I^o*, A and k determine the entry decision and license fees in equilibrium as follows:*

1. Entry is blocked if $(1 + 2\gamma)\, x_I^o \geq A + 2k$.
2. For $A + 2k \geq (1 + 2\gamma)\, x_I^o \geq A + k/2$, entry is restricted with the incumbent charging f_I^M and earning its monopoly profits.)
3. For $A + k/2 > (1 + 2\gamma)\, x_I^o > 2A/5 + k/5$. Entry is restricted with the incumbent charging f_I^R and earning less than its monopoly profits.
4. For $2A/5 + k/5 > (1 + 2\gamma)\, x_I^o$, entry is unrestricted and the firms just charge the unconstrained Stackelberg license fees.

Proof. See Appendix

When the network advantage of the incumbent is not big enough to block entry. the entrant enters the market. However if the advantage is still sufficiently large then the incumbent is able to charge its monopoly fees and make its monopoly profits while restricting the entrant to zero output in the Cournot output game.

Given that the network advantage of the incumbent is not big enough to block entry, we saw in Statement 2 of Proposition 2 that if it is still sufficiently high then the incumbent can restrict entry and make monopoly profits. If its advantage is however not big enough to do that, even then a sufficiently high network advantage allows it to restrict entry. It then charges f_I^R which is different from its monopoly license fee and earns less than its monopoly profits. Thus in this case the incumbent is able to act as a monopolist in the output market but not in license fees.

If the initial network advantage of the incumbent is not very big compared to A and k then not only is it unable to keep the entrant out of the market but it is unprofitable to restrict its entry too. In that case the entrant enters the market and both firms sell positive amounts of output.

As corollaries to Proposition 2 we get the result that there is no entry deterrence and we also get a comparison between the monopoly license fees of the incumbent and its license fees when a potential entrant exists.

Corollary 1. There is no entry deterrence.

At f_I^D the entrant produces nothing and the incumbent just makes the profits it would as a monopolist in the second stage output game. Since f_I^D is the largest license fee for the incumbent that deters entry, if $f_I^M \leq f_I^D$ then there is blocked entry. If $f_I^M > f_I^D$ however, then entry is not blocked. But it also means that the incumbent's profits must be increasing at f_I^D (since the monopoly profits are concave in f_I and from Lemma A.2 we know that in the interval $[f_I^D, f_I^R]$, the incumbent makes monopoly profits). Hence the incumbent will not find it profitable to charge f_I^D or less. Thus entry is not deterred.

As a corollary to Proposition 2 we get a comparison between the monopoly license fees of the incumbent and its license fees when a potential entrant exists.

Corollary 2. At the equilibrium duopoly license fee f_I^*, $f_I^* \leq f_I^M$ *always and sometimes* $f_I^* < f_I^M$

Proof. See Appendix

Thus we see that the presence of another firm makes the incumbent choose at most the license fee it would if it were a monopolist. In other words the incumbent chooses its technology to be at most as closed as that of the monopolist.

If its initial network is not very big then the presence of the other firm makes it want to be more open . The firm is then willing to give up more of the licensing revenue in order to improve quality since that will help it in the second stage output competition. If its network advantage is already very big then it does not need to raise quality to give it a competitive edge in the second stage and it continues charging its monopoly license fees.

Theorem 3. For $(1 + 2\gamma)\, x_I^o < A + 2k$ (i.e., when the entrant enters). there exists x_I^{o*}, such that for $x_I^o > x_I^{o*}$,, $f_I^* > f_E^*$ and for $x_I^o < x_I^{o*}$, , $f_I^* < f_E^*$, i.e., if the incumbent' s network is smaller than x_I^{o*}, then the incumbent chooses to be more open and if the network is bigger than x_I^{o*},, then the entrant chooses to be more open.

Proof. See Appendix

Consider first the scenario where the incumbent has a small network advantage, namely the case of unrestricted entry and restricted entry without monopoly profits. Because of the installed base of consumers that firm I has, firm E is at a disadvantage in the output market so cannot expect to make as large a profit from direct sales as can firm I. Firm I on the other hand, when it has a small network advantage, would want to compound its advantage in the output market by increasing its quality more that firm E. Given this initial imbalance in network advantage, firm E is less willing to afford a loss in revenue licenses in order to improve quality. Thus the incumbent charges a lower license fees than the entrant, in other words, the incumbent is more open than the entrant.

To examine this phenomenon in more detail, consider first the case of unrestricted entry. In this case we can isolate two effects that make the incumbent choose to be more open than the entrant, namely the "Stackelberg" effect and the "network" effect. The "Stackelberg" effect can be discerned by comparing the Cournot license fee (when the two firms choose their license fees simultaneously) with the Stackelberg license fee in the absence of network externalities. In the Cournot case with $x_I^{\,o} = 0$, both firms charge exactly the same fees whereas in the Stackelberg case the incumbent charges a lower fee. Thus part of the reason that the incumbent chooses to be more open is just the "first mover" or Stackelberg effect. Now if we reintroduce the network term, we see that the incumbent chooses to be even more open while the entrant chooses to be less open.

From the Appendix (A .10) we see that starting from an optimal f_I increasing $x_I^{\,o}\,r$ by a small amount increases the marginal effect of f_I on license revenues by less than it decreases the marginal effect of f_I on direct sales. Thus the introduction of $x_I^{\,o}$ requires a reduction in f_I in order to bring the marginal effects of f_I on direct sales revenues and licensing revenues into balance again. For the entrant, we see from the reaction function (equation 15) that both a larger $x_I^{\,o}$ and a smaller f_I , lead E to charge a higher f_E. In the case where there is restricted entry without monopoly profits, the entrant is held down to zero output but the incumbent has to lower its license fee below its monopoly level to do so. The entrant on the other hand is able to charge its full copyright license fee. Thus again, the incumbent chooses to be more open than the entrant.

If, however, the incumbent has a large network advantage so that it can still charge its monopoly license fee and make its optimal monopoly profits, then the entrant has to fight to even stay alive in the market. The bigger the incumbent's network is the more difficult it is for the entrant to stay alive i.e.. the smaller is the license fee it charges . Thus there exists a sufficiently large network advantage $x_I^{\,o*}$ for the incumbent beyond which the entrant charges a lower license fee i.e., chooses to be more open.

7.5. Conclusions and Extensions

This chapter has shown that being "open" could be a very sensible, in fact, optimal equilibrium strategy for profit-maximizing firms in a market with network externalities, for example, the internet and computer related markets. As in most other theoretical models, we could not possibly include all the factors relevant to this recently observed phenomenon. Instead, we construct one way of modelling "open", trying to capture the central idea of why "open" makes sense. We devote this section to discussing what can be done or added on to our model in future research efforts on this topic.

In our model we have excluded the traditional "technology stealing" effect. One might argue that that is precisely why we need copyrights and patents - to prevent the influx of copycats into the market driving profits to zero. However, as we mentioned in the introduction, in a market with network externalities, there is a natural barrier against imitators getting ahead of an innovator with an installed base of consumers, namely that consumers will perceive their product to be not as attractive as the incumbent's, even if they are of the same quality. It would still be interesting to see the result of this business stealing" effect being put back into the model. We would expect it there to still be “open" in equilibrium, though to a lesser extent. The equilibrium now needs to strike a balance between the two opposing effects of going "open", namely, the indirect network effect of quality improvement, and the "technology stealing" effect. We could also make the probability of technology being stolen vary inversely with network size, in which case we would expect the result that the incumbent goes more open to be reinforced.

Another possibility is to introduce competition in the first stage of the game. As of now, the incumbent and the entrant do not compete for downstream firms, each of them faces an identical and independent demand for its licenses. This could be justified if there are numerous downstream firms looking for prospective technologies to develop. A more realistic setting may be one where both the incumbent and the entrant are competing in license fees for downstream firms to buy their licenses. Each downstream firm buys at most one unit of the license.

However, this should not change our results drastically and we should still see "open" as an equilibrium strategy.

In fact, with competition, both the incumbent and the entrant are likely to go more open because now they need to compete to sell their licenses.

We could introduce costs into the technology of the firms. In our current model, we have normalized both firms' costs to zero. Differences in the technologies of the firms may sway our results either way depending on who has the better (less costly) technology. It would also be interesting to see how the coupling of the "technology stealing" effect and positive costs may work. For example, if the incumbent freely distributes its technology then the costs for the entrant may fall because it can now "steal' the technology of the incumbent.

In our model, we don't have entry deterrence but we have restricted entry in which the entrant sells licenses in the first stage, but produces nothing in the second stage. This may seem a bit unrealistic. With positive fixed costs, we should be able to have the standard entry deterrence result. We would still expect restricted entry but one where the entrant is 'restricted" to some positive output level.

Another possible extension is making innovation stochastic, i.e. replacing the link *of* $q_i = q\ (m_i)$ with $q_i = q(m_i, \varepsilon_i)$, where ε_i is stochastic. We argue that this again should not change our results qualitatively so long as the resulting distributions for qualities exhibit second order stochastic dominance - the larger the m, the more likely it is for firm i to have a bigger innovation.

Making the game more dynamic is also another interesting extension. As *of* now, we have two stages in the game. *If* we add in more stages in the game, the network effect may get compounded since it now lasts longer, a big early network carries all the way into later stages too. It is even more essential for firms to build up a network fast to lure in more customers, the "open" result thus may be even more pronounced.

We can bring back expectations in consumers utility. Instead *of only* caring about the initial size of the network, consumers now form expectations on how big the future network size for a firm will be before they make their purchase decisions. We then need to deal with much more complicated algebra and to adopt a more refined equilibrium concept in the second stage to handle this problem. For example, we can use the Fulfilled Expectations Cournot Equilibrium (FECE) as in Katz and Shapiro(1986). We suspect that doing so will not buy us anything new in our results.

References

Arrow, K.J. (1962) 'The Economics of Learning by Doing', *Review of Economic Studies* 29, 155-173

Cane,A. (2004) 'No free lunch, no free software' , *Financial Times*, March 31

Choi, J.P.(1994) 'Network Externality, Compatibility Choice, and Planned Obsolescence', *The Journal of Industrial Economics* 42, 53-72

Dixit, A. K., (1980) 'The Role of Investment in Entry-Deterrence'. *Economic Journal* 90,540-553

Economides. N. (1996) 'The Economics of Networks', *International Journal of Industrial Organization* 14, 788-800

The Economist (2004a) *'An Open-Source Shot in the Arm'*, Technology Quarterly, *June 12*

The Economist (2004b),'*More Balls through Windows', April 15*

Evans, D..K. and Schmalensee,R. (2001) 'Some Economic Aspects of Antitrust Analysis in Dynamically Competitive Industries', National Bureau of Economic Research, Cambridge, Ma. , Working Paper 8268, www.nber.org/papers/w8268

Farrell, J. and Saloner, G. (1985) 'Economic Issues in Standardization', in James Miller, ed., *Telecommunications and Equity: Policy Research Issues*, New York: North Holland, 165-178

Farrell, J and Saloner, G. (1986) 'Installed Base and Compatibility: Innovation, Product Preannouncements, and Predation', *American Economic Review* 76, 940-955

Fudenberg, D. and Tirole, J.(1991) *Game Theory*, Cambridge,Ma.: MIT Press

Gottinger, H. W.(2003) *Economies of Network Industries*, London: Routledge

Gottinger, H.W. (2006) *Innovation, Technology and Hypercompetition*, London: Routledge

Katz, M.. and Shapiro, C. (1985) 'Network Externalities, Competition, and Compatibility', *American Economic Review.* 75 (3), 424-440

Katz, M. and Shapiro, C.(1985) 'On the Licensing of Innovations'. *Rand Journal of Economics* 16, 504-520

Katz, M. and Shapiro, C.(1986) 'Product Compatibility Choice in a Market with Technological Progress', *Oxford Economic Papers* 38, 146-165

Katz, M. and l Shapiro, C. (1986) 'How to License Intangible Property' .*Quarterly Journal of Economics* 103, 180-188

Katz, M. and Shapiro, C.(1992) 'Product Introduction with Network Externalities'. *The Journal of Industrial Economics,* 40, 55-83

Kende, M. (1998) 'Profitability under an Open versus a Closed System', *Journal of Economics and Management Strategy 12, 25-35*

Kristiansen. E.G. (1996) 'R&D in Markets with Network Externalities', *International Journal of Industrial Organization* 14, 531-547

Lerner,J. and J. Tirole (2004), 'The Economics of Technology Sharing: Open Source and Beyond', Harvard Business School Working Paper, Cambridge, Ma.

Regibeau, P. and Rockett , K (1996) 'The Timing of Product Introduction and the Credibility of Compatibility Decisions', *International Journal' of Industrial Organization* 14, 801-823

Shapiro, C. (1989) 'Theories of Oligopoly Behavior', in R. Schmalensee and R.D. Willig (eds), *Handbook of Industrial Organization*, Vol. I, Amsterdam: North Holland, 370-414

Varian, H.R. and Shapiro, C. (2003), 'Linux Adoption in the Public Sector', www.sims.berkeley.edu/papers

APPENDIX

Proof of Theorem 1

When the monopolist has a product of quality q_I and charges a price of p_I the only consumers who buy from it are the ones for whom $r + q_I + \gamma x_I^o - p_I \geq 0$. Therefore demand for the monopolist's product equals

$A + q_I + \gamma x_I^o - p_I$. It's revenue(R) equals $p_I (A + q_I + \gamma x_I^o - p_I)$.. The optimal price for selling its output is thus given by:

$$\partial R / \partial p_I = A + q_I + \gamma x_I^o - 2 p_I = 0$$

or

$$p_I^M = x_I^M = (A + q_I + \gamma x_I^o)/ 2 \qquad \text{(A1)}$$

The monopolist's profit is therefore

$$\Pi_I^M = [(A + q_I + \gamma x_I^o)/ 2]^2 + f_I (k_I + x_I^o - f_I)$$

Π_I^M *is* concave in f_I .

Therefore ,

$$\partial \Pi_I^M / \partial f_I = (A + (1 + \gamma) x_I^o + k - f_I)/2 + k + x_I^o - 2 f_I = 0$$

gives us the optimal f_I:

$$f_I^M =(k + (1 - \gamma) x_I^o - A) /3 \qquad \text{(A2)}$$

If $\gamma > 1$ we see that f_I^M is decreasing in x_I^o whereas $\gamma < 1$, f_I^M is increasing in x_I^o.

Duopoly: With Incumbent and Potential Entrant

We saw in Section 3 that when the firms sell positive amounts of output, the equilibrium price equals the equilibrium output for each firm. Thus the first component of a firm's profit $p_i x_i$ just equals $(x_i)^2$ in equilibrium. The same is true if a firm sells zero output (since then $p_i x_i = (x_i)^2 = 0$) or if a firm sells its monopoly output (as previously analyzed). Thus a firm's equilibrium profits can be written as:

$$\Pi_i = [\,x_i(f_i, f_j)]^2 + f_i m(f_i, x_i^o)\,,\; i \in \{I,E\} \tag{A3}$$

Assuming no constraints on the *x's* and the *f's.*, making use of(A1)-(A3) and substituting , the profits can be written as:

$$\Pi_i = [(A + k + 2\,(1+\gamma)\,x_i^{\,o} - (1+\gamma)\,x_j^{\,o} + f_j - 2f_i/3)]^2 + f_i\,(k + x_i^{\,o} - f_i)\,,$$
$$i \in \{I,E\} \tag{A4}$$

It can be checked that Π_i in the above equation is concave in f_i. *Setting* $\partial \Pi_i / \partial f_i = 0$ *gives us the Cournot reaction function in license fees for firm i, j* $\in \{I,E\}$:

$$f_i = k/2 + (2\,(1+\gamma)\,x_j^{\,o}/5 + (1 - 8\gamma)x_i^{\,o}/10 - 2A/5 - 2f_j/5 \tag{A5}$$

We note from equation (A5) that the reaction functions in license fees are downward sloping. The reason behind this is as follows: From equation (A3) we see that a firm's equilibrium profit has two components , $[\,x_i(f_i, f_j)]^2$,which represents the revenues from direct sales and $f_i m(f_i, x_i^o)$ which is the revenue from licensing. Firm i's reaction function gives us the optimal f_i for every f_j that the other firm might charge.

Assuming that both firms sell positive amounts, increasing f_i by a small amount decreases the profit from the first term (since from the Cournot game, x_i is decreasing in f_i). At the optimal f_i this must be exactly offset by the increase in revenue from licensing. Again, given that both firms sell positive amounts, the equilibrium x_i is increasing in f_j whereas the firm i's revenue from licensing is unaffected by it. Thus if we now increase f_j , then a small increase in f_i from its previous optimal level increases the revenue from the license fees by the same amount as before. However, the decrease in revenue from direct sales is larger since x_i is larger. Thus with the larger f_j profits are decreasing in i's license fees at the previously optimal f_i. Given the concavity of the profit function in a firm's own license fee this requires a lowering of f_i in order to reach equilibrium again. Hence the reaction function is downward sloping.

Lemma A1. There exists f_I^D *for the incumbent such that for all* $f_I < f_I^D$ *the optimal response of the entrant is to stay out of the market and for* $f_I > f_I^D$ *it is to enter.* f_I^D *is thus the largest license fee for the incumbent that deters entry.*

Proof. Let f_I^D be the license fee for which $f_E = 0$ is the smallest license fee that makes $x_E(f_E, f_I^D) = 0$. When $f_E = 0$. $x_E = 0$, and $f_I = f_I^D$ then $\Pi_E = 0$ and $\partial \Pi_E / \partial f_E = 0 + k > 0$. Thus reducing f_E will only make Π_E negative while a bigger f_E is not an acceptable license fee. So entry is deterred at f_I^D.

To calculate f_I^D we set x_E equal to zero and $f_E = 0$ with it.

We then get

$$A + 2(k - f_E) - (k + x_I^{\,o} - f_I^D) - \gamma x_I^{\,o} = 0 \tag{A6}$$

$$\text{Therefore, } f_I^D = (1+\gamma)\,x_I^{\,o} - A - k \tag{A7}$$

Entry is deterred at any $f_I < f_I^D$ too, since then the smallest f_E that makes x_E $(f_E, f_I) = 0$. must be negative ,see (A6). For $f_I > f_I^D$ the smallest f_E that makes x_E $(f_E, f_I) = 0$. is positive, thus there do exist acceptable license fees that give the entrant positive profits. Hence the entrant will enter and so there is no entry deterrence. Thus f_I^D *is* indeed the largest license fee that the incumbent can charge and still deter entry.

Lemma A2. There exists $f_I^R > f_I^D$, such that in the interval $[f_I^D, f_I^R]$ it is optimal for firm E to charge the largest acceptable license fee f_E that makes $x_E = 0$ and for $f_I > f_I^R$ the optimal response for firm E induces it to produce a positive amount.

Proof. From equation (A5) we know that the best response for the entrant to f_I^R *is* given by

$$2\, f_E = k + (4\,(1 + \gamma)\, x_I^o/5 - 4A/5 - 4\, f_I^R\, /5 \qquad \text{(A8)}$$

For x_E to equal zero when $f_I = f_I^R$, f_E must be as given by (A6) with f_I^R *replacing* f_I^D, *i.e.*

$$2\, f_E = A + k - (1 + \gamma)\, x_I^o + f_I^R \qquad \text{(A9)}$$

If there were no restrictions on the x's. then when firm I chose f_I^R and firm E chose its license fee optimally, by definition of f_I^R in the subsequent output game firm E would end up selling nothing. If firm I chose $f_I > f_I^R$ and firm E chose its license fee optimally, then in the subsequent output game firm E would end up selling a positive amount. If however firm I chose $f_I < f_I^R$ and firm E chose its license fee according to its reaction function, then in the subsequent output game firm E would be required to sell a negative amount. Since that is not possible E just sets its license fee at the level that just makes its output in the next stage zero. Hence when there is no entry block, in the interval $[f_I^D, f_I^R]$ firm E charges the largest acceptable license fee f_E that makes $x_E = 0$. Firm I makes profits according to the monopolist's profit function. This is where the inequality $x_i \geq 0$ for the entrant is binding.

For $f_I > f_I^R$ the entrant just plays its unconstrained best response in the Stackelberg game. f_I^R is the smallest license fee for the incumbent above which the entrant plays its unconstrained optimal fees and output in equilibrium.

Proof of Theorem 2

We prove the theorem in a few steps.

Lemma A3. Entry is blocked if $(1 + 2\gamma)\, x_I^o \geq A + 2k$.

We find the smallest f_E that gives us x_E $(f_E, f_I^M) = 0$

From (A6) we get:

$$A + 2(\mathrm{k} - f_E) - (k + x_I^0 - f_I^M) - \gamma x_I^o = 0$$

Substituting the expression for f_I^M f from equation (A2) into the above gives us:

$$f_E^* = A + 2k - (1 + 2\gamma) x_I^o/3$$

f_E^* *is* the largest acceptable license fee for the entrant when the incumbent charges f_I^M.

When $f_E^* \leq 0$, Π_E at f_E^* is non-positive (when $f_E^* \geq 0$, Π_E at f_E^* is non-negative). Further, $\partial\Pi_E/\partial f_E = k - 2f_E^* > 0$.

Given the concavity of Π_E in f_E means that if $f_E^* \leq 0$, there is no acceptable license fee for the entrant that gives it a positive profit. Hence entry is blocked if $f_E^* \leq 0$, i.e. if

$$A+2k< (1+2\gamma)x_I^o$$

$f_E^* = 0$ is the largest f_E^* for which entry is blocked since if $f_E^* > 0$ then there does exist an acceptable license fee for the entrant that gives it positive profit.

Lemma A4:For $A+2k \geq (1 + 2\gamma)\, x_I^o \geq A + k/2$, entry is restricted with the incumbent charging f_I^M and earning its monopoly profits.

We saw earlier that in the interval $[f_I^D, f_I^R]$ firm E charges the smallest f_E that makes $x_E = 0$, firm I makes profits according to the monopolist's profit function.

We know that the incumbent makes the largest possible profits when it is a monopolist charging f_I^M.

Thus if, when there is no blocked entry, $f_I^M \leq f_I^R$ then the optimal license fee for the incumbent is just f_I^M

$$f_I^M \leq f_I^R \iff k + (1-\gamma)x_I^o - A/3 \leq (1+\gamma)\, x_I^o - A$$

which gives us the condition

$$k+2A < 2(1+-\gamma)\, x_I^o$$

Putting together this condition with that for no blocked entry $f_I^D > f_I^M$ *(Lemma A3)* gives us the required result:

$$A+k/2 \leq (1+2\gamma)\, x_I^o \leq A+2k$$

Lemma A5. For $A + k/2 > (1 +2\gamma)\, x_I^o \geq 2A/5 + k/5$. entry is restricted with the incumbent charging f_I^R and earning less than its monopoly profits.

When $k+2A > 2\,(1+\gamma)x_I^{\,0}$ then the optimal monopoly license fee, f_I^M is bigger than f_I^R (Lemma A4.)

Since the incumbent's profits in the range *$[f_I^D, f_I^R]$ coincide with its monopoly profits Π_I^M, its profits must be increasing in $[f_I^D, f_I^R]$.*

Call Π_I^S unconstrained Stackelberg profits for firm I. We get Π_I^S *by substituting* f_E from firm E's reaction function (A5) into firm's I profit function (A4):

$$\Pi_I^S = [A/5 + k/2 + 4(1+\gamma)\, x_I^o/5 - 4f_I/5\,]^2 + f_I(k + x_I^o - f_I)$$

Then, for $f_I > f_I^R$ the incumbent's profits coincide with Π_I^S, and at $f_I = f_I^R$, $\Pi_I^M = \Pi_I^S$ (since x_E in the output game equals zero when $f_I = f_I^R$ and E chooses its best response to f_I^R, thus making $\Pi_I^M = \Pi_I^S$). It can be checked that Π_I^S is concave in f_I.

If Π_I^S is decreasing in f_I at $f_I = f_I^R$ then given the concavity of Π_I^S, the optimal license fee for the incumbent must be f_I^R.

$$\partial \Pi_I^S / \partial f_I = -8/5\,[A/5 + k/2 + 4(1+\gamma)\,x_I^o/5 - 4 f_I/5\,] + k + x_I^o - 2 f_I \qquad \text{(A10)}$$

when $f_I = f_I^R = (1+\gamma)\,x_I^o - A$,

$$\partial \Pi_I^S / \partial f_I = 1/5\,[k + 2A - 5(1+2\gamma)\,x_I^o\,]$$

Π_I^S is decreasing in f_I at $f_I = f_I^R$

if

$$k+2A \le 5(1+2\gamma)\,x_I^o$$

Thus for $2A/5 + k/5 \le (1+2\gamma)\,x_I^o \le A + k/2$, , the optimal f_I is f_I^R and the incumbent earns less than monopoly profits.

Lemma A6. For $2A/5+k/5 > (1+2\gamma)\,x_I^o$, *entry is unrestricted and the firms just charge the unconstrained Stackelberg license fees.*

If $k + 2A > (1+2\gamma)\,x_I^o$ then we infer from Lemmas A2 to A3 that there is no blocked entry, the incumbent's profits are increasing in the range $[f_I^D, f_I^R]$, and are also increasing at $f_I = f_I^R$ .The incumbent's profits are continuous in the relevant range of $f_I \ge f_I^D$ and coincide with Π_I^S for $f_I \ge f_I^R$. Since Π_I^S is concave, the optimal license fee for the incumbent must be given by the one that maximizes Π_I^S. Call this license f_I^S. Setting $\partial \Pi_I^S / \partial f_I = 0$ from (A10) we get

$$f_I^S = [5k - 8A - (7 + 32\gamma)\,x_I^o\,]/18 \qquad \text{(A11)}$$

Given our definition of f_I^R, $f_I \ge f_I^R$ is optimal for $x_E > 0$.

Thus if $k + 2A > 5(1+2\gamma)\,x_I^o$, then the incumbent charges f_I^S, the entrant charges f_E given by its reaction function, and both firms produce positive amounts.

Proof of Corollary 2

From Lemmas *A2* and A3 we infer that for $A + k/2 \le (1+2\gamma)\,x_I^o$, the incumbent charges its optimal monopoly license fee, f_I^M. Hence the statement of the corollary is true in this case. From Lemma A4, when $2A/5 + k/5 \le (1+2\gamma)\,x_I \le A + k/2$. the optimal f_I is f_I^R. But in this scenario monopoly profits are increasing in the interval

$[f_I^D, f_I^R]$ as we saw in Lemma *A4* . Thus it must be the case that $f_I^M > f_I^R = f_I^*$. Finally, when $k + 2A > 5(1+2\gamma)\,x_I^o$, the optimal license fee for the incumbent is given by f_I^S in equation (A11).

$$f_I^S - f_I^M = -[2A + k + 13\,(1+2\gamma)\,x_I^o]\,/18 < 0\,.$$

Thus when $k + 2A > 5(1+2\gamma)\,x_I^o$, $f_I^M > f_I^S = f_I^*$

Proof of Theorem 3

It can be checked that in the cases when there is unrestricted entry and when there is restricted entry without monopoly output, $f_I < f_E$. When there is restricted entry with monopoly profits

$$f_I - f_E = [-k - 2A + (2+\gamma)\, x_I^{\,o}]/3$$

Thus,

$$f_I < f_E \text{ if } k + 2A > (2+\gamma)\, x_I^{\,o},$$

$$f_I > f_E \text{ if } k + 2A < (2+\gamma)\, x_I$$

Hence, $k + 2A = (2+\gamma)\, x_I^{\,o}$

Chapter 8

8. COMPETITION IN INCREASING RETURNS AND NETWORK INDUSTRIES

8.1. INTRODUCTION

This chapter reviews and integrates in a conceptual model heretofore disjointed conceptual contributions that explicitly and implicitly report the notion of increasing returns (IR) to address dynamic polarization phenomena in business competition. In contrast to conventional views which ordinarily associate business competition (and success) with a very reduced number of variables and conceive the growth of the firm, industrial structure and technological competition as independent levels of analysis , the model suggested moves away from this decomposing approach to suggest that competition in IRIs is better characterized by a more comprehensive framework where a variety of IR mechanisms combine to explain simultaneously three likely features of IR competition: (i) big firms with non-negligible market shares cluster around concentrated industrial structures with skewed distribution of firm size and market share, (ii) there is a tendency of certain cases of technology competition to end up in a temporary monopoly,(iii) the competition process usually follows a dynamic, cumulative pattern that starts symmetric and ends up asymmetric.

For an industrial policy toward promoting economic growth it would be of prior importance to complementarize IRIs which would enhance their value creation and competitiveness (McAfee, 2002, Chapt.2)

Most industrial sectors of highly industrialized economies are not perfectly competitive. They are usually formed by a small number of big firms with non-negligible market share. Besides being prevalent in the economy, big firms cluster around concentrated industrial structures which exhibit a skewed distribution of firm size and market share. This situation may be brought about by the intrinsic potential of dynamic technological competition to end up in (temporary) technological monopoly, so in those cases industrial competition may start out symmetric but end up asymmetric.

We show how the competitive process proliferates in increasing returns industries (IRIs) where the total of all unit activities linked together yield a higher return than the sum of the individual unit activities operating separately. For this to be happening we must show that a variety of increasing returns mechanisms combine to enable the effect of an increasing returns industry.

We propose an integrated framework to provide tools and insights for explaining competition among skewed industrial structures. However, it is only a tentative step toward attempting to explain the path-dependent, indeterminate, suboptimal, locking-in nature of technological competition under increasing return.

Because of this we partially review the literature on the dynamics of technological diffusion, substitution, and competition. The purpose of this review is to show that we cannot accurately understand industrial competition without taking into account the self-reinforcing nature of commercial success in most emerging markets. We enrich increasing returns mechanisms by incorporating a set of stronger, yet neglected, increasing returns mechanisms --reputation effects, infrastructure effects and positive network externalities into a preliminary framework model. The resulting theoretical structure, we will argue, captures the interdependent and cumulative character of the three aspects of industrial competition: the number and size of firms, skewed industrial structures, and the nature of technological competition.

The increasing returns discussion in economics has provided important insights into the characteristics and dynamics of modern industrial economies. However, the discussion on policy applications had some misleading features in the literature to conclude that a completely *new economy* is emerging and that it obeys a set of rules, which are totally different from those that apply to traditional sectors of the economy. While it is undeniable that the increasing return paradigms remain fairly new and revolutionary and while there is no doubt that this paradigm is key to our understanding of new industrial sectors, and their sustaining role in productivity growth, we should clarify its proper role in industrial structure and growth of the economy. At this stage we are most concerned about the catalytic role of technological competition in increasing returns industries. Increasing returns industries are nowadays most likely to be identified with high technology industries, in particular with information, communication and health care related industries (Gottinger, 2003). As an example, in a corporate context, how to unlock increasing returns in its global operations, consider General Electric (GE). It constantly evolves its portfolio to drive growth despite its large size and already significant presence in major markets. It encourages its executives and business units to take an expansive view of its markets as a means of unlocking growth initiatives that a product centric view would miss. Often, when its market share exceeds 10 percent, it seeks to redefine the market more broadly to include adjacent products or services . This continual questing lies behind successful moves from manufacturing to services , that has allowed it to keep growing in complementarizing given industrial markets (This even remains true , as nowadays, in financial distress situations where complementarizing growth activities could accelerate a downward cycle).

For those industries Shapiro and Varian (1999) have suggested a combination of supply-side scale economies and demand-side scale economies to explain the intrinsic aspects of technological competition. It appears however that this way of seeing technological competition is too simple to capture the variety and complexity of real-world businesses in those industries Thus we suggest a general framework to describe technological competition in what we are going to call the *increasing returns economy.*

Here is an outline of what follows. Section 8.2 identifies supply-side scale economies as a major ingredient of increasing returns economies. Section 8.3 lists increasing returns properties as part of a Schumpeterian mechanism. The relationship of increasing returns and non-ergodic markets is explored in Section 8.4. Section 8.5 explores technological competitive paths subject to uncertainty of technological outcomes whereas Section 8.6 focusses on technological competition under standard setting. Section 8.7 relates the intensity of technological competition to network externalities, and Section 8.8 provides a summary of increasing returns factors in competitive settings. Section 8.9 provides an example of increasing returns, structural change and development conomics. Finally, Section 8.10 draws conclusions on the systemic connection of increasing returns and technological competition.

8.2. Supply-Side Scale Economies

A first source of increasing returns assuming constant technology identifies a concentrated industry structure as a result of supply-side scale economies. In many cases large firms are more efficient than smaller companies because of its scale: larger corporations tend to have lower unit costs. This efficiency in turn fuels further their growth. However, positive feedbacks based on supply-side economies of scale usually run into natural limits. Past a certain size companies find growth difficult owing to the increasing complexity of managing a large organizational structure. From then on, negative feedback takes over. As traditional supply-side economies of scale generally become exhausted at a scale well below total market dominance, large firms, burdened with high costs, never grow to take the entire market and smaller, more nimble firms can find profitable niches. Shapiro and Varian (1999) conclude that because of this most industrial markets are oligopolies rather than monopolies.

Negative feedback generated by the difficulties of managing large organizations (scale diseconomies) indeed interrupts the growth of the firm and the level of industrial concentration. This situation, nevertheless, may be transient, because firms may be subject to other sources of increasing returns. Large firms that go through increasing returns mechanisms other than scale economies may increase their efficiency and overcome the negative aspects of overgrown organizations. Industries in which scale diseconomies are counterbalanced by other increasing returns mechanisms, then, may begin to head toward the extreme of 'winner-takes-most' situation. The increasing returns mechanisms capable to offset scale diseconomies are usually related to technological progress, so in the following sections we analyze other major causes of the growth of the firm, namely, the Schumpeterian loop, cost reducing learning, learning-by-doing, learning-by-using, and demand-side increasing returns.

8.3. Schumpeterian Mechanism

The most widely accepted theory of technological change in modern economics is Schumpeter's (1942). In the Schumpeterian world, scale economies are present as well, but technology is not a constant. Here the creative role of the entrepreneur allows for the introduction of new technologies capable to displacing the established ones. In the context of IRIs, Schumpeter's main point has been that innovation competition leads to increasing returns economies triggering serial innovations inducing more IRIs (Freeman, 2003). Most of Schumpeter's discussion stresses the advantages of concentrated market structures involving large firms with considerable market share. In his view, it is more probable that the necessary scale economies in R&D to develop new technologies be achieved by a monopolist or by the few large firms of a concentrated industry. Large size firms, besides, may increase their rate of innovation by reducing the speed at which their transient rents and entrepreneurial advantage are eroded away by imitators. In the absence of patent protection large firms may exploit their innovations on a large scale over relatively short periods of time -and in this way avoid rapid imitation by competitors- by deploying their productive, marketing and financial capabilities. Large firms may also expand their rate of innovation by imitating and commercializing other firms' technologies.

Schumpeter's thesis encouraged a large body of empirical literature in the field of industrial organization. Most of this literature focused on two hypotheses associated with Schumpeter's assertion: (1) innovation increases more than proportionally with firm size and (2) innovation increases with market concentration.

The most comprehensive review of the empirical evidence of the relationship between innovation and firm size and market structure dates back to Cohen and Levin (1989). They observe that the empirical results on the Schumpeterian relation are accurately described as fragile. They note that the lack of robust results seems to arise in part from the inappropriate attention to the dependence of these relationships on more fundamental conditions. From their overview Cohen and Levin draw the basic methodological lesson that the omission of important and potentially correlated variables that influence innovation can lead to misleading inferences concerning firm size and concentration.

Following Schumpeter's lead, Richard Nelson and Sidney Winter (1978, 1982) stand out for having formalized and completed many of Schumpeter's original intuitions. Whereas the connection between industrial structure and innovation has been viewed by Schumpeter as going primarily from the former to the latter, in Nelson and Winter (1982) there is a reverse causal flow, too. That is, there is clearly a circular causality suggesting a self-reinforcing mechanism between the innovations and the firm’s growth. Nelson and Winter (1982) stand out not only for having recognized the endogeneous character of innovation and market structure, but also for having pointed out and modeled the mutual causality between technical change and market structure (Nelson, 1986).

Evolutionary economists (like Nelson and Winter) define innovation very broadly. It encompasses product and process innovation, opening up new markets, and acquisition of new sources of raw material. They also describe the nature of technical progress as succession of major discontinuities detached from the past and with quite transitory life span. This process of change is characteristic of certain industries, but it is not the sole kind of technological change. Technological change can also be *continuous.* That is to say, technologies improve constantly in absolute terms after their introduction. The view of technological progress as a continuing, steady accumulation of inumerable minor improvements and modifications, with only very infrequent major innovations, has two sources: (1) the accumulation of knowledge that makes possible to produce a greater volume of output from a given amount of resources and (2) the accumulation of knowledge that allows the production of a qualitatively superior output from a given amount of resources. The former source of technological progress is the result of a *cost reducing learning process,* while the second category is the result of what is known as *learning-by-doing* and *learning-by-using.* Given that both categories of technological progress are important determinants of the number and size of firms in a given industry, we analyze them in the next sections.

Cost Reducing Learning

An important aspect of technological change is costs reducing in nature. As we saw before, Porter (1980) and Henderson (1975), in the strategic field, pioneered the notion of experience curve as a source of cost reductions. In economics, Hirsch (1956) has underlined the importance of repetitive manufacturing operations as a way of reducing direct labour requirements, while Arrow (1962) has explored the consequences of learning by-doing (measured by the cumulative gross investment, which produces a steady rate of growth in productivity) on profits, investment, and economic growth. However, the historical study on the patters of growth and competitiveness of large corporations of Alfred D. Chandler (1990) is a major and detailed contribution to our understanding of the way firms grow by diminishing costs.

Large corporations, according to Chandler, along with the few challengers that subsequently enter the industry, do not compete primarily on the basis of price. Instead they compete for market share and profits through functional and strategic effectiveness. They compete functionally by improving their products, their processes of production, their marketing, their purchasing, and their labour relations. Big corporations compete strategically by moving into growing markets more rapidly and effectively than do their competitors. Such rivalry for market share and profits make more effective the enterprise's functional and strategic capabilities, which, in turn, provide the internal dynamics for continuing growth of the enterprise. In particular, it stimulates its owners and managers to expand into distant markets in its own country and then to become multinational by moving abroad. It also encourages the firm to diversify and become multiproduct by developing and introducing products in markets other than the original ones.

Learning-by-Doing

Some of the writings on industrial competition assumes that firms compete mainly in cost-reducing competitive advantages, especially those achieved through scale economies, scope economies (economies of joint production and distribution), and innovation in production and organizational processes. Here technical progress is implicitly treated as the introduction of new processes that reduce costs of producing essentially unchanging products. Beyond, there is a category of learning known as 'learning-by-doing' (Rosenberg, 1982) which enhances the qualitative aspects of final products.

Western industrial societies today, Rosenberg (1982) argues, enjoy a higher level of material welfare not merely because they consume larger per capita amounts of the goods available. They have also made available improving forms of rapid transportation, instant communication, powerful energy sources, life-saving and pain-reducing medications, and other goods that were undreamed of one or two centuries ago. Therefore, ignoring incremental product innovation and quality improvements in products is to overlook what has been one of the most important long-term contributions of technical progress to human welfare. Many products, such as beverages, toothpaste, soap, clothing, VCRs, TV sets can be subject to improvements. Such improvements, however, are marginal when compared with the amazing rate of development that other products and technologies can reach. Automobiles, aircraft, flight simulators, computers, and nuclear reactors are very complex technologies and, as a consequence of this, have a tremendous capacity of being enhanced. Consequently, the competitive behavior of the firms that produce these technologies consists not only of the innovative acts they perform to improve production, organizational, and distribution processes, but also from the efforts to improve constantly their products.

Learning-by-Using

With respect to a given product, Rosenberg (1982) distinguishes between that kind of learning that is internal to the production process (learning-by-doing) and that which is generated as a result of subsequent use of that product (learning-by-using). The later category of learning begins only after a certain new product is used. In an economy where complex new technologies are common, there are essential aspects of learning that are a function not of the experience involved in producing a product but of its *use* by the final consumer.

The optimal performance of durable goods (especially complex systems of interacting components) often is achieved only after intensive and prolonged use. In the aircraft industry, for instance, the attainment of high standards of reliability is a major concern, in particular during the development stage. But it is only through extensive use of aircraft by airlines that faults are discovered and eliminated and detailed knowledge is gained about metal fatigue, weight capacity, fuel consumption of engines, fuselage durability, minimum servicing, overhaul requirements, maintenance costs, and so on.

Demand Side Increasing Returns

In the economy there are increasing returns mechanisms that come from the demand side of the market, not just from supply side. For the average (risk adverse and imperfectly informed) consumer it becomes more attractive to adopt a widespread technology or product. Minimizing the risk of purchasing a defective technology or the cost of searching for an adequate one introduces a reputation or informational feedback that may produce a disproportionately high selection of the best-selling option. Informational or reputational feedback effects occur in various situations that could be reinforced through network externalities. First, when the complexity of the technology or product in question is such that consumers try to reduce uncertainty by asking previous purchasers about their experience with these technologies (Arthur and Lane, 1993). Second, in other situations the source of uncertainty is not the complexity of the technology, but the large quantity of options the consumers face. One is bound to choose, and the best way to do so is by confining one's attention to the best-assessed items in the consumer report. Third, in a market where the quality or value of a product is defined on the basis of arbitrary and short-living conventions, rather than strictly on the basis of lasting objective value, consumers usually tend to follow the expert's opinion. This kind of easy-to-manipulate, reputation-driven market success is typical of markets for highly symbolic products (e.g. many art markets, fashion wear and luxury items) , which also will result in a disproportionately high selection of one of the options.

Finally, the most preeminent and common kind of reputation effects in the economy, arise plainly as a result of a well-timed and very aggressive advertising campaign. This self-reinforcing mechanism -and the lasting market dominance that it causes- might be quite unrelated to relative added value, but it certainly might produce an excessive predilection for one of the options.

By moving beyond the Schumpeterian hypotheses and focus on a more complete model of industrial competition we have identified other fundamental determinants of technological change that affect the mutual link between firm size and market structure (Aghion and Howitt, 1998).

These determinants --which in our analysis take the form of increasing returns mechanisms -- are usually studied as if they work independently from the other. But there are not many cases of industries where one single mechanism acts in isolation from the other sources of increasing returns. Therefore, the growth of the firm and the evolution of skewed industrial structure, more than the result of a single self-reinforcing mechanism, are the effect of the combination of several sources of increasing returns, which overlap and feed back upon one another..

The unification of the resource-based loop, the Schumpeterian loop, scale economies, the different categories of learning, and demand-side increasing returns (reputation) – loops A, B, and C, respectively, in Fig.1—constitutes a simple but useful model capable to explain endogeneously the number and growth of firms in a given industry, and in a wider context, the gap of economic performance in a given industrial sector.

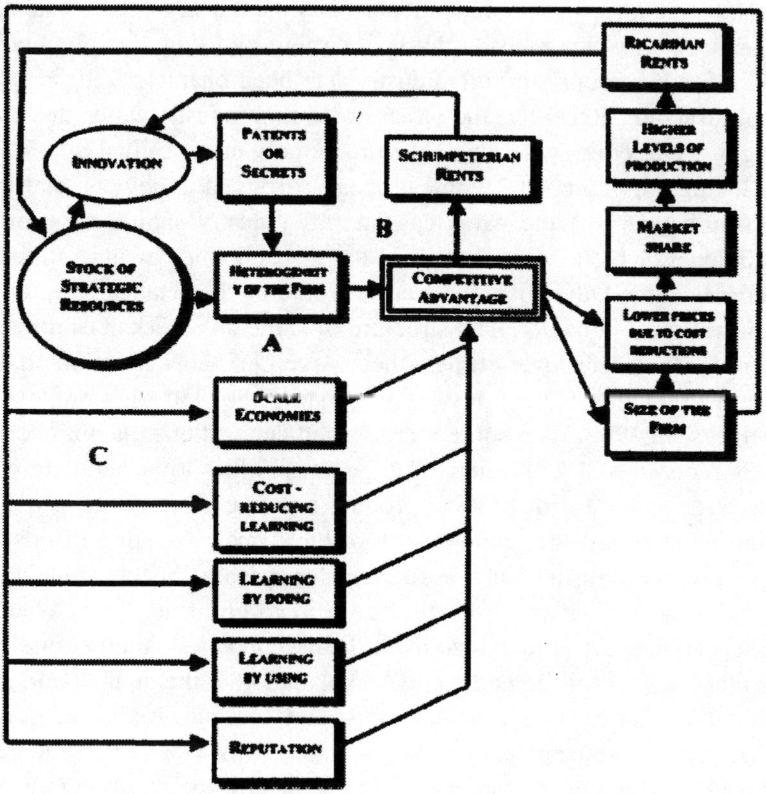

Figure 1. Increasing Returns Mechanism: A Qualitative Model of Industrial Competition.

In the model sketched in Figure 1 the positive relationship that runs from industrial structure to efficiency operates through the accumulation of rare resources, innovations, scale economies, reputation, and the different aspects of learning. This dynamics, over time, makes costs fall as learning accumulates, new technologies are developed and improved, and firm-specific factors are amassed and exploited due to output increases. As a result of this mutual causality, market share and production levels increase, price falls, profitability rises, and with which relatively profitable firms expand continually while unprofitable ones contract uninterruptedly.

A relevant aspect of the structural determinants of the number and size of firms in an industry suggested in this model is that, when one of them is exhausted, causing a slowdown in the growth of the firm, the other mechanisms may be activated, which may allow for a further period of continued rapid growth. When the firms of a given industry are capable to accumulate firm-specific resources, innovations, costs reducing learning, qualitative product innovation based on learning-by-doing and learning-by-using, and reputation, these firms usually use them as strategic weapon. In doing so, they are capable not only to neutralize but also to overwhelm the negative effects of complex, overgrown, hard-to-manage organizational structures that arise from their constant growth. The process can take a long period of time, but eventually the sources of increasing returns can drive markets toward increasingly skewed industrial structures.For instance, in the commercial aircraft industry competition principally involves considerable development costs, continuous improvements in aircraft models, technology and product support, so this industry exhibits substantial scale economies, large scope for learning-by-doing, learning-by-using, and reputation effects. Because of this, the commercial aircraft industry has been characterized by an increasing skewed industrial structure. Recently, the structure of this industry, after the acquisition of McDonnell Douglas by Boeing, was reduced to a monopoly in the United States. In the world aircraft market Boeing only competes with European Airbus. It is obvious that the merge of the two main manufacturers of the American aircraft industry should have brought about some gain in efficiency, which counterbalanced the diseconomies owing to the managing a more complex organization. Otherwise, the merger would not have taken place or would have been the result of irrational behavior. The structure of some industries does not seem to head toward monopoly. However, over time, their level of concentration has increased substantially. The world automobile industry, for instance, in 1970 was composed of at least 40 major competitors. In 1998, with some mergers and acquisitions, the number of the main manufacturer was reduced to 17. Because of large possibilities to accumulate cost reducing learning and the large scope for qualitative product improvements in the world automobile industry, both the number and the homogeneity of the firms competing in this industry are expected to decrease even further in the future. Here, again, benefits due to both costs reducing learning and qualitative product innovations brought about by mergers and acquisitions are larger than any cost created by scale diseconomies. Another interesting aspect of this model is that it also offers an endogenous explanation of the number and size of firms. In contrasts with the traditional economic views---that see industrial structure (number of firms) as an exogenous variable and assume homogenous firms--- and the strategic paradigms -which are focused first and foremost in explaining heterogeneity among firms within an industry-,this model recognizes that the strategic choices and acts of the firms have an effect not only on the performance and size of the firm itself, but also on the structure of market. In summary, industrial structure is caused by a combination of various increasing returns mechanisms. Here, then, the combination of accumulation of resources, product innovation, scale economies, cost reducing learning, learning-by-doing, learning-by-using or reputation enhances the performance of the firm and determine, to a great extent, the level of skewness of the structure of the industry where it competes.

8.4. INCREASING RETURNS AND ERGODIC MARKETS

Traditioanal neoclassical economics has tended to portray most economic situations as something analogous to a large Newtonian system, with a unique and stable equilibrium solution predetermined by a given pattern of resources, preferences, and technological possibilities. Brian Arthur and his group (Arthur, 1994b; Arthur et al., 1987), however, have shown that this conventional way of seeing economic reality overlooks important and frequent economic situations where increasing returns are conspicuous. In order to distinguish economic situations characterized by decreasing returns from those where increasing returns are dominant, Arthur, Ermilov and Kaniovski (1987) developed the theory of *non-linear Polya processes,* which describes the long-run self-organizing structures that emerge from dynamic processes where proportions are involved. The general non-linear Polya scheme can be pictured by imaging an urn of infinite capacity to which balls of several colors are added .In the simplest case, where decreasing and constant returns prevail, the probability of a ball of a given color to be chosen the next time is independent of proportions of colors at the moment of the addition. In this simple sequential process, the strong law of large numbers predicts that, over time, the proportion of balls of color i has a fixed probability, where $\Sigma_i q(i) = 1$. Therefore, it has a unique, predetermined outcome. Sequences of choices in these simple cases are important at the beginning of the process. However, as the process advances, different sequences of choices are averaged away by the economic forces, which are subject to constant or decreasing returns. So, no matter the sequences of choices, the system will always -- with probability one – end up into the same pattern. For instance, in a coin-tossing experiment the event "head" is independent of previous tosses, then the expectation of a "head" in each toss is 0.5 no matter how many times the experiment is repeated. Likewise, the proportion of 6's in a dice-casting experiment will tend to 1/6. The process by which firms in an industry concentrate in different regions is like the coin-tossing or the dice-casting experiment, if the geographic preferences of each firm is not modified by the preferences of the other firms. In more general cases -where increasing returns are present- the dynamics is completely different and the standard strong law is inapplicable. In this regime, the next ball to be added into the urn is not known, but the probability of adding one ball of specific colour depends on the present proportions of colours in the urn. In other words, the probability of an addition of the colours becomes a function of the proportions of ball of each colour at each time of choice. The case of firms deciding where to settle down illustrate this kind of non-linear Polya processes. Here increasing returns can be incorporated within the model by introducing agglomeration effects. Because of agglomeration effects, additions to a specific region are not independent of previous locational choices and firms are added incrementally to regions with probability exactly equal to the proportions of firms in each region at the time. Under increasing returns, then, the process becomes *path-dependent.*

Arthur et al. (1987) show that at the outset of the process proportions are not stable, but once the industry settles into a vector of proportions, locational patterns become constant at that vector with probability one. However, the constant vector is selected randomly from uniform distribution over all possible shares that sum to 1.0. This means that each time this locational process is rerun under different historical events, it will in all likelihood settle into a different pattern. Therefore, it is possible to predict that the locational pattern will tend toward a constant proportion, but it cannot be foreseen at *which* proportion it will settle down.

The interpretation of economic history is different under different regimes. Under constant and diminishing returns, the evolution of the system is *ergodic*. Ergodic structures emerge when repeated random events -that are drawn from the same distribution and are independent from previous ones- have a long-term average that approach their expected value, that is a long-run persistent random cycle (Feller,1957,410). The typical example of an ergodic system is coin tossing. If a fair coin is tossed indefinitely, the proportions of heads varies considerably at the outset, but settles down to 50 per cent with probability one. The evolution of an ergodic system, therefore, follows *a convex* probability function, which has expected motions that lead toward a unique, determinate outcome. In this regime "historical chance" cannot influence the evolution of the systems so history is reduced to a mere deliverer of the inevitable and the known.

Under increasing returns, by contrasts, the process is *nonergodic,* because small historical events become magnified by positive feedback. A nonergodic system follows a nonconvex probability function, so two or more outcomes are possible and "historical chance" determines which of these is ultimately selected. History becomes all-important. There are some cases of nonergodic systems in which , from the multiplicity of structures that may emerge, there are some "corner solutions" with a single option monopolizing the choices. In this specific kind of nonergodic systems, while information on preferences, endowments and transformation possibilities allows locating and describing the various possible corner equilibria, it is usually insufficient to determine which one will be selected. In these cases, as Arthur (1994b,13) has pointed out 'there is an *indeterminacy* of outcome'.

Adoption of technologies that compete under diverse regimes can be appropriately modeled as a nonlinear Polya process (cf. Arthur, 1989, 1990a, 1990b; Arthur et al., 1987). In the simplest regime, when technological competition is characterized by constant and decreasing returns, the probability of a technology of being chosen depends on its current market share. As each adoption is independent of the previous one, market share should converge to a point where they equal probability. Therefore, under constant and decreasing returns two technologies or products performing the same function will end up sharing the market according to each technology's intrinsic value and technical possibilities. Therefore, markets characterized by constant and decreasing returns can be called *ergodic markets*.

Under increasing returns to adoption, the probability of adoption depends on the numbers of adoptions holding each technology at a particular time. Markets of this kind can be called *nonergodic* markets. Within this kind of markets there are those where increasing returns may drive the outcome toward a single dominant technology, with small events early on selecting the technology that takes over. This particular type of nonergodic markets can be termed *tipping or indeterminate markets.* This indeterminacy relates to the “selection problem” – how one allocation outcome is “selected” over time by small historical events when there are several possible long-term results.

8.5. TECHNOLOGICAL COMPETITION UNDER UNCERTAINTY AND INERTIA

In high technology markets the commercial success of emerging new technologies is both highly uncertain and inertial. As regards uncertainty, in addition to the problem trying to discern the true potential of a new generic technology, there is also the difficulty of foreseeing the precise direction in which the said technology will evolve. Indeed, as depicted in Figure 8.2, the emergence of a new generic technology generally opens the door not just to one specific technological path, but rather to a whole variety of possible trajectories in product design and process technology.

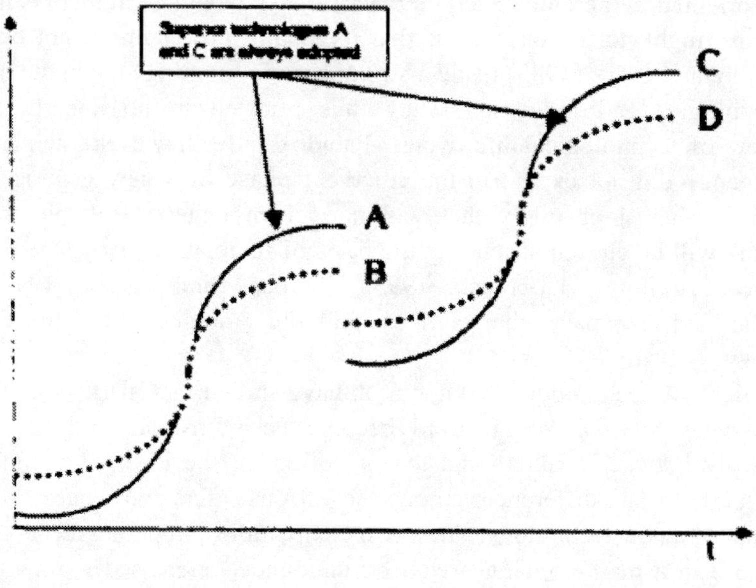

Figure 8.2. Uncertain and Inertial Technological Trajectory: superior technologies A and C are always adopted.

On the other hand, the inertial forces unleashed by commercial success are a lot more powerful than the classical models of diffusion suggests. Abernathy and Utterback (1978), Abernathy and Clark (1985), Teece (1986) and Hughes (1994), among others, have rightly underlined that in addition to the rigidities which may affect individual workers or machines and individual intermediaries or users, there are *systemic rigidities* of a much greater scope and importance. Every successful generic technology has a complex web of complementary technologies woven around its core. Once such an integrated and expensive, in terms of purchasing and using, technological system is in place, its momentum becomes enormous. Consequently, once a specific new technology becomes part of a dominant system, it will become increasingly difficult to dislodge, even by more worthy alternatives. This is depicted in Figure 8.2 where technology B (the inferior one) is foreclosed by the entrenchment of technology A (the superior one), which will only be displaced by the much superior technology C.

Uncertainty and inertia can combine to cause decisive first-mover advantages, which may grant an unassailable market dominance to an early technological trajectory. And yet, these authors do not go far enough in recognizing that in the real world, optimal technological cycles, trajectories and discontinuities, such as options A and C in Figure 8.2, are not unalterable realities. They largely ignore and or minimize the self-reinforcing (and not simply inertial) nature of commercial success and the consequent unpredictability of technological evolution in general and of "dominant designs" in particular. With this, they also overlook that a technology's success is tributary to the competitive decisions (often arbitrary and myopic) of the major players in an industry, as they are to any set of exogenous technical parameters.

Abernathy and Utterback did not believe in the research lab as an optimal selector of new technologies and they did question the optimality of selection by the market, but only to a small degree. The early articles written together by Abernathy and Utterback are thoroughly ergodic markets-oriented (Abernathy and Utterback, 1978). Nowhere in them is it hinted that *a dominant design* might not be optimal or that its lasting power might not be inevitable. Later on, Abernathy and Clark (1985) made a strong case for contingency in the maturity and decline of technologies and industries. They thus rejected in no uncertain terms the deterministic view of technological life cycles. Paradoxically, however, their emphasis on historical contingency did not extend to the emergent phase of a new generic technology. They continued to suggest or imply that within a given generic technology, a specific "dominant design" will be chosen strictly on the basis of its relative merit. As for Utterback, in his more recent writings (Utterback, 1993; Utterback and Suarez, 1994), he fully acknowledges that indeterminacy characterizes both the emergence and the decline of a generic technology.

Our observations on technological competition have shown that markets, in the presence of *increasing returns to adoption,* tend to become very unstable and tipping -i.e., to discriminate sharply between winners and losers-, often on the basis of minimal, perhaps almost random, market share differences among the various offers and regardless the relative merit and potential of a new technology. From two comparable competing technologies A and B (see Figure 8.3) in a market characterized by unbounded increased returns to adoption, only one will win the race for dominance (lock-in). But, *a priori,* it is hard to determine which technology will tip the market (indeterminacy). Furthermore, it is not always sure that the market will select the superior option (sub-optimality). Then, the market is not necessarily an optimal selector of optimal technologies.

Another aspect the work on technological competition under increasing returns has shed light on is related to the implications of market instability for the management of risk.

Ergodic models tacitly assume that new technologies are cheap to develop, hard to improve, stand alone, easy to appraise, easy to use, and strongly protected through patents. This implies technologies arrive at the market full developed before diffusion and that the process of development and the diffusion itself can be separated from each other. Ergodic models, then, introduce a very limited level of uncertainty.

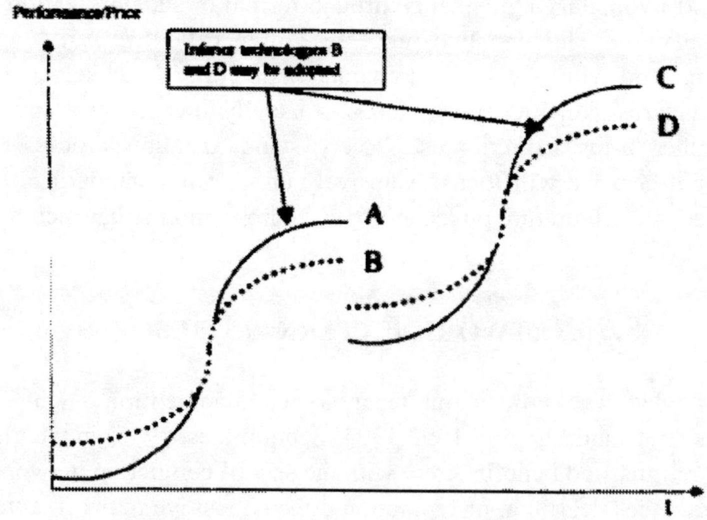

Figure 8.3. Indeterminate Technological Trajectory: Inferior Technologies B and D may be adopted.

In the models of indeterminate technological change, in contrast, new technologies are expensive to develop, subject to further improvements, often due to systemic nature, difficult to appraise and use and with weak patent protection. Therefore, their adoption become self-reinforcing not only for the *reputation effect* of market success, but also for the significant improvements that technologies accumulate during their spreading As the *diffusion process confers value* to technologies and not only conspicuousness, a technology that initially did not deserve being chosen may end up meriting it. Consequently, according to Foray (1989) , the market becomes not only a selector of adequate technologies, but a creator of dominant, superior ones. Under these circumstances, technological sponsors do not face an information problem. but an indeterminate scenario, as Arthur (1994) has indicated. Thus the most effective way to manage totally contingent and unpredictable results in unstable environments is to invest aggressively in market share as the market takes off.

8.6. STANDARDS AND INCREASING RETURNS

Early models of technology diffusion explicitly recognized the general notions of adoption externalities and self-reinforcing dynamics. The epidemic model specified that the diffusion of a new technology, much as that of a potent virus, would be a self-reinforcing process since every user of the respective technology would turn into one of its ardent promoters. What these models, however, failed to recognize was that diffusion can increase considerably the value , and not simply the reputation, of the new technology. In other words, the early models were too focused on the information externalities and neglected to take into account another source of selfreinforcing in diffusion, namely, *increasing returns to adoption.*

In recent years, technological competition and the emergence of a technological monopoly over a whole market has been the privileged topic of the literature on standards (David and Greenstein, 1990). This literature has identified three processes by which technological standardization can be attained through (a) government regulation through mandated standards, (b) voluntary agreements through formal or standardization committees, and (c) market competition. The first two processes, often called *de jure* standardization, usually result in a standard with public-good characteristics. Standards selected through the market *-de facto* standards-, on the other hand, are usually owned by a firm, which can therefore exclude other firms from its use. Every standardization process has its own theoretical interest, but here we will focus exclusively on *de facto* standardization, which is identified with the economic literature on technological competition under increasing returns.

8.7. NETWORK EXTERNALITIES

At the basis of what we know about technological competition is the literature on network externalities (Katz and Shapiro, 1992,1994; Economides, 1996) in which market size relates to increasing returns, and benefits grow with the size of competing networks.

Just as scale economies, learning, or reputation effects, positive network externalities are a self-reinforcing diffusion dynamic. Network effects, however, differ from the other self-reinforcing mechanisms in several important respects: First, while the benefits of scale economies, learning and (some) reputation effects can only be reaped at the time of purchasing the product in question, most of the benefits accruing from network externalities can be enjoyed well past the point of purchase and throughout the entire life cycle of the product. Second, network effects are considerably *forward looking* and *less bounded* and therefore more powerful than scale and learning effects. In fact, because they cast a shadow into the future, network effects can combine with reputation effects to create extremely powerful and lasting self-reinforcing dynamics in market success. Since most of the benefits accruing from network externalities can be enjoyed throughout the full life cycle of a product, new users faced with a multiplicity of competing technical options will have to make their choices not simply in function of what the majority of post purchasers have already chosen, but also in function of what the majority of *inter-face* users are likely to choose. Interestingly, while very pessimistic user expectations about an overall emerging market can be self-dampening, optimistic expectations about the success of a specific technical format in a battle of standards could easily become *self-fulfilling*. The greater the number of people who think that a given technical option is likely to become dominant, the more new users will side with it and the more likely and pronounced the dominance will in fact become. Third, while scale economies and learning can only be a source of increasing returns to adoption and while users' learning costs (or switching costs) can exclusively be a source of inertia, both reputation effects and network externalities, in contrast, can act as both strong inertial and increasing returns to adoption.

8.8. A SUMMARY ON INCREASING RETURNS IN INDUSTRIAL COMPETITION

The analysis so far done has gradually recognized the central role of increasing returns mechanisms in generating and sustaining dominant firms and technologies. Clearly, while scale economies, the resource-based loop, the Schumpeterian (innovation-based) loop, reputation, and the different categories of learning help to explain some of the most basic occurrences of dominant firms and slanted industrial structures, only increasing returns to adoption – a notion intrinsically connected to Schumpeterian economics - can explain most of the instances of technological dominance which we see in contemporary high-technology markets. Thus the integration of all these increasing returns mechanisms, as Figure 8.1 shows, results in a quite complete explanation of industrial competition.

Such an explanation combines the self-reinforcing loops based upon resources and innovations (loops A and B), scale economies, learning, and reputation (loops C) with the loops based upon increasing returns to adoption. These loops are of two kinds. A set of further loops, composed of a mesh of scale economies, learning, reputation effects, infrastructure effects, and network effects, links increasing competitive advantages with increasing returns to market share. A last set of loops indicates that, if increasing returns to adoption are present and considerable, market share becomes a strategic asset well worth investing on in an aggressive manner through vigorous production capacity expansion, price reductions, infrastructure development, and alliances with manufacturer of complementary technologies, products, and services.

As a model of increasing returns mechanism in industrial dynamics, the one described here seems to be rather comprehensive. It can explain the polarized outcomes that are common in most industrial sector and describe business competition as a dynamic and cumulative process. A final, but not less interesting, feature of this model of industrial competition is that it is general, in the sense that it is capable to describe simultaneously the three levels of industrial competition. It elucidates how technological adoption, the number and growth of firms, and industrial structure combine and cause each other. In other words, the general model of industrial competition gives a picture of how industrial competition is a process in which technological competition affects the size of the firms competition in a given industry and how the growth of the firms, in turn, influences the structure of that industry. That is why technological adoption goes between conduct and performance in the chain of causality that leads from the size of the firms to industrial structure.

8.9. Increasing Returns, Structural Change and Development Paths: An Example

The seminal article formalising the "big push" theory of industrialisation is that of Murphy, Shleifer and Vishney (1989). In their model, firms choose between a constant returns and an increasing returns of technology based on their expectations of demand.

However, these choices spill over into aggregate demand creating a strategic interaction among sectors in their technology adoption decisions. Thus, under certain conditions, there exist two equilibria: with all firms choosing the constant returns or all choosing the increasing returns technology. Clearly, in the latter equilibrium, all households are better off.

While the Murphy, Shleifer and Vishny model shows how increasing returns (and a wage effect) aggregate to strategic complementarity among sectors, it does not lend itself readily to the debate concerning the degree of balance in industrialisation policy.

First, the static content leaves open the question of whether the intervention should take the form of anything more than indicative planning. Second, the most commonly discussed policy instrument in the industrialization debate is the subsidisation of investments.

However, in the Murphy, Shleifer and Vishny example, use of this instrument biases one toward a more unbalanced policy. To see this, observe that it is the role of the government to facilitate a move to the industrialising equilibrium. This means that the government must subsidise a sufficient amount of investment to make it profitable for all sectors to adopt the modern technology. Given the binary choice set, there then exists some minimum critical mass of sectors that must be targeted to achieve a successful transition. A greater range of successful industrialisation policies might be more plausible, however, if firms had the choice of a wider variety of technology to choose from. One might suppose that targeting a large number of sectors to modernise a little and targeting a small number of sectors for more radical modernisation might both generate a big push. Thus, to consider the balanced approach properly, a greater technological choice space is required.

What would be the choice variables available to the government provided it would be able to pick up what is likely to be increaing returns industries in the future? First, in each period, the government can choose the set of firms that it targets for structural change.

Second, for each targeted firm , the government can choose a target level for 'increasing returns industry' modernisation in the period. Along this vein, the government could choose to target the same number of firms in each period but induce those firms to modernise gradually over time. Or in contrast, the government chooses a single level of modernisation to occur across all firms and all periods. It then targets a mass of firms each period for entry and modernisation. This means that industrialisation policy is solely characterised by the critical mass of sectors targeted , and the target level of modernisation. Given a parametrised development path , the most significant parameter represents the strength of increasing returns in the technology adopted by industrial sectors which generates a rationale for 'big push ' intervention.

8.10. Conclusions: Increasing Returns Mechanisms and Technological Competition

The strategic importance of increasing returns to technology adoption is unquestionable. In a strictly ergodic market technological options eventually obtain the share of the market they deserve in proportion to their value and technical possibilities. In non-ergodic situations, in a tipping market, on the other hand, the winner takes all or most and the losers (no matter how worthy and how many of them there are) loses all or much. Because of this , the introduction of factors causing tipping markets determines the outcomes of technological competition. This framework not only captures the interplay of institutional arrangements, resources and network of firms and industries in industrial competition, but also delineates very concrete regularities, which can provide us with a simple but powerful tool to explain endogeneously, and in a dynamic way the firm's growth, industrial structure , and technological competition.

This chapter suggests a Schumpeterian model of industrial competition. In contrast to the approaches that underline a specific aspect of industrial competition and/or base their explanation on a reduced number of factors and against conventional economics that overlooks increasing returns mechanisms, this model links the increasing returns mechanisms that determine endogenously inter-firm asymmetries and the kind of industrial structure which emerges during this competition process. This framework also emphasizes the fact that the emergence of dominant firms and the evolution of industrial structure are strongly intertwined with the process of technological change and diffusion.

One of the most important contributions of the work on increasing returns is its having shown that the emergence and persistence of technological monopolies is not an exogenous datum, largely determined by scientific and technical parameters, but is strongly influenced by vibrant market forces stemming from self-reinforcing mechanisms. In the presence of strong, global and long lasting increasing returns, the actions and omissions of the main actors in the industry in question affect considerably the final result of technological competition. To the extent to which these actors are capable of fully perceiving and exploiting strong increasing returns in emerging markets. they can ensure the entrenchment of their technology as the industrial standard by investing in those strategies that bring about market share. Once entrenched, and to the extent they are capable to exploit inertial forces, established firms can ensure the persistence of their technologies well beyond the time warranted by their relative technical value.

This chapter showes that technological monopoly should be attributed to increasing returns in general, but it is network externalities in particular what has caused some important markets to be dominated by a technological monopoly. In fact, at the level of technological competition, the only thing the other sources of increasing returns to adoption do is to exacerbate the implications of network effects, but they do not turn, isolated from network effects, a market tipping. The most obvious and direct reason for technological monopoly is that the components of a given network are compatible and constantly interconnected. The telephone and the fax are examples of networks where physical interconnection and compatibility have led to technological monopoly.

Winner-takes-all markets are associated with cases where there is (often intense) competition in innovative activity but the future market is such that competition in it is, over a reasonable timeframe, not sustainable. Thus firms compete to attain a position of dominance.

Perhaps the most famous example of a winner-takes-all market is that for operating systems for desktop PCs. It is instructive to recognise that this market benefits from massive economies of scale in production protected by intellectual property rights (very low marginal cost of supply compared with very large fixed costs of initial product development) and substantial economies of scale in consumption (due in large part to the network effects associated with the relationships between the operating system market and the related applications software markets).

Identification of such markets is important because it affects the focus of competitive concerns.

Most obviously, if there are strong grounds to believe that a future market is a winner-takes-all market, it is perhaps not appropriate for a competition authority to block a merger or agreement between firms on the basis that this will create a dominant position or lessen competition in this future market. By definition, the nature of the market is such that its existence guarantees that a firm will be dominant on it, at least in the medium term. (This illustrates an important point relevant to wider issues in competition policy: it is typically better to have a situation where a firm is dominant in a relevant market than for that market not to exist at all.) Instead, any intervention must be based on the premise that the merger (agreement) lessens or distorts competition on some other, perhaps related market , or in competition in the innovative activity associated with the winner-takes-all market.

Similarly in dominance cases, if we anticipate that a market is subject to winner-takes-all properties, then it is difficult to establish a case that a firm has abused its dominant position in monopolising this market - the market is naturally prone to monopolisation. Rather, analysis of an alleged abuse of dominance associated with this market should focus on how a dominant position in a related market (perhaps an access market) could be used to distort competition in the innovative activity associated with the winner-takes-all market, or how a dominant position in the winner-takes-all market could be abused to maintain that position - in effect used to distort competition in the innovative activity associated with the future generation of that market.

Indirect network effects may also tilt the market in favor of one of the competing technologies. In the videofilm industry, for instance, because of strong, long lasting, and global network externalities, technological monopoly emerged and product cycle has lasted about 20 years. The strength, duration and scope of increasing returns in the videofilm markets are the direct consequence of particular technical characteristics of the competing VCR technologies. These technologies were quite similar and mature, the usage cycle of their compatible content -videofilms-- is very short, and their potential substitutes have not had large enough advantages so as to replace. them. In the video game industry, in contrast, because of weak, short lasting, and local network externalities due to incomparability of videogame technologies, long usage cycle of videogames, and the proliferation of new, more powerful new formats, different technologies have tended to share the market according to their intrinsic value.

A comparison between the videogame industry and the videofilm industry, then, allows us to show that compatibility constraints are not a sufficient condition for a virtual network technology to become a monopoly: it is necessary, besides, that usage life of content is short and core technologies are incomparable. But when the usage cycle of content is long and core technologies are comparable, any virtual network technology becomes less systemic. As the strength, duration, and scope of network externalities are reduced considerably because of long-lasting usage cycle and technology comparability, competing virtual network technologies end up sharing the market in proportion to their value.

In this chapter we also advanced our understanding of the technical and institutional factors which are likely to affect the nature of technological competition. In doing so, we add to the dimensions of *strength* and *duration,* the dimension of *scope* of increasing returns. The distinction between strength, duration and scope is useful to realize that, contrary to popular and academic literature, a market for virtual network technologies with content dimensions not necessarily will end up with a technological monopoly. With this distinction in mind and against those who think that strong indirect network externalities always act as tipping mechanisms, we also can show that strong indirect network externalities are compatible with fairly ergodic market dynamics, if the scope of such externalities happens to be rather narrow.

By taking the telecommuncations or the videofilm industry, for example, we can show that strong network externalities are *necessary* but not *sufficient* conditions to produce technological monopoly. Short usage life of content and technology incomparability are technical and necessary conditions for technological monopoly in software intensive virtual network technologies to happen. But these technical aspects of virtual network technologies are not a sufficient condition to produce technological monopolies. In chapter 4 we showed that network externalities require not only to have high levels of strength. but also to be global in scope. Under certain institutional condition strong indirect network externalities may be rather localized, which leads to very ergodic market results. In these conditions markets are shared by the competing technologies according to their intrinsic value.

Technical and institutional factors causing different levels of strength. duration and scope of increasing returns to adoption are relevant to determine whether a market is tipping or ergodic. This has some implications. A first implication is that not all network technology is equally systemic. If there are strong network externalities but with a local scope, the systemic nature of a network becomes rather limited. In this case the systemic nature of the VCR network would be rather local compared with the actual network, which is global in nature.

Strength, duration, and scope of increasing returns are also useful to determine in a more detailed way the nature of *cooperation.* When network externalities are strong and global, content-intensive virtual network technologies become rather systemic. In these circumstances, the main sponsors of the competing technologies may produce some components of the system. but the rest of it may be out of their reach. For instance, a PC producer may be incapable to produce software or microprocessors; and microprocessor producers may not be able to produce software or hardware. VCR producers cannot produce films, in the same way as film producers cannot produce VCRs. Consequently, technological competition in markets characterized by strong and global increasing returns is more in connection with complex networks of firms than with conventional industrial array of firms producing homogeneous products. In contrast, in markets with weak and local network externalities, competition takes place mainly between firms than between networks of firms. This is so, because in this kind of markets products are not systemic.

REFERENCES

Abernathy, W.J. and J.M. Utterback (1978), 'Patterns of Innovation in Technology', *Technology Review* 10, 40-47.

Abernathy. W. J. and K. B. Clark (1985). 'Innovation: Mapping the Wind of Creative Destruction', *Research Policy* 14, 3-22.

Aghion, E. and E. Howitt (1998), *Endogeneous Growth Theory*, Cambridge, Ma.: MIT Press

Arrow, Kenneth (1962), 'The Economic Implications of Learning by Doing', *Review of Economic Studies* 29, 155-173.

Arthur, W. B. (1989), 'Competing Technologies, Increasing Returns and Lock-in by Historical Events', *The Economic Journal.* 99, 116-131.

Arthur, W. B.(1990a), 'Positive Feedbacks in the Economy, *Scientific American*, February 22, 92-99.

Arthur, W. B. (1990b) 'Silicon Valley' Location Cluster. When Do Increasing Returns Imply Monopoly' ,*Mathematical Social Science* 19, 235-51.

Arthur. W. B. (1994) ,*Increasing Returns and Path Dependence in the Economy.*
Ann Arbor: The Univ. of Michigan Press

Arthur W. B., Ermoliev,Yu. M. and Yu. M. Kaniovski (1987), 'Path-dependent Processes and the Emergence of Macro-structure', *European Journal of Operational Research.* 30, 294-303.

Arthur, W. B. and D. A. Lane, 1993, 'Information Contagion', *Structural Change and Economic Dynamics* 4, 81-104.

Chandler, A. D.(1990*), Scale and Scope: Dynamics of Industrial Capitalism.* Cambridge. Ma.: The Belknap Press of Harvard University Press

Cohen, W. M. and R. C. Levin. (1989). 'Empirical Studies of Innovation and Market Structure', in Richard Schmalensee and Robert D. Willig. eds., *Handbook of Industrial Organization*. Amsterdam: North-Holland

David ,P. and S. Greenstein (1990), 'The Economics of Compatibility Standards: an Introduction to Recent Research', *Economics of Innovation and New Technology* 1, 3-41.

Economides. N.(1996), 'The Economics of Networks'. *International Journal of Industrial Organization* 25, 1-18

Feller, W.(1957), *An Introduction to Probability Theory and its Applications*, Vol. I, New York: John Wiley & Sons

Foray, D. (1993),'Standardisation et Concurrence: Des Relations Ambivalentes', *Rev. d'Economie Industrielle* 63, 30-45

Freeman, C. (2003) ,'A Schumpeterian Renaissance ? ', Science and Technology Policy Research Unit, Univ. of Sussex, Brighton, SEWPS #102, July

Gottinger, H.W. (2003), *Economies of Network Industries* , London :Routledge

Henderson, B.D. (1975), 'The Market Share Paradox', in Y. Brozen, ed. *The Competitive Economy*, Morristown: General Learning Press, 286-287

Hirsch, W.Z (1956), 'Firm Progress Ratios', *Econometrica* 24, 136-143

Katz, M. and C. Shapiro (1992), 'Product Introduction with Network Externalities', *The Journal of Industrial Economics* 40, 55-84

Katz, M. and C. Shapiro (1994), 'System Competition and Network Effects', *Journal of Economic Perspectives* 8, 93-115

McAfee, R.P.(2002), *Competitive Solutions,* Princeton: Princeton Univ. Press

Murphy, K.M., Shleifer, A. and R.W. Vishny (1989), 'Industrialization and the Big Push", Journal of Political Economy 97, pp.1003-1026

Nelson, R. and S. G.Winter (1982), *An Evolutionary Theory of Economic Change*, Cambridge, Ma.: Harvard Univ. Press

Nelson, R.(1986), Evolutionary Modeling of Economic Change, in Stiglitz, J. and G. F. Matthewson, eds. , *New Developments in the Analysis of Market Structure*, Cambridge, Ma.: MIT Press

Porter, M. E. (1980)*, Competitive Strategy*, New York: Free Press

Rosenberg, N. (1982), *Inside the Black Box: Technology and Economics*, Cambridge :Cambridge Univ. Press

Schumpeter. J.A.. (1942), *Capitalism. Socialism. and Democracy*, New York:Harper

Shapiro, C. and H. R. Varian (1999), *Information Rules*, Boston: Harvard Business School

Teece,D.(1986),'Profiting from Technology Innovations', *Research Policy* 15(6), 285-305

Utterback,J.M.(1994), *Mastering the Dynamics of Innovation*, Boston; Harvard Business School Press

Utterback, J.M. and Suarez,F.F. (1993), Innovation, Competition and Industry Structure, *Research Policy* 22, 1-21

Chapter 9

NETWORK ECONOMIES FOR THE INTERNET

'...the Internet is in its essence an economy, a game , an arena where agents act selfishly and are affected by everybody's decisions...'

Hall, Nikolova and Papadimitriou,in Deng and Graham (2007)

9.1 INTRODUCTION

With advances in computer and networking technology, numerous heterogeneous computers can be interconnected to provide a large collection of computing and communication resources . These systems are used by a growing and increasingly heterogeneous set of users which are identified with the present Internet. A macroscopic view of distributed computer systems reveals the complexity of the organization and management of the resources and services they provide. The complexity arises from the system size (e.g. no. of systems, no. of users) and heterogeneity in applications (e.g. online transaction processing, e-commerce, multimedia, intelligent information search) and resources (CPU, memory, I/O bandwidth, network bandwidth and buffers, etc.)

The complexity of resource allocation is further increased by several factors. First, in many distributed systems, the resources are in fact owned by multiple organizations. Second, the satisfaction of users and the performance of applications is determined by the simultaneous application of multiple resources. For example, a multimedia server application requires I/O bandwidth to retrieve content, CPU time to execute server logic and protocols, and networking bandwidth to deliver the content to clients. The performance of applications may also be altered by trading resources. For example, a multimedia server application may perform better by releasing memory and acquiring higher CPU priority , resulting in smaller buffers for I/O and networking but improving the performance of the communication protocol execution .

Finally, in a large distributed system , the set of systems, users and applications is continuously changing. In this chapter, in line with identifying the strategic factors of Internet enterprises, we address some of the issues of Quality of Service (QoS) and pricing, and efficient allocation of resources (computational resources) in networks and systems.

We review and consider problems of Quality of Service (QoS) provisioning, resource allocation and pricing in computer networks and information systems. We consider such complex systems as economies where multiple classes of users (consumers) compete for resources and services from suppliers: network providers and information providers (servers). The resources under contention are network bandwidth and buffers, server processing rate and memory.

We model and solve problems using economic principles of market mechanism, where resources are priced by suppliers based on demand, and users buy resources to satisfy their Quality of Service (QoS) needs. We focus on the issues of QoS provisioning, and the reasons in choosing economic paradigms to solve some of the problems.

Massive complexity makes traditional approaches to resource allocation impractical in modern distributed systems such as the Internet. Traditional approaches attempt to optimize some system-wide measure of performance (e.g. overall average response time, thruput etc.) Optimization is performed either by a centralized algorithm with complete information , or by a decentralized consensus based algorithm.

The current and future complexity of resource allocation problems described makes it impossible to define an acceptable system-wide performance metric. What single, system-wide performance metric adequately reflects the performance objectives of multimedia server and an online transaction processing system? Centralized or consensus based algorithms are impractical in dynamic systems owned by multiple organizations. Resource allocation complexity due to decentralizations and heterogeneity is also present in economic systems. In general, modern economies allocate resources in systems whose complexity overwhelms any algorithm or technique developed for computer systems. Here we discuss the similarities between complex distributed systems and economies. Competitive economic models could provide algorithms and tools for allocating resources in distributed computer systems (Deng and Graham, 2007). The tools used are algorithmic mechanism design, dynamic game theory, complexity and computational equilibrium.

There is another motivation that has come about due to the commercialization of the Internet. The debate has begun in the area of multiple QoS levels and pricing. How should pricing be introduced to provide many service levels in the Internet? Should pricing be based on access cost or should it be based on usage and QoS received by the end user? Will usage based pricing help the Internet economy grow, and help in accounting and improve the efficiency of the Internet, and make users benefit much more? Similar issues are being investigated in the ATM networking community. We address some of the issues of QoS and pricing, and efficient allocation of resources (computational resources)in networks and systems.

9.2 Internet Resources

The evolution of Internet pricing poses interesting resource allocation problems. Flat-rate pricing has been a key condition that allowed the Internet to expand very fast. In the initial stages of the Internet flat rate pricing has been more prevalent in the US than in Europe which partially explains higher user diffusion rates in the US than in Europe or Japan among private users.

But as the net has grown in size and complexity, not discounting engineering advances in network (management) technologies, it is becoming more obvious that other pricing schemes being able to cope with severe congestion and deadlock should come forward. New pricing schemes should not only be able to cope with a growing Internet traffic but also be able to foster application development and deployment vital to service providers. Usage-based pricing of this new kind should make the internet attractive to many new users. Casual users will find it more affordable, while business users will find a more stable environment.

Without an incentive to economize on usage , congestion could become quite serious. The problem is more serious for data networks like the Internet than for other congestible transportation network resources because of the tremendously wide range of usage rates. A single user at a modern workstation can send a few bytes of email or put a load of hundreds Mbps on the network, for example, by downloading videos demanding as much as 1 Mbps. In the 1990s the maximum thruput on given backbones used to be only 45 Mbps, so it it was clear that even a few users with relatively inexpensive equipment could block the network. There was witness of these problems after American Online introduced a flat fee for its internet services and experienced a massive and persistent breakdown with disgruntled customers. A natural response by shifting resources to expand technology will be expensive and not a satisfactory solution in the long run. Aside from breakthrough technological advances such as broadband that could mitigate but not eliminate the problem many proposals rely on voluntary efforts to control congestion. Many participants in congestion discussions suggest that peer pressure and user ethics will be sufficient to control congestion costs. But as MacKie-Mason and Varian (1995) suggest we essentially have to deal with a problem like the 'the tragedy of the commons', that is overgrazing the commons, e.g. by overusing a generally accessible communication network. A few proposals would require users to indicate the priority they want each of the sessions to receive, and for routers to be programmed to maintain multiple queues for each priority class. The success of such schemes would depend on the users' discipline to stick to the assigning of appropriate priorities to some of their traffic. On the other hand, priority scheduling flies in the face of 'network neutrality' requested, that is, that all internet traffic should be delivered at the same speed and reliability. There are no effective sanction and incentive schemes that would control such traffic, and therefore such a scheme is liable to be ineffective. This is why pricing schemes have gained increasing attention and various approaches and models have been discussed in the network community (Shenker et al., 1995; Wang et al.,1997)

Quality of Service (QoS)

With the Internet we observe a single quality of service (QoS): „best effort packet service". Packets are transported first come, first-served with no guarantee of success. Some packets may experience severe delays, while others may be dropped and never arrive. Different kinds of data place different demands on network services (Shenker, 1995) Email and file transfer requires 100 percent accuracy, but can easily tolerate delay. Real-time voice broadcasts require much higher bandwidth than file transfers, and can tolerate minor delays but they can tolerate significant distortion. Real-time video broadcasts have very low tolerance for delay and distortion. Because of these different requirements , network allocation algorithms should be designed to treat different types of traffic differently but the user must truthfully indicate which type of traffic he/she is preferring, and this would only happen through incentive compatible pricing schemes .

Network pricing could be looked at as a mechanism design problem (Nisan and Ronen, 2001). The user can indicate the 'type' of transmission and the workstation in turn reports this type to the network. To ensure truthful revelation of preferences , the reporting and billing mechanism must be incentive compatible.

Pricing Congestion

The social cost of congestion is a result of the existence of network externalities. Charging for incremental capacity requires usage information. We need a measure of the user's demand during the expected peak period of usage over some period, to determine the share of the incremental capacity requirement. In principle, it might seem that a reasonable approach would be to charge a premium price for usage during the pre-determined peak periods (a positive price if the base usage price is zero), as is rountinely done for electricity pricing (Wilson, Chapt.10, 1993). However, in terms of internet usage , peak demand periods are much less predictable than for other utility services. Since the use of computers would allow to schedule some activities during off-peak hours, in addition to different time zones around the globe, we face the problem of shifting peaks. By identifying social costs for network externalities the suggestion by MacKie-Mason and Varian (1995) was directed toward a scheme for internalizing this cost as to impose a congestion price that is determined by a real-time Vickrey auction. The scheme requires that packets should be prioritized based on the value that the user puts on getting the packet through quickly. To do this , each user assigns his/her packets a bid measuring his/her willingness-to-pay (indicating effective demand) for immediate servicing. At congested routers, packets are prioritized based on bids. In line with the design of a Vickrey auction, in order to make the scheme incentive compatible, users are not charged the price they bid, but rather are charged the bid of the lowest priority packet that is admitted to the network. It is well-known that this mechanism provides the right incentives for truthful revelation (Nisan and Ronen, 2001). Such a scheme has a number of desirable characteristics. In particular, not only do those users with the highest cost of delay get served first , but the prices also send the right signals for capacity expansion in a competitive market for network services. If all of the congestion revenues are reinvested in new capacity, then capacity will be expanded to the point where its marginal value is equal to its marginal cost.

9.3 Quality of Service Parameters

Internet Communication Technologies: ATM and B-ISDN

The Internet and Asynchronous Transfer Mode (ATM) have strongly positioned themselves for defining the future information infrastructure. The Internet is successfully operating one of the popular information systems, the World Wide Web (WWW), which suggests that the information highway is forming on the Internet. However, such a highway is limited in the provision of advanced multimedia services such as those with guaranteed quality of service (QoS). Guaranteed services are easier to support the ATM technology. Its capability far exceeds that of the current Internet, and it is expected to be used as the backbone technology for the future information infrastructure. ATM proposes a new communications paradigm. ATM allows integration of different types of services such as digital voice, video and data in a single network consisting of high speed links and switches. It supports a Broadband Integrated Services Digital Network (B-ISDN), so that ATM and B-ISDN are sometimes used interchangeably, where ATM is referred to as the technology and B-ISDN as the underlying technical standard. ATM allows efficient utilization of network resources, and simplifies the network switching facilities compared to other proposed techniques in that it will only require one type of switching fabric (packet switch). This simplifies the network management process (Ackermann et al. 2007). The basic operation of ATM, and generally of packet-switched networks, is based on statistical multiplexing. In order to provide QoS, the packets need to be served by certain scheduling (service) disciplines. Resource allocation algorithms depend heavily on the scheduling mechanism deployed. The scheduling is to be done at the entrance of the network as well as the switching points. The term „cell" designates the fixed-size packet in ATM networks. ATM allows variable bit rate sources to be statistically multiplexed. Statistical multiplexing produces more efficient usage of the channel at the cost of possible congestion at the buffers of an ATM switch. When the congestion persists, buffer overflow occurs, and cells are discarded (or packets are dropped). Therefore, resources (i.e. bandwidth and buffer space) need to be carefully allocated to meet the cell loss and the delay requirements of the user. The delay and the cell loss probability that the user wishes the network to guarantee are referred to as the QoS parameters. Overall, QoS is usually defined in terms of cell loss probability, delay bounds and other delay and drop-off parameters. How can one provide such QoS with guarantees? The general approach is to have an admission or performance algorithm that takes into account the traffic characteristics of the source and assigns suitable amounts of resources to the new connection during channel establishment. The admission algorithm is responsible for calculating the bandwidth and buffer space necessary to meet the QoS requirements specified by the user. The algorithm depends on how the traffic is characterized and the service disciplines supported by the switches.

Although the Internet is capable of transporting all types of digital information, it is difficult to modify the existing Internet to support some features that are vital for real time communications. One important feature to be supported is the provision of performance guarantees. The Internet uses the Internet Protocol (IP), in which each packet is forwarded independently of the others. The Internet is a connectionless network where any source can send packets any time at speeds that are neither monitored nor negotiated. Congestion is bound to happen in this type of network. If congestion is to be avoided and real-time services are to be supported, then a negotiation (through pricing or rationing) between the user and the network is necessary. ATM is a connection-oriented network that supports this feature. A virtual channel is established, and resources are reserved to provide QoS prior to data transfer. This is referred to as channel establishment.

Traffic in B-ISDN

In a B-ISDN environment high-bandwidth applications such as video, voice and data are likely to take advantage of compression. Different applications have different performance requirements, and the mechanisms to control congestion should be different for each class of traffic. Classification of these traffic types is essential in providing efficient services. There are two fundamental classes of traffic in B-ISDN: real-time and non real-time (best effort) traffic. The majority of applications on the Internet currently are non-real-time ones (Paxon, 1994) based on TCP /IP. TCP/IP is being preserved with an ATM technology (Chao, 1994). The Internet can support data traffic well but not real-time traffic due to the limitations in the functionality of the protocols. B-ISDN needs to support both non-real-time and real-time traffic with QoS guarantees. Most data traffic requires low cell loss, but is insensitive to delays and other QoS parameters. Applications such as Telnet require a real-time response and should therefore be considered real-time applications, the same applies to Voice of Internet Protocol (VOIP). Video is delay-sensitive and, unlike Telnet, requires high bandwidth. High throughput and low delay are required of the ATM switches for the network to support video services to the clients. This puts a constraint on the ATM switch design in that switching should be done in hardware and the buffer sizes should be kept reasonably small to prevent long delays. On the other hand, best effort traffic tends to be bursty, and its traffic characteristics are hard to predict. This puts another, opposite constraint on an ATM switch, which requires large buffers at the switching point, further complicating its design.

Congestion Control

Statistical multiplexing can offer the best use of resources, however, this is done at the price of possible congestion. Congestion in an ATM network can be handled basically in two ways: reactive control and preventive control . Reactive control mechanisms are commonly used in the Internet, where control is triggered to alleviate congestion after congestion has been detected. Typical examples of reactive control are (i) explicit congestion notification (ECN), (ii) node to node flow control and (iii) selective cell discarding. In the more advanced preventive control approach, congestion is avoided by allocating the proper amount of resources and controlling the rate of data transfers by properly scheduling cell departures. Some examples of preventive control mechanisms are (i) admission and priority control , (ii) usage parameter control and (iii) traffic shaping.

Reactive and preventive control can be used concurrently, but most reactive controls are unsuitable for high-bandwidth real-time applications in an ATM network, since reactive control simply is not fast enough to handle congestion in time . Therefore, preventive control is more appropriate for high speed networks.

Service Discipline

Traffic control occurs at various places in the network. First, the traffic entering the network is controlled at the input, second, the traffic is controlled at the switching nodes. In either case, traffic is controlled by scheduling the cell departures. There are various ways how to schedule departure times, and these mechanisms are part of service disciplines. The service discipline must transfer traffic at a given bandwidth by scheduling the cells and make sure that it does not exceed the buffer space reserved (or the delay bound assigned) for each channel. These functions are usually build into the hardware of the ATM switch and into the switch controller. When implementing a service discipline in an ATM network, it is important to choose it simple enough that it can be easily integrated into an ATM switch. However, the discipline must support the provision of quality of service guarantees. This also means that the service discipline is responsible for protecting „well-behaved" traffic from the „ill-behaved" traffic and must be able to provide certain levels of QoS guarantees. The service discipline also needs to be flexible enough to satisfy the diverse requirements of a variety of traffic types, and to be efficient, that is, to permit a high utilization of the network. Various service disciplines have been proposed, and many of them have been investigated thoroughly and compared. An important class is that of disciplines used in rate-allocating servers.

Bandwidth-Buffer Tradeoff

A simple example on the representation of QoS parameters is the bandwidth-buffer tradeoff. Bandwidth can be traded for buffer space and vice versa to provide the same QoS. If a bandwidth is scarce, then a resource pair that uses less bandwidth and more buffer space should be used (Gottinger, 1997). Resource pricing is targeted to exploit this tradeoff to achieve efficient utilization of the available resources. The pricing concept for a scarce resource is well-known in economics, but in the context of exploiting the bandwidth-buffer tradeoff , Low and Varaiya (1993) use non-linear optimization theory to determine centralized optimal shadow prices in large networks. With respect to large scale application, however, the complex optimization process limits the frequency of pricing updates, which causes inaccurate information about available resources. In order to make pricing in the context of a buffer-bandwidth tradeoff more adjustable and flexible it should be based on decentralized pricing procedures according to competitive bidding in large markets where prices will be optimal prices if the markets are efficient. This would also allow flexible pricing which results in accurate representation of available resources in that prices are updated as the instance connect request arrives. The subsequent procedure is based on distributed pricing as a more feasible alternative to optimal pricing.

9.4. The Rationale of Economic Models in Networking

There are intrinsic interfaces between human information processing and networking that show the usefulness of economic modeling.

Decentralization: in an economy, decentralization is provided by the fact that economic models consist of agents which selfishly attempt to achieve their goals. There are two types of economic agents: suppliers and consumers. A consumer attempts to optimize its individual performance criteria by obtaining the resources it requires, and is not concerned with system-wide performance. A supplier allocates its individual resources to consumers. A supplier's sole goal is to optimize its individual resources to consumers. A supplier's sole goal is to optimize its individual satisfaction (profit) derived from its choice of resource allocation to consumers. Models of economic agents are summarized in the Appendix.

Limiting Complexity: economic models provide several interesting contributions to resource sharing algorithms. The first is a set of tools for limiting the complexity by decentralizing the control of resources . The second is a set of mathematical models that can yield several new insights into resource sharing problems.

Pricing and Performance: most economic models introduce money and pricing as the technique for coordinating the selfish behavior of agents. Each consumer is endowed with money that it uses to purchase required resources. Each supplier owns a set of resources, and charges consumers for the use of its resources. The supplier prices its resources based on the demand by the agents , and the available supply. Consumers buy resources or services such that the benefit they receive is maximized. Consumer-agents buy resources based on maximizing performance criteria. As a whole the system performance is determined by some combination of the individual performance criteria.

Usage Accounting, Billing and Dimensioning: by using economic models for service provisoning in distributed systems, accounting for QoS becomes an important task for suppliers, as they have to keep track of the resource usage in order to price the resources, and thereby charge or bill the users for QoS. In addition, pricing can be used to understand the user demands and thereby dimension systems appropriately.

Administrative Domains: often large distributed systems and computer networks spread over several domains, the control of resources is shared by multiple organizations that own distinct parts of the network. In such an environment , each organization will have a set of services that it supports. Economic principles of pricing and competition provide several valuable insights into decentralized control mechanisms between the multiple organizations and efficient service provisioning.

Scalability: a key issue in designing architectures for services in large computer networks and distributed systems is scalability. With the ever growing demand for new services , flexible service architectures that can scale to accommodate new services is needed. Economic models of competition provide, in a natural fashion, mechanisms for scaling services appropriately based on service demand and resource availability.

9.5 Modelling Approaches

Most studies of resource allocation mechanisms have used a performance model of the resource, where the very concept of the resource is defined in terms of measurable qualities of the service such as utilization, thruput, response time (delay) and so on. Optimization of resource allocation is defined in terms of these measurable qualities. One novelty introduced by the economic approach is to design a system which takes into account the diverse QoS requirements of users, and therefore use multiobjective (utilities)optimization techniques to characterize and compute optimum allocations. Economic modeling of computer and communication resource sharing uses a uniform paradigm described by two level modeling: QoS requirements as inputs into a performance model that is subject to economic optimization.

In the first step, one transforms QoS requirements of users to a performance (example: queueing service model).This model establishes quantifiable parameterization of resource allocation. For example, average delay QoS requirement, when based on a FIFO queueing model, is a function of resources, bandwidth and buffer, and user traffic demands. These parameters are then used to establish an economic optimization model. The question of whether the resource is a piece of hardware, a network link, a software resource such as a database or a server, or a virtual network entity such as a TCP connection is not of primary importance. The first modeling transformation eliminates the details and captures the relevant behaviors and the optimization parameters.

Our approach evolves in the following sequence. Many users present QoS demands, which are translated into demands on resources based on a performance model. The suppliers compute the optimal allocations based on principles of economic optimization and market mechanisms. Once the optimization is done, the results provide inputs to mechanisms for QoS provisioning, such as scheduling of resources and admission of users in networks and load balancing in distributed systems. We present briefly an overview of the problems and contributions

Optimal allocation and QoS

We motivate and solve a problem of allocating resources and providing services (QoS) to several classes of users at a single link. The resources at the link are buffer space and bandwidth. The link (network provider) prices per unit buffer and bandwidth resources. The consumers (user traffic classes), via economic agents, buy resources such that their QoS needs are satisfied. The network provider prices resources based on demand from the consumers. The ingredients are as follows:

- Economic models: we use competitive economic models to determine the resource partitions between user traffic classes, which compete to obtain buffer and bandwidth resources from the switch suppliers.
- Optimal allocations using economic principles: we look for Pareto optimal allocations that satisfy QoS needs of agents. Agents represent QoS via utility functions which capture the multiple performance objectives.
- Pricing based on QoS : we compute equilibrium prices based on the QoS demands of consumers. Prices are set such that the market demand and supply are met. Prices help in determining the cost of providing a service.
- Priorities: using the economic framework, we show a simple way to support priority service among the user-classes (or agents).
- Decentralization: we show a natural separation between the interactions of the user-classes (represented by agents) and the network switch suppliers. The interaction is purely competitive and market based. This decentralization promotes scalable network system design.

Scheduling and pricing mechanisms

We consider a dynamic system where sessions arrive and leave a traffic class, and demand fluctuates over time. In such a setting, we investigate practical mechanisms, such as packet level scheduling to provide bandwidth and buffer guarantees, admission control mechanisms to provide class QoS guarantees, practical pricing to capture the changing demand, and charging mechanisms for user sessions within a class.

- Scheduling algorithms for class based QoS provisioning: we provide novel scheduling mechanisms, which allocates bandwidth and buffer for meeting the demand from traffic classes. The scheduling mechanism allocates bandwidth, which is computed from the economic optimization.
- Admission Region and Control: we compute the admission control region of the agents on the economic model. Due to the natural separation between who controls the admission of sessions into the traffic class, the admission region can be determined.
- We propose simple pricing models which capture the changing demand, and are easy to implement. We also propose novel QoS based charging mechanisms for sessions in a class with applications to charging in ATM Networks and Integrated Services Internet.

We first consider a network economy, of many parallel routes or links, where several agents (representing user classes) compete for resources from several suppliers, where each supplier represents a route (or a path) between a source and destination. Agents buy resources from suppliers based on the QoS requirements of the class they represent. Suppliers price resources, independently, based on demand from the agents. The suppliers connect consumers to information providers, who are at the destination; the flow of information is from information providers to the consumers. We formulate and solve problems of resource allocation and pricing in such an environment.

We then consider a server economy in a distributed system. Again, we use a similar model of interaction between agents and suppliers (servers). The servers sell computational resources such as processing rate and memory to the agents for a price. The prices of resources are set independently by each server based on QoS demand from the agents. Agents represent user classes such as transactions in database servers or sessions for Web servers that have QoS requirements such as response time. Using such economic models, our contributions are as follows:

- We propose a decentralized model of network and server economies, where we show efficient QoS provisioning and Pareto allocation of resources (network and server resources) among agents and suppliers, which are either network routes or servers (content providers).
- We show how prices for resources are set at the suppliers based on the QoS demands from the agents.
- We propose alternative dynamic routing algorithms and admission control mechanisms based on QoS preferences by the user classes for the network economy, and we propose a simple way to perform transaction routing. We also show static optimal routing policies by the agents for the network and server economies.

Network and Server Economies.

Consider a large scale distributed information system with many consumers and suppliers. Suppliers are content providers such as web servers , digital library servers, multimedia database and transaction servers. Consumers request for and access information objects from the various suppliers and pay a certain fee or no fee at all for the services rendered.

Consider that third party suppliers provide information about suppliers to consumers in order to let consumers find and choose the right set of suppliers.

Access and dissemination: consumers query third-party providers for information about the suppliers , such as services offered and the cost (price). Likewise, suppliers advertise their services and the costs via the third party providers in order to attract consumers. Consumers prefer an easy and simple way to query for supplier information, and suppliers prefer to advertise information securely and quickly across many regions or domains. For example, consider a user who wishes to view a multimedia object (such as a video movie). The user would like to know about the suppliers of this object, and the cost of retrieval of this object from each supplier.

Performance requirements: users wish to have good response time for their search results once the queries are submitted. However, there is a tradeoff. For more information about services offered, advanced searching mechanisms are needed , but at the cost of increased response time. In other words, users could have preferences over quality of search information and response time. For example , users might want to know the service costs in order to view a specific information object. In large networks , there could be many suppliers of this object, and users may not want to wait forever to know about all the suppliers and their prices. Instead, they would prefer to get as much information as possible within a certain period of time (response time).

From the above example, in order to let many consumers find suppliers , a scalable decentralized architecture is needed for information storage , access and updates.

Naming of services and service attributes of suppliers becomes a challenging issue when hundreds of suppliers spread across the globe. A simple naming scheme to connect consumers, across the internet, with information about suppliers is essential. The naming scheme must be extensible for new suppliers who come into existence. A name registration mechanism for new suppliers and a de-registration mechanism (automatic) to remove non-existent suppliers is required. In addition, naming must be hierarchical , domain based (physical or spatial domains) for scalability and uniqueness. Inter-operability with respect to naming across domains is an additional challenging issue not covered here.

The format of information storage must be simple enough to handle many consumer requests quickly within and across physical domains. For better functionality and more information, a complex format of information storage is necessary, but at the cost of reduced performance. For example, a consumer, in addition to current service cost, might want to know more information such as the cost of the same service during peak and off-peak hours , the history of a supplier, its services , and its reputation, in order to make a decision. This information has to be gathered when requested. In addition, the storage formats must be inter-operable across domains .

Performance: a good response time is important to make sure consumers get the information they demand about suppliers within a reasonable time period, so that decision-making by consumers is done in a timely fashion. In addition, the design of the right architectures for information storage and dissemination is necessary for a large scale market economy to function efficiently. Using the previous example , consumers and suppliers would prefer an efficient architecture to query for and post information. Consumers would prefer good response time in obtaining the information , and suppliers prefer a secure and fast update mechanism to provide up-to-date information about their services.

Security in transferring information and updating information at the bulletin boards (name servers) is crucial for efficient market operation and smooth interaction between consumers and suppliers. For this the third party suppliers (naming services) have to provide authentication and authorization services to make sure honest suppliers are the ones updating information about their services.

Allocation and Pricing Models

In economic models, there are two main ways to allocate resources among the competing agents. One of them is the exchange based economy and the other is the price based economy. In the exchange based economy, each agent is initially endowed with some amounts of the resources. They exchange resources until the marginal rate of substitution of the resources is the same for all the agents. The agents trade resources in the direction of increasing utility (for maximal preference). That is, two agents will agree on an exchange of resources (e.g. CPU for memory) which results in an improved utility for both agents. The Pareto optimal allocation is achieved when no further, mutually beneficial, resource exchanges can occur. Formally, an allocation of resources is Pareto optimal when the utility derived by the competing economic-agents is maximum. Any deviation from this allocation could cause one or more economic agents to have a lower utility (which means the agents will be dissatisfied).

In a price based system, the resources are priced based on the demand, supply and the wealth in the economic system. The allocations are done based on the following mechanisms. Each agent is endowed with some wealth. Each agent computes the demand from the utility function and the budget constraint. The aggregate demand from all the agents is sent to the suppliers who then compute the new resource prices. If the demand for a resource is greater than its supply, the supplier raises the price of the resource. If there is surplus supply, the price is decreased. The agents again compute their demands given the current prices and present the demand to the suppliers. This process continues iteratively until the equilibrium price is achieved where demand equals the supply.

Bidding and auctioning resources is another form of resource allocation based on prices. There are several auctioning mechanisms such as the Sealed Bid Auction, Dutch Auction, and English Auction. The basic philosophy behind auctions and bidding is that the highest bidder always gets the resources, and the current price for a resource is determined by the bid prices.

What are the economic based problems?

Some of the interesting problems encountered when designing an economic based computer system are discussed and stated.

- How do agents demand resources? This is a fundamental question regarding the agents preferences on the resources they consume. Are there smooth utility functions that can capture the agents preferences of the resources? Are there utility functions that can capture the diversity of the agents preferences?
- How are the prices adjusted to clear the economy or to clear the markets? In an economic model, efficient allocation of resources occurs when the demand equals the supply at a certain equilibrium price vector.
- What rational pricing mechanisms do the suppliers adopt? This question raises issues on pricing mechanisms that will attract agents (consumers).
- How do suppliers provide price guarantees to agents? This is a fundamental question in advertising and providing price guarantees to agents. Delays in information about prices, and surges in demand can cause prices to vary. Therefore agents can make bad decisions.
- What are the protocols by which the consumers and suppliers communicate to reserve resources?
- What are the general allocation principles? Can economic models give insight into the allocation mechanisms that can cause the computer system to reach equilibrium? Can these principles be used practically to evolve the computer system in a way that price equilibrium can be achieved?

9.6 NETWORK ECONOMY

The economic model consists of the following players: Agents and Network Suppliers. Consumers or user classes: Consumers (or user classes) request for QoS. Each user class has several sessions (or user sessions). Users within a class have common preferences. User classes have QoS preferences such as preferences over packet-loss probability, max/average delay and thruput. Users within a class share resources.

(Two variations of the model are referred to the Appendix).

Agents and Network Suppliers: Each user class is represented by an agent. Each agent negotiates and buys services (resource units) from one or more suppliers. Agents demand for resources in order to meet the QoS needs of the user classes. Network providers have technology to partition and allocate resources (bandwidth and buffer) to the competing agents. In this competitive setting network providers (suppliers) compete for profit maximization.

Multiple Agent-Network Supplier Interaction: Agents present demands to the network suppliers. The demands are based on their wealth and QoS preferences of their class. The demand by each agent is computed via utility functions which represent QoS needs of the user classes. Agents negotiate with suppliers to determine the prices. The negotiation process is iterative, where prices are adjusted to clear the market; supply equals the demand. Price negotiation could be done periodically or denpending on changes in demand.

Each agent in the network is allocated a certain amount of buffer space and link capacity. The buffer is used by the agent for queueing packets sent by the users of the class. A simple FIFO queueing model is used for each class. The users within a class share buffer and link resources.

Agent and supplier optimality: Agents compete for resources by presenting demand to the supplier. The agents, given the current market price, compute the affordable allocations of resources (assume agents have limited wealth or budget). The demand from each agent is presented to the supplier. The supplier adjusts the market prices to ensure demand equals supply.

The main issues form the economic model are:

- Characterization of class QoS preferences and traffic parameters via utility functions, and computation of demand sets given the agent wealth and the utility function.
- Existence and computation of Pareto optimal allocations for QoS provisioning, given the agent utility functions.
- Computation of equilibrium price by the supplier based on agent demands, and conditions under which price equilibrium exists. Price negotiation mechanisms operate between the agents and suppliers.

Problem formulation

Network model: The network is composed of nodes (packet switches) and links. Each node has several output links. Each output link is associated with an output buffer. The link controller, at the output link, schedules packets from the buffers and transmits them to other nodes in the network. The switch has a buffer controller that can partition the buffer among the traffic classes at each output link. We assume that a processor on the switch aids in control of resources.

We have confined ourselves to problems for a single link (output link) at a node, but they can be applied to the network as well. Let B denote the output buffer of a link and C be the corresponding link capacity. Let $\{c_k,b_k\}$ be the link capacity and buffer allocation to class k on a link, where k ε [1,K]. Let $\mathbf{p} = \{p_c,p_b\}$ be the price per unit link capacity and unit buffer at a link, and w_k be the wealth (budget) of traffic class k. The utility function for TC_k is $U_k = f(c_k,b_k,\mathbf{Tr}_k)$. The traffic of a class is represented by a vector of traffic parameters ($\mathbf{Tr}_k$) and a vector of QoS requirements (such as packet loss probabilities, average packet delay and so on.).

Agent (TC: traffic class) buys resources from the network at the given prices using its wealth. The wealth constraint of agent TC_k is: $p_b * b_k + p_c * c_k \leq w_k$. A budget set is the set of allocations that are feasible under the wealth constraint (budget constraint). The budget set is defined as follows:

$$B(\mathbf{p}) = (x : x \, \varepsilon \, X, \mathbf{p}\, x \leq w_k\} \qquad (1)$$

Computation of demands sets : The demand set for each agent is given by the following:

$$\Phi\,(\mathbf{p}) = (\, x : x \, \varepsilon \, B(\mathbf{p}) \,, U(x'), \forall x' \, \varepsilon \, B(\mathbf{p})\} \qquad (2)$$

The goal of TC_k is to compute the allocations that provide maximal preference under w_k and $\mathbf{p}$. Each TC_k performs the following to obtain the demand set (defined above):

Find: $\{c_k, b_k\}$ (3)

such that: $\max U_k = f(c_k, b_k, \mathbf{Tr}_k)$

Constraints: $p_b\, b_k + p_c\, c_k \leq w_k$

$c_k\ \varepsilon\ [0,C]\ ,\ b_k\ \varepsilon\ [0,B]$

Utility Parameters

In the previous section, we show a general utility function which is a function of the switch resources; buffer (b) and bandwidth (c). The utility function could be a function of the following:

- Packet loss probability $U_t = g(c,b,\mathbf{Tr})$
- Average packet delay $U_d = h(c,b,\mathbf{Tr})$
- Packet tail utility $U_t = v(c,b,\mathbf{Tr})$
- Max packet delay $U_b = f(b,b_T)$
- Thruput $U_c = g\ (c,c_t)$

The variables b and c in the utility functions refer to buffer space allocation and link bandwidth allocation. In the utility functions U_b and U_c; the parameters b_T and c_T are constants. For example, the utility function $U_b = f(b,b_T)$ for max packet delay is simply a constant as b increases, but drops to 0 when $b = b_T$ and remains zero for any further increase in b.

We look at utility functions which capture packet loss probability of QoS requirements by traffic classes, and we consider loss, max-delay and thruput requirements. After this we proceed to utility functions that capture average delay requirements, followed by utility functions that capture packet tail utility requirements. We also could give examples of utility functions for agents with many objectives; agents have preferences over several QoS parameters as shown below.

$$U = f(U_l, U_d, U_t, U_b, U_c) \qquad (4)$$

Packet Loss

The phenomenon of packet loss is due to two reasons: the first, packets arrive at a switch and find that the buffer is full (no space left), therefore, are dropped. The second is that packets arrive at a switch and are buffered , but they do not get transmitted (or scheduled) in time, then they are dropped. A formal way of saying this: for real-time applications, packets, if delayed considerably in the network, do not have value once they reach the destination.

We consider K agents, representing traffic classes of M/M/1/B type, competing for resources from the network provider. The utility function is packet loss utility (U_l) for the user classes. We choose the M/M/1/B model or traffic and queueing for the following reasons:

- The model is tractable, where steady state packet loss utility is in closed-form, and differentiable. This helps in demonstrating the economic models and the concepts
- There is a renewed interest in M/M/1/B or M/D/1/B models for multiplexed traffic (such as video), where simple histogram based traffic models capture the performance of queueing in networks (Kleinrock, 1975; Wolff, 1989)

For more complex traffic and queueing models (example of video traffic)we can use tail utility functions to represent QoS of the user class instead of loss utility.

In the competitive economic model, each agent prefers less packet loss, as the more packet loss, the worse the quality of the video at the receiving end. Let each agent TC_k have wealth w_k, which it uses to purchase resources from network provider.

Let each TC transmit packets at a rate λ (Poisson arrivals), and let the processing time of the packets be exponentially distributed with unit mean. Let c,b be allocations to a TC. The utility function U for each TC is given as follows:

$$U = f(c,b,\lambda) = \begin{cases} \dfrac{(1-\frac{\lambda}{c})(\frac{\lambda}{c})b}{1-(\frac{\lambda}{c})^{+1+b}} \\ \dfrac{1}{b+1} \\ \dfrac{(-1+)(\frac{\lambda}{c})(\frac{\lambda}{c})^{b}}{-1+(\frac{\lambda}{c})^{1+b}} \end{cases} \text{for } \lambda < c, \lambda = c, \lambda > c \text{ resp.} \qquad (5)$$

The above function is continuous and differentiable for all c ε [0,C], and for all b ε [0,B]. We assume that b εR for continuity purposes of the utility function.

9.7 Equilibrium Price and Convergence

Pareto efficient allocations are such that no traffic class can improve upon these allocations without reducing the utility of one or more traffic classes. The more formal definition of Pareto efficiency is given in Varian (1993). The set of Pareto allocations that satisfy the equilibrium conditions forms the Pareto surface.

Each agent computes the demand set, which is a set of allocations, that maximizes the preference under the wealth constraint. The demand set is obtained by minimizing the utility function under the budget constraint. The Lagrangian is given below with L as the Lagrange multiplier.

$$\min[f(c,b,\lambda) - L*(p_c*c + p_b - w)] \qquad (6)$$
$$c \geq 0,\ b \geq 0$$

The function f(c,b,λ) is smooth, strictly convex and compact, thus the demand set is just one element [1,2]. Using the Kuhn-Tucker optimality conditions, the optimal resource allocation vector is obtained, where L is the Lagrange multiplier

$$\frac{\partial U}{\partial c} = L*p_c, \frac{\partial U}{\partial b} = L*p_b \qquad (7)$$

From this the equilibrium condition is obtained. This condition states that the marginal rate of substitution is equal among the competing traffic classes. The economic problems are to establish competitive equilibrium, compute the equilibrium prices p_c^*, p_b^* and Pareto optimal allocations. The equilibrium condition is shown as follows:

$$\frac{\partial U/\partial c}{\partial U/\partial b} = \frac{p_c^*}{p_b^*} \qquad (8)$$

Using the utility function given by equation (5), the price ratio is given below. From the equation, it is evident that the price ratio is a function of the resource allocations and the traffic parameter λ.

$$\frac{p_c}{p_b} = g(\lambda, c, b) = \frac{-\lambda + \lambda\frac{\lambda^b}{c} - \lambda b + cb}{(\lambda - c)c\log(\frac{\lambda}{c})} \qquad (9)$$

This equation can be rewritten in the following way, where function N has a nice interpretation. It is the ratio of the effective queue utilization (ρ(1-U)) to the effective queue emptiness (1 – ρ *(1-U)), where ρ = λ/c.

$$\frac{p_c}{p_b} = \frac{N-b}{c\log\rho} \text{ where } N = \frac{\rho*(1-U)}{1-\rho*(1-U)} \qquad (10)$$

This can also be interpreted as the effective number in an equivalent M/M/1 queueing system, where the system utilization is ρ = ρ (1-U). For an M/M/1 system, the average number in the system is $\frac{\rho}{1-\rho}$.

The following gives the equilibrium condition for K agents competing for resources from a single network provider. From this condition, and the resource constraints. the Pareto allocations and the corresponding equilibrium price ratios can be computed.

$$-\frac{p_c}{p_b} = \frac{b_1 - N_1}{c_1 \log(\rho_1)} = \frac{b_2 - N_2}{c_2 \log(\rho_2)} = \ldots = \frac{b_K - N_K}{c_K \log(\rho_K)} \quad (11)$$

Using the buffer constraint $b_1 + b_2 + b_3 + \ldots + b_k = B$, the equilibrium price ratio and optimal buffer allocation for each agent i can be represented by the following equations:

$$\frac{p_c^*}{p_b^*} = \frac{\sum_i N_i - B}{\sum_i (c_i \log(\rho_i))} \quad (12)$$

$$b_i = N_i - \frac{(\sum_i N_i - B)(c_i \log(\rho_i))}{\sum_i (c_i \log(\rho_i))}) \quad (13)$$

The issue of determining the equilibrium prices, so that supply equal demand for different types of utility functions can use convex optimization tools (Chen, Ye and Zhang, 2007)

Competitive Pricing Algorithm

1 Set initial prices : $p_c = p_c^0, p_b = p_b^0$

2 Compute demand set, ie. find minimum of min $[U_i = f_i(c_i, b_i, \lambda_i)]$ $\forall i \varepsilon$ [1,K] given $p_c c_i + p_b b_i \leq w_i$ (wealth constraint)

3 Demand: $D_c = \sum_{i=1}^{i=K} c_i, D_b = \sum_{i=1}^{i=K} b_i$.

4 If $(D_c - C)$ <(>) 0, then, $p_c = p_c - (+)\Delta_c$

If $(D_b - B)$ <(>)0, then, $p_b = p_b - (+)\Delta_b$

Go back to step (2)

5 Else if $D_c = C$ at p_c, and $D_b = B$ at p_b, then the equilibrium is attained and prices are at equilibrium

The algorithm computes iteratively the equilibrium prices in a competitive economy using the utility functions. Given the wealth in the economy, the prices converge to a point on the Pareto surface, which can be computed using the first-order conditions. There is a minimum price p_ε, that each traffic class has to pay, if the equilibrium prices are lower than p

$_i$. Once the prices are computed, the network service provider releases the resources to the agents.

9.8 EXAMPLE OF TWO AGENTS AND ONE SUPPLIER

We consider two agents, representing traffic classes of the M/M/1/B model. The utility function is shown in equation 5. The agents have wealth w_1 and w_2 respectively. The agents compete for resources, which then are used to provide services to users.

Two Classes: We consider two competing traffic classes. Using the equilibrium conditions, the equilibrium price ratio is given by,

$$\frac{P_c^*}{P_b^*} = \frac{N_1 - b_1}{c_1 \log \rho_1} = \frac{N_2 - b_2}{c_2 \log \rho_2} \tag{14}$$

The above equation states that at equilibrium, the log of the ratio of utilizations of the two traffic classes is equal to the ratio of the time to evacuate the residual buffer space of the traffic classes. Rewriting the above equation:

$$\frac{\log \rho_1}{\log \rho_2} = \frac{N_1 - b_1}{c_1} \cdot \frac{c_2}{N_2 - b_2} \tag{15}$$

By using the resource constraints $c_1 + c_2 = C$ and $b_1 + b_2 = B$, the equilibrium conditions become a function of just two variables. The Pareto surface is the set of allocations that satisfy equation (14). The function N_i and U_i (for all i ε {1,2}) have several interesting properties for different values of ρ_i. We study the properties of these functions for various regions of ρ_1 and ρ_2, where ρ_1 and ρ_2 are utilizations of TC_1 and TC_2 respectively.

- $\rho_1 < 1$, $\rho_2 < 1$: As the buffer is varied to infinity, the utility function (loss utility) becomes 0, and the effective average number (N_1,N_2) become the average number in an M/M/1 queue. The $\lim_{b1 \to \infty} N_1 = \dfrac{\rho_1}{1-\rho_1}$, $\lim_{b1 \to \infty} U_1 = 0$. The quantity $b_1 - N_1 \geq 0$ for b_1 ε$[0, \infty)$.
- $\rho_1 > 1$, $\rho_2 > 1$: The allocated capacity is less than the mean rates of TC_1 and TC_2. We consider the case where the buffer tends to infinity. $\lim_{b1 \to \infty} N_1 = \infty$, $\lim_{b1 \to \infty} U_1 = 0$. The quantity $b_1 - N_1 < 0$ for b_1 ε$[0, \infty)$.
- $\rho_1 \to 1$, $\rho_2 \to 1$: The quantity is $N_1 = b_1$, $N_2 = b_2$. The equilibrium condition for offered loads equal to 1 is $\dfrac{b_1 * (b_1 + 1)}{2 * \lambda_1} = \dfrac{b_2 * (b_2 + 1)}{2 * \lambda_2}$.

Several other cases such as $\rho_1 > 1$, $\rho_2 = 1$ are omitted, but are essential in determining the Pareto surface.

For the two competing traffic classes, the following relation between the utility functions of the traffic classes with respect to the Pareto optimal allocations is obtained:

$$\frac{\log U_1}{\log U_2} = \frac{(b_1 - N_1)}{c_1} \cdot \frac{c_2}{(b_2 - N_2)} \tag{16}$$

$$\frac{\log U_1}{\log U_2} = \frac{(b_1 - N_1)}{(b_2 - N_2)} \cdot \frac{c_2}{c_1} \tag{17}$$

This relation has an interesting physical meaning: The loss of the ratio of the utilities of the traffic classes is equal to the ratio of the time to evacuate the residual buffer in the queues. The residual buffer is simply: $b_i - N_i$, where N_i is given by equation (10).

9.9 Conclusion

We demonstrate the application of economic tools to resource management in distributed systems and computer networks. The concepts of analytical economics were used to develop effective market based control mechanisms, and to show the allocation of resources are Pareto optimal.

Methodologies of decentralized control of resources, and pricing of resources are based on QoS demand of users. We bring together economic models and performance models of computer systems into one framework to solve problems of resource allocation and efficient QoS provisioning. Such a scheme can be applied to pricing services in ATM networks and Integrated Services Internet of the future.

There are drawbacks to this form of modeling where several agents have to use market mechanisms to decide where to obtain service (which supplier?). If the demand for a resource varies substantially over short periods of time, then the actual prices of the resources will also vary causing several side effects such as indefinite migration of consumers between suppliers. This might potentially result in degradation of system performance where the resources are being underutilized due to the bad decisions (caused by poor market mechanisms) made by the users in choosing the suppliers.

Unlike economies, the resources in a computer system are not easily substitutable. The future work is to design robust market mechanisms and rationalized pricing schemes which can handle surges in demand and variability, and can give price guarantees to consumers over longer periods of time. Another drawback is that resources in a computer system are indivisible resulting in non-smooth utility functions, which may yield sub-optimal allocations, and potential computational overhead.

In summary, economic models are useful for designing and understanding internet-type systems. The Internet currently connects hundreds of millions of users and thousands of sites. Several services exist on many of these sites, notably the World Wide Web (WWW) which provides access to various information sources distributed across the Internet. Many more services (multimedia applications, commercial transactions) are to be supported in the Internet. To access this large number of services, agents have to share limited network bandwidth and server capacities (processing speeds). Such large-scale networks require decentralized mechanisms to control access to services. Economic concepts such as pricing and competition can provide some solutions to reduce the complexity of service provisioning and decentralize the access mechanisms to the resources.

REFERENCES

Ackermann, H., Briest,P., Fanghänel, A. and B. Vöcking (2007), 'Who Should Pay for Forwarding Packets', in Deng, X. and F.C. Graham (2007*), Internet and Network Economics*, Third International Workshop, WINE 2007, San Diego, Berlin, New York: Springer, 208 - 219

Bohn, R., Braun, H.- W., Claffy, K. C. and S. Wolff (1994), 'Mitigating the coming Internet Crunch: Multiple Service Levels via Precedence', Technical Report, Supercomputer Center, San Diego, Ca., March 22.

Chao, J. and D. Ghosal (1994), 'IP on ATM on Local Area Networks', *IEEE Communications Magazine* 12

Chen, L., Ye, Y. and J. Zhang (2007), 'A Note on Equilibrium Pricing as Convex Optimization', in: Deng, X. and F.C. Graham (2007), *Internet and Network Economics*, Third International Workshop, WINE 2007, San Diego, Berlin, New York: Springer, 7 – 16

Clearwater, S. (1995), *Market based Control: A Paradigm for Distributed Resource Allocation*, Singapore: World Scientific Publishing

Deng, X. and F.C. Graham (2007), *Internet and Network Economics*, Third International Workshop, WINE 2007, San Diego, Springer: Berlin, New York

Gottinger, H.W (1997)., 'Telecommunication, Internet, Regulation and Pricing', Chapt. 5 in: Takashima, M. , Gottinger,H.W. and C. Umali, *Economics of Global Telecommunications and the Internet,* Nagasaki Univ. Report, 107-126

Gupta A. and D.O.Stahl ,(1995), 'An Economic Approach to Networked Computing with Priority Classes', MIT Press, Cambridge, March

Iong,S., Man-Cho-So, A. and M. Sundararajan (2007), 'Stochastic Mechanism Design', in: Deng, X. and F.C. Graham (2007), *Internet and Network Economics*, Third International Workshop, WINE 2007, San Diego, Berlin, New York: Springer, 269 - 280

Kahin, B. and Keller J. (1995) ,eds, *Public Access to the Internet*, Cambridge, Ma.: MIT Press

Kleinrock., L. (1976) *Queueing Systems* ,Volume 2, New York : Wiley

Low, S. and P. Varaiya (1993), ' A New Approach to Service Provisioning in ATM Networks', *IEEE Trans. on Networking* 1, Nov.

MacKie-Mason, J.K. and H.R. Varian (1995), 'Pricing the Internet', in *Public Access to the Internet* , Cambridge, Ma.: MIT Press, 269-314.

Minzer, S. (1989), 'Broadband ISDN and Asynchronous Transfer Mode(ATM)' *,IEEE Communications Magazine* 7, Sept.

Nisan, N. and A. Ronen (2001), ' Computationally Feasible VCG Mechanisms', *Games and Economic Behavior* 35, 166-196

Paxon, V. (1994), 'Growth Trends in TCP/IP', *IEEE Communications Magazine*, 12, April

Shenker, S. (1995), 'Service Models and Pricing Policies for an Integrated Services Internet', in *Public Access to the Internet*, Cambridge, Ma. : MIT Press ,315- 337.

Shenker, S. (1994)'An Architecture for the Future Internet', *Hot Interconnect* II, Aug.

Shenker. S., Clark D., Estrin, D. and S. Herzog(1995), 'Pricing in Computer Networks: Reshaping the Research Agenda', *Journal of Telecommunications Policy* 20 (1)

Varian, H.R. (1993), *Microeconomic Analysis*, New York: Norton

Wang,Q, Peha,J.M and Sirbu, M.A. (1997), 'Optimal Pricing for Integrated Services Network', in L.M. McKnight and J.P.Bailey ,eds., *Internet Economics*, Cambridge: MIT Press, 353-376

Wilson, R. (1993), *Nonlinear Pricing*, Oxford: Oxford Univ. Press

Wolff, R.W.(1989), *Stochastic Modeling and the Theory of Queues*, Prentice Hall, Englewood Cliffs, New Jersey, 1989.

APPENDIX

A. The Network Economy

The network consists of V nodes (packet switches) and N links. Each node has several output links with an output buffer. The resources at output link are transmission capacity (or link capacity) and buffer space. The link controller at the output link schedules packets from the buffer. This is based on how the buffer is partitioned among the traffic classes and the scheduling rule between the traffic classes. Sessions are grouped into traffic classes based on similar traffic characteristics and common QoS requirements. Sessions that belong to a class share buffer and link resources, and traffic classes compete for resources at a packet switch. Each session arrives to the network with a vector of traffic parameters Tr, vector of QoS requirements and wealth. A session is grouped or mapped to a corresponding traffic class. A traffic class has common QoS requirements, and we consider QoS requirements per traffic class rather than per session. Once a session is admitted along a path (a route), it will continue along that path until it compeletes.

Each agent k performs the following to obtain the demand set on each link. The allocations are buffer (b)and bandwidth (c) on each link for each agent. The wealth is distributed across the links by each agent to buy resources.

That is, the problem is to find pairs $\{c^*_k, b^*_k\}$ such that max $U_k = f(c_k, b_k, Tr_k)$, constraints $p_b b_k + p_c c_k \leq w_k$.

In the above formulation , each agent k buys resources from each link. The allocation for agent k is $c^*_k = \{ c_k^{*1}, c_k^{*2}, \dots, c_k^{*N} \}$ and $b^*_k = \{ b_k^{*1}, b_k^{*2}, \dots, b_k^{*N} \}$. An agent can invest wealth in either some or all the links. We assume that at each link there is competition among at least some of the agents for buying resources. As previously, Gottinger [1999] , we show a general utility function which is a function of the switch resources : buffer(b) and bandwidth(c) . A utility function of the agent could be a function of:

- Packet loss probability $U_t = g(c,b,Tr)$
- Average packet delay $U_d = h(c,b,Tr)$
- Packet tail probability $U_l = v(c,b,Tr)$

- Max packet delay $U_b = f(b)$
- Thruput $U_c = g(c)$

We consider that an agent will place demands for resources based on a general utility function , which is a combination of the various QoS requirements:

$$U = f(c,b,Tr) = x_l U_l + x_d U_d + x_b U_b + x_c U_c + x_t U_t$$

where U_l is the packet loss probability utility function, U_d is the average delay utility function , U_t is the packet tail probability , U_b is the utility function for max-delay requirements, and U_c is for bandwidth (throughput) requirements. x_l , x_d , x_b, x_c , x_t are constants. Agents could use such a utility function . As long as the convexity property with respect to buffer b and bandwidth c holds. Pareto optimal allocations and price equilibria exist. However, if they are not convex , then depending on the properties of the functions , local optimality and price equilibrium could exist. To show the main ideas for routing and admission control, we use packet loss probability as the main utility function (U_l) , which means we assume that x_l from the above equation are the only constant and the rest are zeros. For doing this , we need first some further specifications of the loss probability. We later show results for Pareto optimality and price equilibrium , and then we propose routing and admission control algorithms. In general, one can assume that agents, on behalf of user classes , demand for resources from the link suppliers based on the utility function shown above. The agent uses the utility function to present the demand for resources over the whole network of parallel links.

Loss Probability Specifications. At each output link j the resources are buffer space B^j and link capacity C^j .

Let $\{c^j_k, b^j_k\}$ be the link capacity and buffer allocation to class k on link j where $k \varepsilon [1,K]$. Let p^j_c and p^j_b be the price per unit link capacity and unit buffer respectively at link j, and w_k be the wealth (budget) of a traffic class k. For a link j from the source to the destination , the packet loss probability (utility) for traffic class k is given by the following

$$U_{lk} = P_{loss} = 1 - \Pi_{j=1}^{N} (1 - P_k^j)$$

where P_k^j is the packet loss probability at link j of agent k.

The goal of the agent is to minimize the packet loss probability under its wealth or budget constraints . If the traffic classes have smooth convex preferences with respect to link capacity and buffer allocation variables at each link , then the utility function U_{lk} is convex with respect to the variables.

B. The Server Economy

We now discuss the server economy where servers offer processing resources and memory to agents representing user classes. The agents compete for these resources and buying as much as possible from suppliers. The agents perform load balancing based on the OoS preferences of the class it represents.

The economic model consists of the following players: Agents and Server Suppliers, Consumers or user classes and Business. User sessions within a class have common preferences. User classes have QoS preferences over average delay and throughput , and in some cases completion times of sessions (deadlines). Users within a class share resources at the servers.

Agents and Network Suppliers: Agents represent user classes. An agent represents a single user class. Agents negotiate with the supplier and buy resources from service providers. Agents on behalf of user classes demand for resources to meet the QoS needs. Suppliers compete to maximize revenue. Suppliers partition and allocate resources (processing rate and memory) to the competing agents.

Multiple Agent Network Supplier Interaction: Agents present demands to the suppliers . The demands by agents are based upon their wealth and user class preferences. The demand by each agent is computed via utility functions which represent QoS needs of the class. Agents negotiate with suppliers to determine the prices . The negotiation process is iterative where prices are adjusted to clear the market. Price negotiation could be done periodically or depending on changes in demand.

The agent and network supplier become service providers in the market. The role of the supplier is to provide technologies to sell resources (buffer and bandwidth units) and to partitioning them flexibly based on the demand by the agents. The agents transform the goods (buffer and bandwidth) and provide QoS levels to the user-classes. The agents strive to maximize profits (minimize buying costs) by using the right utility functions and the right performance models in order to provide QoS to the user-class. More users within a user-class implies more revenue for the agent. The agent is decoupled from the traffic class and the supplier .

In this economy, user classes are transaction classes that send transactions to database servers for processing . The transaction processing time at each of the server is based on the type of transaction . Consider K classes of transactions and each class is represented by an agent (economic agent). In the economy, the agents negotiate with the servers for server capacity. We assume that transactions of any class can run on any of the database servers. Therefore, agents negotiate with all the servers for server throughput (or processing speed). A model where K agents compete for services in a transaction processing system , each class could do the following based on its preferences on average delay and throughput: (i) each agent i can minimize its average response time under throughput constraints, (ii) each agent i can maximize throughput of its transactions under an average delay constraint , (iii) each agent i can look at a combination of QoS requirements and have preferences over them.

Therefore, each class can choose either one of these preferences and let the agent control the flow of transactions through the system. The problem now becomes a multi-objective optimization problem as every agent is trying to maximize its benefit in the system based on the class of QoS preferences. Consider that the classes wish to choose various objectives, the the utility function assumes $U = x_d U_d + x_l U_l$ where U_d is the utility function for average delay and U_l is the utility function for throughput , and x_d and x_l are constants. Consider that there are requirements for transaction completion time. Instead of scheduling transactions to meet deadlines , we try to minimize the number of transactions that have missed the deadlines (in a stochastic sense). Consider that each transaction class is assigned a service queue at each server , then we try to minimize the probability of the number of transactions of a class exceeding a certain threshold in the buffer. This is the tail probability

P(X >b) where X is the number of transactions of a class in a queue at a server , and b is threshold is threshold for the number in the queue, beyond which transactions miss deadlines. If we include this QoS requirement , then the above utility function will be $U = x_d U_d + x_l U_l + x_t U_t$ where U_t is the tail probability utility function and x_t is a constant.

Pareto Optimality: We now have a simple formulation for classes competing for server capacity (processing rate) in order to minimize average delay (or average response time). The utility function is simply $U = x_d U_d$ as the rests of the constants are zero. Let p_j be the price per unit processing rate at server j. The maximum processing rate at server j is C_j . The problem therefore for each agent is the following: find $\{c_{ij}^*\}$ such that min $U_d = \{ \sum_{j=1}^{N} W_{ij}\}$ with constraints $\sum_{j=1}^{N} \lambda_{ij} = \gamma_i \ \forall i , \sum_{1}^{N} c_{ij} * p_j \leq w_i \ \forall i$

In the above problem definition , each agent will try and minimize the utility function under the wealth conbstraint and under the throughput constraint. This constraint is necessary to make sure that positive values of throughput are obtained as a result of the optimization. The transaction agents compete for processing rate at each server , and transaction servers compete for profit. The objectives of the transaction classes are conflicting as they all want to minimize their average response time. In the above formulation $W_{ij} = \lambda_{ij} / (c_{ij} - \lambda_{ij})$ this is

The average number of class i transactions in queue at system j. The average delay in the system for each class i is simply the average number in the system divided by the overall throughput $\sum_{j=1}^{N} \lambda_{ij}$.

The main goal of the agent representing the transaction class is to minimize a utility function which is simply the average number in the overall system . This will also minimize the average delay or average response time of the transaction class.

Proposition 1. The utility function U_d is convex with respect to the resource allocation variable c_{ij} where $\lambda_{ij} \in [0,c_{ij})$, and $c_{ij} \in (0, C_j]$

The proof follows from Gottinger [1997] .

The utility function U_d is discontinuous when $\lambda_{ij} = c_{ij}$.

Demand Set. The demand set for an agent i, given the prices (p_j of server j) of the processing rates (or capacities) at the servers is $\{ c_{i1} , c_{i2}, \ldots , c_{iN} \}$ over all the servers. We use the standard techniques of optimization to find the demand set , which is given as follows for all $j \in [1,N]$

$$c_{ij} = \lambda_{ij} + ((w_i - \textstyle\sum_{j=1}^{N} \lambda_{ij} p_j) / \textstyle\sum_{j=1}^{N} \sqrt{\lambda_{ij} p_j}\,) \sqrt{\lambda_{ij} / p_j} \ .$$

Price Equilibrium: Once the demand set is obtained, then using the wealth constraints , we can solve for the equilibrium price . This is not easily tractable. However, numerical results can be computed using the tatonnement process whereby agents compute the demand set, given the processing rate prices by each server.

An iteration process between the agents and the servers takes place. This will converge to an equilibrium price , when demand equals the supply which is $\sum_{i=1}^{K} c_{ij} = C_j$.

We now state formally the result for K agents competing for processing resources from N servers.

Proposition 2 . Consider K agents competing for processing resources from N servers . If the utility function of these agents is U_d and the performance model at the servers is an M/M/1 model, then price equilibrium and Pareto optimality exist.

The proof of this proposition is the same as described in Gottinger [1997]. The utility function U_d is continuous and decreasing convex with respect to the allocation variables c_{ij}. The function is discontinuous when $\lambda_{ij} = c_{ij}$.

Due to this, Pareto allocations or price equilibrium may not exist. However, we solve this problem by stating that the agents , when they present their demands , have to make sure that the transaction throughput rate λ_{ij} at a server has to be lower than the capacity allocation c_{ij} . If this is not met , then the price iteration process or the tatonnement process will not converge. We assume that the servers know the transaction throughput or arrival rate from each agent during the iteration process. //

INDEX

U

V

W